THE DUBIOUS MORALITY OF
MODERN
ADMINISTRATIVE LAW

RICHARD A. EPSTEIN

ROWMAN & LITTLEFIELD
Lanham • Boulder • New York • London

Published by Rowman & Littlefield
An imprint of The Rowman & Littlefield Publishing Group, Inc.
4501 Forbes Boulevard, Suite 200, Lanham, Maryland 20706
www.rowman.com

6 Tinworth Street, London SE11 5AL, United Kingdom

British Library Cataloguing in Publication Information Available

Library of Congress Cataloging-in-Publication Data

978-1-5381-4149-6 (cloth)
978-1-5381-4150-2 (electronic)

∞™ The paper used in this publication meets the minimum requirements of
American National Standard for Information Sciences—Permanence of Paper for
Printed Library Materials, ANSI/NISO Z39.48-1992.

To my colleagues, friends, and students,
who have made my every day in the
academic profession an adventure

CONTENTS

ACKNOWLEDGMENTS

This book was written in less than one year, thanks crucially to my student research assistants at the New York University School of Law. Their contributions went beyond the careful attention to detail that is necessary to round any manuscript into shape. They also pushed me to cover subjects that I had either slighted or overlooked. In so doing, these students helped me to expand a short essay into a systematic volume that looks at administrative law, not only as a body of separate doctrine but as an area of rich interconnections to private and public law. So a heartfelt thanks to Tiberius Davis, William Dawley, Kenneth Hershey, Kenneth Lee, Matt Pociask, Jeremy Rozansky, Joseph Scopelitis, Benjamin Silver, and Nathaniel Tisa.

I also want to thank Larry Mone and Reihan Salam of the Manhattan Institute for sponsoring this book. The Institute's James Copland, Rafael Mangual, Howard Dickman, and Troy Senik were instrumental in urging me to finish the task in a timely fashion. Thanks to Jana Weinstein and Janice Meyerson for their meticulous copyediting of a manuscript that was, until the final moments, in a constant state of flux. Thanks as well to Jamie Meggas, Manhattan Institute's senior designer.

And last, I want to thank my wife, Eileen, who has learned over the years to live with a distracted husband, and my children, their spouses, and their children for all the moral and social support over the years. As William Rainey Harper has said, "we are one in spirit, not necessarily in opinion."

ABOUT THE MANHATTAN INSTITUTE

The Manhattan Institute for Policy Research develops and disseminates new ideas that foster greater economic choice and individual responsibility. Since 1977, the institute has helped change the United States and its cities for the better: welfare reform, tort reform, proactive policing, and economic growth are at the heart of MI's legacy. Today, the institute continues to develop new ways to advance its message in the battle of ideas.

The Manhattan Institute is a 501(c)(3) nonprofit organization. Contributions are tax-deductible to the fullest extent of the law.

ABOUT THE AUTHOR

Richard A. Epstein is the Laurence A. Tisch Professor of Law at the New York University School of Law; the Peter and Kirsten Bedford Senior Fellow at the Hoover Institution; and the James Parker Hall Distinguished Service Professor of Law Emeritus at the University of Chicago Law School, where he is a Senior Lecturer. He has taught a wide array of both public and private law courses and has published numerous articles on a wide range of topics. Among his many books are *Takings: Private Property and the Power of Eminent Domain* (1985), *Simple Rules for a Complex World* (1995), *How Progressives Rewrote the Constitution* (2006), and the *Classical Liberal Constitution: The Uncertain Quest for Limited Government* (2014). He has been a member of the American Academy of Arts and Sciences since 1985 and received the Bradley Prize in 2011, as well as honorary degrees from the University of Ghent (2003) and the University Siegen (2018), and was designated an honorary professor at the Peruvian University of Applied Sciences I 2003. His column "The Libertarian" has appeared weekly in the *Defining Ideas Journal* of the Hoover Institution since 2008, and he has published widely in such places as the *Atlantic*, the *New York Times*, and the *Wall Street Journal*. He podcasts include *Law Talk* with John Yoo and Troy Senik, the *Libertarian* with Troy Senik, *Reasonable Disagreements* with Adam White, and is a regular guest on the *John Batchelor Show*.

INTRODUCTION:
AN ACCIDENTAL BOOK

A year ago, I was approached by James Copland of the Manhattan Institute, who requested that I write a short critique of modern American administrative law. I have taught administrative law several times and long been a critic of the modern developments in this field.[1] But I did not regard myself as a true expert on the many wrinkles and interstices of the Administrative Procedure Act (APA) of 1946[2] and the huge volume of judicial interpretation and academic commentary that it has generated over the course of its 70-plus years of existence. However, I have encountered large chunks of administrative law in connection with modern substantive subjects such as environmental law, food and drug law, labor law, securities law, and water law.

After agreeing to write only a short essay on the topic, my first task was to find a foil to my own skeptical orientation. An article by Professors Cass Sunstein and Adrian Vermeule, "The Morality of Administrative Law,"[3] filled that role because it relied on the now classic book *The Morality of Law*, written by Lon Fuller in 1964,[4] and later revised in 1969, for their defense of modern administrative law. Sunstein and Vermeule argue that the basic concerns about the morality of law addressed by Fuller in the 1960s help justify the mature body of administrative law that developed during the first part of the 21st century. I was immediately skeptical of this claim and started to prepare a short essay that explained why Fuller's various conditions for the coherence of any legal system are not satisfied by modern American administrative law. Fuller's steely insistence on legal coherence, clarity, and consistency, coupled with his strong condemnation of retroactive laws, does not mesh with modern administrative law.

While developing the defense of my view, it quickly became

1

apparent that I not only had to update Fuller's account to apply to modern law, but I also had to address the various substantive defenses of modern administrative law, all of which are closely tied to an endorsement of the post–New Deal regime. A vigorous defense of this regime was written by Professor Gillian Metzger in "1930s Redux: The Administrative State Under Siege,"[5] published only months before Sunstein and Vermeule's article.

To respond properly to Metzger's defense, I found it necessary to expand the scope of my project. First, I had to offer a systematic account of the key differences in aspiration and techniques between the 19th-century version of administrative law and the modern administrative state, which was cemented by the 1936–37 watershed term of the U.S. Supreme Court. For a thorough account of this important term, I relied in part on Professor Aditya Bamzai's informative article "The Origins of Judicial Deference to Executive Interpretation."[6] Studying the cases from that term revealed a compact and disciplined body of administrative law that addressed such critical issues as land and patent grants, pensions, and tariffs. So one of the major themes of this book is to contrast the pre–New Deal and post–New Deal versions of administrative law.

One central conclusion that emerges is an explanation for the rise of judicial deference to administrative action that appears with far greater strength after the New Deal. Earlier cases were consistent with the relatively constrained substantive ambitions of the earlier law, which may be reduced to rules. For example, in *J. W. Hampton, Jr. & Co. v. United States*,[7] the Supreme Court cabined discretion by using mathematical formulas to determine adjustments that should be made in tariff levels for certain goods coming in from certain countries.

In the post–New Deal period, that level of precision is frequently not attainable because today's legislative schemes require extensive administrative discretion, especially in the award of public benefits, to fulfill their lofty ambitions. Perhaps the most notable illustration is *NBC v. Federal Communications Commission*,[8] in which Justice Felix Frankfurter, an ardent supporter of the New Deal, upheld the level of discretion given to the Federal Communications Commission (FCC) under the "public convenience and necessity standard," which, he proudly noted, allowed the administrative agency not only to set property boundaries between frequencies—a classical liberal function—but also to determine the "composition of the traffic"—a subject that neither Frankfurter nor the FCC knew anything about. In cases where it is not possible to articulate an administrable standard, discretion with respect to the disposition of any individual case becomes a far more attractive alternative.

Yet there is often no need to tolerate the degree of judicial deference given to administrative bodies in connection with the implementation of other statutes with more traditional regulatory goals. The key explanation for why such a high level of discretion is applied by courts is an uncritical belief that administrative agencies will act in the public interest and resist pleas for partisan outcomes. In all too many cases, that optimistic assumption is false. On many issues, the party in power will determine the scope of action, as was the case, for example, in *Bowles v. Seminole Rock & Sand Co.*,[9] which dealt with price controls, and *Auer v. Robbins*,[10] which dealt with overtime regulations.

Before diving into the substance of this book, a word of caution is urgently needed. The purpose of this book is not to slam administrative agencies for all that they do—for indeed, they do many things well. Instead, it is to conduct a closer, case-by-case analysis of the development of administrative law, identifying those cases where agencies have done their tasks well and those cases where they have not. It turns out that it is not possible to undertake that normative inquiry without some detailed knowledge of both the procedural standards for review under the APA and the substantive provisions of the statute.

This book starts with procedure. One of the inveterate dangers of modern administrative law is that it assumes that its procedural commands can be understood by looking—and not too carefully at that—at administrative agencies as though the correct legal regime in question has to be constructed de novo, without drawing upon the analogous issues that arise in civil procedure, where, roughly speaking, a trial court stands in the position of an administrative agency. The common tendency in modern administrative law is to assume that it somehow sets up a unique relationship between administrative agencies and judicial oversight.

Ironically, the opposite is actually true. The watershed event in administrative procedure was the adoption of APA in 1946, which was passed as a conscious effort by Congress to rein in some of the perceived excesses of the administrative state. APA was enacted only eight years after the new Federal Rules of Civil Procedure, which went a long way toward modernizing standard practice in federal courts, were adopted. The connection between these two major events should not be minimized. The clear impetus of APA was to try to integrate the rules of administrative procedure with the general body of procedural rules, one of whose major functions is to organize some kind of appellate review of the determinations of fact and law made by the legal authority that first hears the case.

That issue arises both with ordinary trials, which can be very complex, and with administrative hearings, which are sometimes quite straightforward. Complexity aside, the key principles should be the same. On any question of law, a trial court has no special competence that gives it any systematic advantage over an appellate court in answering such a legal question. In ordinary civil matters, all questions of law are subject to de novo review. I see no relevant difference in the distribution of powers when initial legal determinations are made by an administrative agency, rather than a trial court.

In *Chevron U.S.A. Inc. v. Natural Res. Def. Council,*[11] however, the Supreme Court ignored this obvious parity when it held that in cases involving an ambiguous statute, a court owes to an administrative agency the level of deference that it would never confer on a trial court. Justice John Paul Stevens made this determination without once citing the relevant provision of APA, Section 706, and it has resulted in an abject neglect of legal duty, in many cases, and a risky compromise of the judicial branch's independent authority to make final determinations on questions of law. No amount of institutional reliance should prevent this flawed decision from being overruled.

Apart from questions of law, the second class of cases involves so-called "ultimate issues of fact"—whether the evidence gathered shows that a defendant was negligent or that certain statements were false and misleading. Here the level of scrutiny increases until, roughly speaking, the ultimate determination made below must be supported by substantial evidence. Once again, there is no reason to think that administrative agencies, with all their supposed expertise, should be less able to meet this standard than ordinary district court judges or juries—subject, of course, to the control of district court judges.

It is just at this juncture that the implementation of APA goes badly astray, on questions of fact as well as law. In its 1983 decision *Motor Vehicles Manufacturers Ass'n v. State Farm Ins.*,[12] the Supreme Court read the phrase "arbitrary and capricious" to authorize a hard look review, at least in some cases—though, in other cases, those same words are read so laxly that virtually any government action will pass muster. What makes matters worse is that the choice of standards turns on covert substantive issues, especially in such critical areas as product safety or environmental regulation.

Yet a double standard is at work. Let the agency approve some project, and the sharp knives come out to find whether there is any defect in the proceedings below, and the case can be sent back for yet another round of review that can be so costly and time-consuming that the project is effectively dead. But if the agency blocks a project, no matter how frivolous its reasons, the agency decisions are routinely upheld. Just this standard took hold to destroy the nuclear power industry. There are strong signs that the same disastrous approach may take hold with respect to pipeline permits, although it is too soon to make a final judgment. Sadly, both extremes err, and the more sensible approach, often ignored, is to hold that so long as the agency tries to respond to both sides of the question, on these matters its decisions should be upheld.

Finally, many initial determinations about evidentiary matters are allowed to stand unless, roughly speaking, that determination is either clearly or plainly erroneous. On these issues, there is a rule that limits oversight to determinations that are clearly erroneous—an issue on which civil and administrative procedure are roughly in accord.

After procedure, the book takes up substance. The constant judicial preoccupation with standards of review has a second dire consequence. Courts are so often anxious to defer to agency determinations on both questions of law and ultimate issues of fact that they do not think hard about the substantive merits of a case or the quality of agency performance. And that quality can vary. In some cases, an agency does an outstanding job, and its decisions do not need the benefit of a huge presumption in its favor. In such cases, the agency should be able to persuasively explain the situation to a court, not because of some artificial judicial presumption but because of the intellectual clarity of its arguments. In other cases, the only way that a sloppy administrative rule can survive judicial scrutiny is through an uncritical dose of excessive deference. Allowing deference to save such flawed rules permits administrative agencies to warp or invert Congress's initial statutory design.

Here is one example. In conventional administrative law discussions, cases like *Seminole Rock* and *Auer* are yoked together as if they represent a continuous and consistent application of administrative law, when, in fact, they don't. *Seminole Rock* is a model of sound administrative interpretation regarding a general pricing regulation introduced at the height of World War II. *Auer* is a wholly indefensible rendition of the Fair Labor Standards Act, which, ironically, is a less controversial statute today.

Important implications follow from the unwise decision to view these two cases and statutes as equivalent. The new fetish with various flavors of administrative deference on key questions of law and fact survives precisely because judges at both the trial and appellate levels choose not to take a hard look at different statutory design, purpose, and text. The common mode of judicial activity today thus seeks to develop a substantive-free administrative law. But that effort to understand administrative law on the cheap is bound to fail. It is always necessary to make a systematic effort to understand regulatory challenges, the appropriate statutory responses, and the applicable administrative implications. There can be no shortcuts. For example, to do administrative law on securities regulation, as in *SEC v. Chenery Corporation (Chenery I)* [13] and *SEC v. Chenery Corporation (Chenery II)*, [14] you have to know something about securities legislation. To deal with the various exceptions for executive, administrative, or professional employees under the Fair Labor Standards Act, it is critical to know something about the chain of command in complex organizations. To deal with nuclear power or pollution requires knowledge of the best system for safety regulation of the former and pollution emissions on the latter. It is always dangerous to assume that an administrative agency possesses expertise that it lacks, or to deny expertise that an administrative agency has developed.

On this point, I have a comparative advantage in thinking about administrative law, because I come to the field with a strong working knowledge of the various substantive fields to which it is applied. Thus, as this book evolved, I did not content myself just with analysis of how the jurisprudence of Lon Fuller carries over to administrative law, or to a historical understanding of the evolutionary arc of administrative law from early to modern times. I have also gone into significant detail to examine particular statutory schemes in order to understand how the administrative process captured the purpose and structure of the schemes, or utterly ignored relevant statutory commands.

To summarize, the purpose of this book is to examine administrative law from three different perspectives. The first addresses basic rule-of-law considerations, from both a theoretical and historical perspective. The second deals with the procedural workings under APA when checked against ordinary rules of civil procedure. And the last perspective more closely looks at the substantive fields of law that come into contact with the administrative state. Analyzed holistically, the overall picture is not uniformly bad. But there is much space for improvement in its operation—which is why this book seeks to identify and correct the dubious morality of the modern administrative state.

The situation in administrative law took a turn for the better just as this book was about to go to press, when the Trump Administration issued two executive orders, both of which are intent on promoting the rule of law. Speaking very broadly, these executive orders seek to cut back on administrative agencies' all-too-common practice of issuing "guidances" that can be held over the heads of private parties without going through the usual notice-and-comment rulemaking as required under the Administrative Procedure Act. Guidances allow agencies to often hold, in the words of the first executive order, an "implicit threat of an enforcement action if the regulated public does not comply."[15] The new executive orders hold, in the words of the second executive order, that "[a]n agency may not seek judicial deference to its interpretation of a document arising out of litigation"[16] unless it has been properly vetted. The exact import of these orders is as yet unclear, but it is not too early to say that their publication represents an important effort to rein in the modern administrative state.

ENDNOTES

1. *See, e.g.,* Richard A. Epstein, DESIGN FOR LIBERTY: PRIVATE PROPERTY, PUBLIC ADMINISTRATION, AND THE RULE OF LAW, 149-171 (Harvard U. Press, 2011).

2. 5 U.S.C. §§ 551–559.

3. Cass R. Sunstein and Adrian Vermeule, *The Morality of Administrative Law,* 131 HARV. L. REV. 1924 (2018).

4. Lon L. Fuller, THE MORALITY OF LAW (2d ed. 1969) (Yale U. Press, 1964).

5. Gillian Metzger, *1930s Redux: The Administrative State Under Siege,* 131 HARV. L. REV. 1 (2017).

6. Aditya Bamzai, *The Origins of Judicial Deference to Executive Interpretation,* 126 YALE L.J. 908, 912–13, 912 n.5 (2017).

7. 276 U.S. 394 (1928) (discussed *infra* Part 2, at 48-49).

8. 319 U.S. 190 (1943).

9. 325 U.S. 410 (1945).

10. 519 U.S. 452 (1997).

11. 467 U.S. 837 (1984).

12. 463 U.S. 29 (1983).

13. 318 U.S. 80 (1943).

14. 332 U.S. 194 (1947).

15. Executive Order 13891 of Oct. 9, 2019, Promoting the Rule of Law Through Improved Agency Guidance Documents, 84 Fed. Reg. 55235 (Oct. 15, 2019), *available at* https://www.federalregister.gov/presidential-documents/executive-orders/donald-trump/2019.

16. Executive Order 13892 of Oct. 9, 2019, Promoting the Rule of Law Through Transparency and Fairness in Civil Administrative Enforcement and Adjudication, 84 Fed. Reg., 55239 (Oct. 15, 2019), *available at* https://www.federalregister.gov/presidential-documents/executive-orders/donald-trump/2019.

PART 1

THE DEBATE OVER THE MODERN ADMINISTRATIVE STATE

T he current status of modern administrative law is the subject of intense and protracted intellectual debate. This debate is not over small issues or legal niceties. It is the latest and most prominent manifestation of a deep and long-simmering disagreement.

On one side lie the modern progressives, who by and large champion a large administrative state and are determined to ensure that certain key agencies retain broad discretion to implement major social and institutional reforms. On the other side lie the defenders of what I call the classical liberal tradition, whose belief in private property, freedom of contract, and limited government lead them to take the opposite position. In the view of the latter, administrative agencies should be closely monitored in their actions to reduce the likelihood that they will initiate reforms that further undermine key elements of a sound social and legal polity. So understood, the debate over administrative law is a continuation of the debate over the legitimacy of the constitutional revolution that culminated in the transformative Supreme Court decisions of the 1936–37 term.[1]

The issue today is not just one of academic speculation but one that has spilled over into the realm of high politics. The recent appointments of Justices Neil Gorsuch and Brett Kavanaugh signal a willingness on the part of major elements of the conservative and libertarian movements to return to first principles in examining the foundations of the administrative state. The most tangible signs that this major shift is afoot are found in the roster of cases now before the Supreme Court.

During the 2018–19 term, a divided Court handed down two major decisions: *Gundy v. United States*,[2] which leaves the status of the non-delegation doctrine very much up for grabs in the coming years; and *Kisor v. Wilkie*,[3] in which a divided Court first reexamined, and then transformed, two of the Court's previous major administrative law decisions—*Auer v. Robbins*[4] and *Bowles v. Seminole Rock & Sand Co.*[5]—so that today it is no longer clear that they unfailingly instruct the courts to defer to administrative agencies' interpretations of their own rules. Left undisturbed, at least for now, are other basic legal pillars of the administrative state, which have also been subject to renewed attack. This list includes the most storied decisions in modern administrative law: *Chevron U.S.A. Inc. v. Natural Resources Defense Council*,[6] *National Cable & Telecommunications v. Brand X Internet Services*,[7] and *Motor Vehicle Manufacturers Association v. State Farm Mutual Automobile Insurance Co.*[8] The first two decisions instruct courts to defer to administrative agencies' interpretations of ambiguous statutes. The third instructs courts to give a "hard look" at complex factual findings made by administrative agencies.

Even before his elevation to the Supreme Court, now-Justice Neil Gorsuch attacked both *Chevron* and *Brand X* in uncompromising form. In his opening salvo in *Gutierrez-Brizuela v. Lynch*, he declares:

> There's an elephant in the room with us today. We have studiously attempted to work our way around it and even left it unremarked. But the fact is *Chevron* and *Brand X* permit executive bureaucracies to swallow huge amounts of core judicial and legislative power and concentrate federal power in a way that seems more than a little difficult to square with the Constitution of the framers' design. Maybe the time has come to face the behemoth.[9]

On the academic side, perhaps the most insistent and vociferous critic of the modern administrative state has been Professor Philip Hamburger. He has vigorously questioned the very lawfulness of the administrative state,[10] describing it as "unlawful," "extralegal," and "supralegal," resulting in the "exercise of power outside and above the law."[11] In a somewhat more cautious vein, Peter Wallison has argued in his recent book, *Judicial Fortitude: The Last Chance to Rein in the*

Administrative State,[12] that modern administrative law is fast approaching a tipping point beyond which it may not be possible to rein in the administrative state. Consistent with other critics, Wallison argues that the progressive preference for powerful administrative agencies leads to a dangerous combination of legislative and executive power that the courts are unwilling to control, notwithstanding the serious threat that this combined power poses to individual liberty and the rule of law.[13] I have also expressed my dissatisfaction with many features of the administrative state, most notably its excessive use of guidance documents that are said to instruct but instead often bind.[14] I have also criticized the use of ad hoc tribunals located inside administrative agencies to decide questions that should be, and would be better, decided by independent tribunals in the form of Article I or Article III courts.[15]

Not surprisingly, the conservative and libertarian critique of the modern administrative state has been met by spirited defenses of the status quo. Professor Gillian Metzger titled her foreword to the November 2017 issue of the *Harvard Law Review* "1930s Redux: The Administrative State Under Siege."[16] Her reference to the 1930s invokes memories of what she perceives as the bad old days, before the New Deal constitutional revolution—before the three key decisions that transformed the structure of modern American constitutional and administrative law. The first of these decisions was *Humphrey's Executor v. United States*, in 1935, which bestowed a constitutional blessing upon independent federal agencies.[17] Two years later, the Supreme Court handed down *NLRB v. Jones & Laughlin Steel Corp.*[18] and *West Coast Hotel Co. v. Parrish*[19] during its epic 1936–37 term. The former rubber-stamped a vastly expanded federal power under the Constitution's Commerce Clause, and the latter sharply reduced the level of constitutional protections afforded to economic liberties. Taken together, these three cases ushered in an age of vastly expanded federal authority. The cases' full impact was felt only after the conclusion of World War II, with the overwhelming passage by a voice vote of the Administrative Procedure Act of 1946 (APA).[20] In line with most academics, Metzger throws her lot in with the post–New Deal status quo.

A more philosophical defense of the modern administrative state has been offered by Professors Cass Sunstein and Adrian Vermeule in their article "The Morality of Administrative Law."[21] Their firm (if qualified) defense of administrative law invokes Professor Lon L. Fuller's influential book, *The Morality of Law*.[22] Fuller was much concerned with the general question of the minimum requisites of the rule of law, provided in the first instance by his imaginary lawgiver "Rex." Although administrative law was not Fuller's main focus, Sunstein and Vermeule extend the author's general analysis of the "internal morality" of law to administrative agencies. In so doing, they acknowledge inconsistencies between Fuller's minimum requisites and modern administrative law but insist nevertheless that many of these gaps are justified by the special imperatives of the administrative state.

The possible permutations on the matter of administrative law also include the forthcoming article "Neoclassical Administrative Law," by Professor Jeffrey Pojanowski, the title of which explains how much deference a court should grant the decisions of an administrative agency, and why.[23] In putting forward his position, Pojanowski separates his view from what he identifies as the three regnant traditions of modern administrative law. The first is the unapologetic embrace of the large administrative state, a camp to which he correctly assigns the work of Metzger.[24] At the opposite pole, Pojanowski places the administrative skeptics such as Hamburger, who insists that "courts are obliged to fulfill their judicial duty to say what the law is, even if (or especially if!) doing so undermines the regnant administrative state."[25] Thinkers of this sort uniformly reject *Chevron* and also show a rising uneasiness with "half-measures," including *Skidmore* deference.[26]

The third variant, which Pojanowski calls "administrative pragmatism," requires the most explication. The notion invokes a "Legal Process–style development of administrative common law doctrine that implements or supplements positive law like the APA or the Constitution."[27] Incremental improvements by consensus is a technique celebrated by, and closely associated with, the legal-process school of the 1950s, embodied chiefly in the work of Henry Hart and Albert Sacks,[28] who stressed the importance of matching the right institution with the right policy choice—a principle that they applied as much, if not more, to ordinary private-law disputes.

One case examined by Hart and Sacks is *Norway Plains Co. v. Boston & Maine Railroad*,[29] in which Chief Justice Lemuel Shaw reviewed the common law liability rule for common carriers in situations where goods are lost or damaged after they reach their destination. As explained by William Eskridge, Jr. and Philip Frickey, Hart and Sacks' exercise was to trace "the evolution of carrier liability rules as established by private behavior, common law regulation in and after *Norway Plains* legislation, and, finally, administrative regulation."[30] That is, they suggest Hart and Sacks' material studied the lineage between common law rules and their encoding or modification in statute. In the cases Hart and Sacks covered, the statutory variations are often incremental changes to a particular rule, often based upon some perceived industry or public awareness of the incompleteness or inadequacy of the common law rule. Incremental change, not legal revolution, is the dominant theme. Clearly, this narrative speaks of an important set of transformations in law, but precisely because of its emphasis on legal process, the efficiency properties of the various rules are not its main focus. This approach will not work well, however, with comprehensive statutory schemes like those now in place for environmental and employment law, which are not designed to flesh out common law principles but instead largely reject and replace them.

In working through these legal-process materials, Pojanowski does not rely on the notion—made current by Aditya Bamzai, and consistent with *Norway Plains*—that 19th-century administrative law acted in harmony with the dominant common law. The notion of such shared principles placed great weight on consistent administrative interpretations of statutory and regulatory language,[31] which made courts deeply suspicious of any administrative reversals of past practice—the polar opposite of the flip-flops allowed under *Chevron* and *Auer*. Instead, Pojanowski seeks to move down a fourth neoclassical path. In contrast to the earlier traditions, his version of administrative law gives greater weight to separation-of-powers and rule-of-law concerns. He thus puts his own position forward as follows:

> In short, the neoclassical approach to judicial review of legal questions divvies up what conventional administrative law deems [*Chevron*] "Step Two" into domains of (1) de novo or *Skidmore* review and (2) deferential review of policymaking. The neoclassicist extends the domain of [*Chevron*] "Step One" to absorb legal questions upon which reasonable

parties could disagree, while shifting over to the domain of arbitrary-and-capricious review questions unamenable to formal legal craft.[32]

A few comments are in order. His reference to "Step Two" review shows that Pojanowski accepts the conventional wisdom that no deference is owed to any administrative agency when the law is clear and unambiguous. But, as always, that proposition still leaves open the question of meta-ambiguity: Is there any agreement on when a particular statutory or regulatory text is so clear that Step Two can be avoided? Once he gets into that domain, though, his solution takes what I regard as an initial correct step when it separates the analysis into two parts. The first deals with the possibility of ambiguity on questions of law, and the second deals with the myriad uncertainties on matters of fact, with mixed questions of fact and law hovering in between. And his use of the term "neoclassical" clearly appeals to my own sensibilities because it shows a systematic uneasiness with the continued expansion of the administrative state.

Nonetheless, the major shortcoming of Pojanowski's approach is its acceptance of a fatal ambiguity in the standard of review for legal questions. De novo review is flatly inconsistent with so-called *Skidmore* deference that asks courts to show respect for the considered interpretations of administrative agencies. But the traditional separation between questions of law and questions of fact requires, in my view, that *all* questions of law be decided de novo, whether the issues arise out of contract, regulation, statute, or constitution. His approach avoids the need to figure out the so-called *Chevron* "Step Zero" question and seeks to determine which kinds of government documents deserve judicial discretion and which do not.[33] By way of example, the dispute in *United States v. Mead Corp.*[34] arose out of a classic 19th-century-type question over the tariff classification of day planners. The non-momentous issue was whether loose-leaf binders should be placed in the same tariff category as bound diaries. This classic legal-classification dispute is generally regarded as a question of law. Nonetheless, Justice David Souter held that *Chevron* deference was not required for these writings. Instead, they were owed *Skidmore* deference, meaning the agency "is entitled to claim respect according to its persuasiveness,"[35] a standard so fluid that it is just easier to treat the issue as a matter of law. Where the government's position is strong under the law, it does not need to seek deference. And where it is weak, the government should not receive it.

At this point, it is critical to mention a single systematic error that pervades all these approaches: the high level of abstraction at which the analysis is conducted. Some of the cases at issue are small matters that are, and should be, resolved as part of the vast mass of routine administrative actions outside the purview of the courts. Others are momentous decisions in which the application of deference norms can radically transform the operation of major economic or social programs within the United States.

There is no simple way to get at this issue, and the constant exchanges in scholarly journals about applicable standards taken out of context do nothing to inform the debate. The proper study of administrative law does not flit from doctrinal peak to doctrinal peak. It must connect abstract doctrines with the concrete realities of individual cases, their facts, and the applicable statutory and regulatory frameworks. Once that is done, it becomes clear that the modern invocation of the deference principle, whether under the guise of *Chevron* or *Skidmore*, is far greater than commonly acknowledged. The basic legal currency is debased by a crude form of linguistic skepticism that expands the area of arguable ambiguity and thus enhances the power of administrators who have powerful social agendas of their own.

All this activity takes place against a social background in which the growth of the administrative state followed hard on the heels of the triumph of New Deal progressivism. As the major constitutional impediments to the growth of the administrative state were removed, a general uneasiness with the newly expanded federal government led to APA. Inspired in part by James Landis's transformational 1938 book, *The Administrative Process*,[36] Congress enacted APA in June 1946, even though all serious consideration of administrative law was put on hold during the war. But that matter returned to the top of the political agenda thereafter—given the need to introduce some judicial oversight to deal with the manifold actions of the modern administrative state, which had attracted prolonged criticisms from Republicans and Southern Democrats.

Indeed, it is best to think of APA as a quasi-constitutional settlement in the wake of the constitutional revolution put into place a decade earlier. There was some retrenchment of the power of the administrative state, but the three major developments of the previous decade remained intact: the gaining of independence by administrative agencies; the expansion of federal power under the Commerce Clause; and the trimming down of the protection afforded to economic liberties.

In this study, I do not take—because I do not believe in—a revivalist position that calls for the wholesale abolition of the administrative state. Even with my strong classical liberal orientation, I consider the existence of some degree of an administrative state to be, and to have been from the beginning, an indispensable part of any mature system of law. But this approach does not endorse the system of administrative law that we have today. It is important to stress that a defense of the *existence* of the administrative state should never be confused with a defense of all the *practices* deployed in the modern administrative state, many of which, in my view, should be sharply curtailed.

Long before the recent wave of judicial and academic criticism, Landis himself expressed many misgivings about the turn of administrative law in the years following the adoption of APA. He came to believe that the convoluted flyspecking of administrative directives was inconsistent with the more modest ambition of APA procedures, which was to alert relevant parties as to the kinds of claims that were to be made by an agency, not to give the reviewing court a complete syllabus of each and every source of information that would, or might, be introduced to deal with the problem.[37]

Yet just that tendency was most evident in the U.S. Court of Appeals for the D.C. Circuit, which, at its peak influence during the 1970s, routinely engaged in these activities when hearing appeals from administrative actions. Section 553(b) of APA states only that any notice of proposed rulemaking should contain "3) either the terms or substance of the proposed rule or a description of the subjects and issues involved." Given its natural meaning, this simple injunction requires, at most, a one- or two-sentence explanation of the topic under study, so that people can then submit evidence that they think relevant to the agency inquiry. But early interpretations of APA transformed this modest provision into an open warrant for constant second-guessing of agencies on technical and factual matters that Congress generally left to administrative determination. On these matters, agencies are entitled to more deference than when they are addressing the interpretation of statutes and regulations, where de novo review is contemplated by Section 706 of APA.[38]

My main focus here is not on the serious constitutional objections to the modern administrative state based on principles of the separation of powers; I have recently addressed these concerns elsewhere and, by and large, have agreed with Justice Neil Gorsuch.[39] Rather, this persistent constitutional unease with modern administrative law rightly should, and does, call for a closer examination of the fundamental organization of the administrative state as it has emerged in the decades since the passage of APA more than 70 years ago.

My thesis is that modern administrative law has taken major false steps in every area of judicial oversight of administrative action. Put bluntly, the seminal cases of *Chevron* and *State Farm* get the basic distribution of powers between courts and agencies precisely backward: courts are too deferential on questions of law and too interventionist on matters of fact.

To demonstrate this thesis, this book proceeds as follows: Part 2 sets out the framework. I accept Fuller's claim that rule-of-law virtues are critical to the soundness of any legal system. But I reject Fuller's further claim that the rule of law is agnostic between different substantive legal systems and can, in practice, work equally well across all forms of substantive law. The rule of law, I explain, meshes more closely with the more limited government found in traditional legal systems than with the modern administrative state.

In Part 3, I examine the historical practices of the administrative state prior to the rise of New Deal constitutionalism and largely acquit them of any charge of the aggrandizement of administrative power.

The core of the book lies in Part 4, which deals with all the various approaches that are taken to questions of law under APA. This section of the book deals with *Chevron* and the variations on that doctrine raised by the major question doctrine. Thereafter, Part 4 covers other forms of deference associated with such key cases as *Seminole Rock, Auer v. Rob-*

bins, *Gloucester County*, and, most recently, *Kisor v. Wilkie*, which may well upend the entire deferential structure to which that very case paid lip service.

In Part 5, I examine in detail modern administrative law and the various hot-button issues that give it its shape: bias and notice, nondelegation, deference, consistency and retroactivity, and standards of arbitrary and capricious review of agency decision making.

The overall critique rests on two key propositions. The first is that on questions of law, the current doctrine affords powerful administrators too much latitude in interpreting the rules that allow them to issue regulations and enforce statutes. The second proposition is that on questions of fact, the current doctrine often makes the opposite mistake: it allows unreasonable second-guessing by courts of factual determinations that are better made by administrative agencies.

Reduced to a single sentence, the appropriate response to these diverse issues is to think of administrative agencies as a functional substitute for district courts, whose legal determinations are subject to de novo review but whose factual determinations are generally upheld so long as there is substantial evidence in their favor. There are obvious differences between courts and agencies, but the key correspondence between the two is that they both hear a case at first instance, and thus interact in the same fashion with the appellate courts that oversee their decisions. If administrative agencies are as expert at matters of law as is claimed—and sometimes they are—they do not need the benefit of special rules to make their case. They can defend themselves on the merits without the benefit of deference to their legal judgments.

A FRAMEWORK FOR ALL ADMINISTRATIVE LAW

Rule-of-Law Basics

One of the virtues of the Sunstein-Vermeule approach is that it offers a conceptual framework by which to evaluate the rules of the administrative state. Sunstein and Vermeule use Fuller's *The Morality of Law* as a benchmark for understanding modern administrative law. Fuller asserts that the moral framework for evaluating the rule of law should be independent of any assessment of the substance of the rules in question. He writes: "In presenting my analysis of the law's internal morality I have insisted that it is, over a wide range of issues, indifferent toward the substantive aims of law and is ready to serve a variety of such aims with equal efficacy."[40] There is little doubt that one of the attractions of Fuller's rule-of-law thinking is that it purports to be consistent with every system of political thought. But the underlying reality is different. I shall first explain the strengths and omissions of Fuller's rule-of-law discussion. Thereafter, I shall explain how Fuller's rule-of-law requirements are more easily satisfied under a classical liberal system of contract, property, tort, and eminent domain than under any modern progressive system.

Fuller on the Rule of Law

Fuller develops his rule-of-law framework by imagining a mythical but inept ruler, Rex, who introduces a misguided system of reforms with the best of intentions:

> Rex's bungling career as a legislator and judge illustrates that the attempt to create and maintain a system of legal rules may miscarry in at least eight ways; there are in this enterprise, if you will, eight distinct routes to disaster. The first and most obvious lies in the failure to achieve rules at all, so that every issue must be decided on an ad hoc basis. The other routes are: (2) a failure to publicize, or to least make available to the affected party, the rules he is expected to observe; (3) the abuse of retroactive legislation, which cannot itself guide action, but undercuts the integrity of rules prospective in effect, since it puts them under the threat of retrospective change; (4) a failure to make rules understandable; (5) the enactment of contradictory rules or (6) rules that require conduct beyond the powers of the affected party; (7) introducing such frequent changes in the rules that the subject cannot orient his action

by them; and, finally, (8) a failure of congruence between the rules as announced and their actual administration.[41]

Under Fuller's framework, then, any system of law—however well-intentioned—will fail because it makes these common errors. Yet in one sense, his list of failures is incomplete. But for the moment, it is sufficient to note that the modern administrative state, more often than not, is guilty of these failures. The basic elements of the indictment are clear enough. Often, administrative agencies engage in ad hoc decision making; fail to give adequate notice of the applicable law; burden private parties with inordinate demands for information of, at best, tangential relevance to the agency's statutory mission; and impose rules or commands that are often unclear, erratic, contradictory, or unduly burdensome.

Worse still, the modern administrative state thrives on the very sort of retroactive rules that Fuller deplores: "Taken by itself, and in abstraction from its possible function in a system of laws that are largely prospective, a retroactive law is truly a monstrosity."[42] He goes on to state:

> Surely the very essence of the Rule of Law is that in acting upon the citizens (by putting him in jail, for example, or declaring invalid a deed under which he claims title to property) a government will faithfully apply rules previously declared as those to be followed by the citizen and as being determinative of his rights and duties. If the Rule of Law does not mean this, it means nothing.[43]

To be sure, Fuller did not think that the prohibition against retroactive legislation was absolute, but his exceptions only confirm the basic injustice of the redistributive practices that he attacks. For example, Fuller identifies several narrow uses of "curative laws" as legitimate exercises of retroactivity. These curative laws are designed to correct earlier inadvertent mistakes in "conveyancing"[44]—the transfer of legal title to real property—and are the kinds of rules that merit his support "because they heal infringements of the principle that like cases should receive like treatment."[45]

There is another way to put the point. The great risk of retroactive changes in the law is that they will introduce an illicit wealth transfer between parties, which operates like a taking without just compensation. Thus, if X owes Y \$100, the government is not free to cancel that debt by implementing a retroactive change in the law that blocks any collection by the creditor. Under Fuller's worldview, this action would be no different from a rule that permitted Y to collect the debt from X, and thereafter decreed a \$100 tax or impost on Y, the proceeds of which would then have to be paid to X. The situation would not be improved if this were made into a general rule for all persons similarly situated as X and Y; the generalization would only compound the error.[46] In contrast, curative laws have precisely the opposite effect—namely, to reinforce the system of private rights by protecting them from inadvertent error.

Fuller's Notable Omissions

Oddly, however, Fuller does not pay attention to certain key structural issues that are relevant to the rule of law but are noticeably lacking in modern administrative decision making. He omits two of the most ancient and hardy maxims in the rule-of-law literature that date back to Roman times. The first is *Nemo judex in causa sua*: "No one should be a judge in his own case." This maxim generalizes into a prohibition against bias in a decision maker, so that government officials should not be allowed to adjudicate a case in which they have a personal, financial, or institutional stake in the outcome, a situation that is all too often the case for mission-driven administrative law judges. The second core maxim that Fuller ignores is *Audi alteram partem*: "Hear the other side." In other words, a court or tribunal should hear from both sides to a dispute before rendering its decision. This simple procedural protection helps guard against hasty and erroneous decisions based on incomplete information. And that ideal, in turn, requires that administrative agencies develop institutional arrangements that are adequate to the task at hand, including representation by counsel and the right to cross-examination.

These Roman maxims are echoed in Enlightenment thought about the status of the social contract. For example, John Locke famously wrote that the state of nature "wants an *establish'd*, settled and known *law*, received and allowed by . . . common measure to decide all controversies between [men]."[47] There is thus a need for rules that are "plain and intelligible,"[48] which can achieve their goal only if applied before a "*known and indifferent Judge*, with authority to determine all differences according to the established law."[49] Many of these same themes are echoed in the work of Friedrich Hayek.[50] Thus, while a close affinity between the rule of law and classical liberal beliefs in private property, freedom of contract, and limited government is not logically necessary, it is also not wholly fortuitous. Rather, the source of the connection lies in the relative ease with which it is possible to implement the rule of law in legal systems that place a strong emphasis on private property, voluntary contract, and robust eminent-domain protections as the key considerations of social organization.

The Empirical Link Between Substance and Procedure

As I will describe in Part 3, the traditional systems of administrative law did well under the various rule-of-law measures articulated by Fuller. As I go on to show, modern administrative law often fails under these same tests. But it is far from obvious whether modern administrative law *can* meet Fuller's constraints, and it is important to see why.

One great attraction of Fuller's nonsubstantive rules is their universal appeal across the political spectrum. Virtually no one of any political persuasion thinks that the operation of any legal system could be improved by omitting any of the precautions that he identifies. But to that list must be added the elementary procedural due-process rules that he omits, relating to bias and the opportunity to be heard. So it is that all sides in the political debate seek to seize the high ground by announcing that they are for the rule of law.

It is true that adhering to the rule of law makes any legal system better than it might otherwise be. But there is a very different question of whether the *effectiveness* of the rule-of-law constraint is, or can be, kept *independent* of the substantive rights protected by the system, which are characterized chiefly by the rules of property, contract, and tort. A second question, to which Fuller pays scant attention, is how these rules translate into the administrative setting.

Property

Turning to the first of these substantive issues, there is a historical affinity of classical liberal writers to the rule of law, which is a center-piece in the writing of such eminent thinkers as Locke and Hayek. As noted earlier, this connection is neither necessary nor fortuitous. Empirically, the source of the connection lies in the relative ease with which it is possible to implement the rule of law in legal systems that place a strong emphasis on private property, voluntary contract, and robust eminent-domain protections.

The interconnection between property rights and the rule of law runs as follows: the rules of private property give one person the exclusive rights to possess, use, and dispose of any tangible thing. These rights bind everyone else in the world, and hence are commonly called "rights in rem," from the Latin, meaning rights "in the thing," by which is meant rights that bind all the world with respect to the thing over which there is a determinate owner. Once that exclusive ownership is created, rules of contract allow individuals to pick their own trading partners in ways that allow for social gains from exchange and the co-operation of capital and labor within this framework. Two or more contracting parties may alter their entitlements among themselves as they see fit, so long as they do not thereby truncate the rights of any third parties. Their exchanges thus produce, as a first approximation, gains for themselves as well as positive opportunities for third parties. There are obvious complications with certain forms of common property, including key resources such as water, which require limitations on freedom of contract in areas vulnerable to monopolization or cartelization. But I ignore those complications here in order to get to the key implications for the rule of law, which, in dealing with private property, consist of three salient virtues that match Fuller's concern for a well-functioning legal system: property rights must be well established, invariant with respect to changes in wealth, and scalable.[51]

First, the legal regime must be constant over time in its demand that all other persons forbear from entrance upon or destruction of the property of another. The forbearance claim—"Keep off, don't pollute"—is easy to understand, so notification to the world is safely presumed and need not be especially advertised. No one needs to be told, time and again, "Thou shalt not kill or steal." Hence for these prohibitions, the maxim *Ignorantia juris non excusat*—"Ignorance of the law is no excuse"—easily dovetails into a sound legal order. Since everyone knows the norm, there is no need to announce specially the general prohibitions. But when it comes to various statutory commands—for example, that people register with the local police office when they move into a new community—the concern with excusable ignorance now becomes a salient issue, giving rise to serious rule-of-law concerns.[52]

Second, any system of property rights must be largely *invariant* to changes, up or down, in individual or social wealth. The forbearance norm works well in all cases, so that the specification of the rights rarely has to change as a function of the state of relative economic or technological development. The rule is not universal, but the needed adaptations are few, which include the adoption of an overflight rule with the advent of plane transportation.

Before the advent of commercial flights, the *ad coelum* rule held that the owner of any piece of property also owned the depths below the surface as well as the skies above it, such that an airplane passing overhead would constitute a trespass. That rule remains largely in effect with a minimum height below which aircraft cannot fly and a new set of property rights for overflights. In effect, this transformation is a powerful confirmation of Harold Demsetz's famous thesis, which explains how property-rights systems evolve in order to "internalize" externalities that existed in previous regimes but have been made more costly because of technological change.[53] In this case, that transformation is driven by the need to prevent the endless holdouts and blockades that would emerge if the ownership of small plots of land, which make eminently good sense for productive uses like farming and manufacture, were projected into the upper airspace. Preventing these holdouts carries with it little social danger because the transformation produces such huge net benefits that no one need inquire into its distributional consequences—everyone benefits from the right to fly over everyone else's property, so there is no need to compensate those who have suffered such minor "trespasses" because they have already received implicit in-kind compensation.[54]

To treat the property right here as absolutely inviolable and require consent or compensation for these small-scale, often imperceptible, trespasses would create an insoluble coordination problem that would make all commercial flight unviable. But most ordinary familial and commercial transactions do not raise those types of formidable coordination problems, so that the basic bundle of property rights of exclusive possession, use, and disposition is as serviceable today as it was in Roman times, notwithstanding the enormous changes in social wealth that have occurred.

Third, private property must be fully *scalable*. Standard obligations to forbear apply to any social organization larger than the family clan. But the rules remain remarkably constant, whether the relevant polity has a thousand members or is 10 million strong. Accordingly, there is no reason to identify any transition point between different sets of rules or to specify what those different rules should be as societies grow or shrink.

It is now an easy matter to see how this fundamental property system maps onto the foundation of the rule of law. It is not ad hoc; it imposes no burdens of notice; it does not allow for retroactive changes. It is easily understandable; it contains no internal contradictions; it makes no exceptional demands on ordinary individuals; it reduces the slippage between articulation and administration; and, of course, it makes it easier to administer the rules without bias and reduces the number of disputed issues for which a hearing is required.

Freedom of Contract

The second part of the classical liberal system involves the creation and enforcement of contract rights. In contrast to rights in rem, these contractual rights are often called "rights in personam" because, unlike property rights, they impose a denser set of obligations on a narrower set of persons—namely, only those who voluntarily assume them. Because the parties to a contract voluntarily select one another, there is an increased likelihood that they will abide by the same nonlegal norms and sanctions, which encourages high levels of cooperation and thus contractual compliance. This, in turn, reduces the likelihood of a dispute taking place. A simple set of formalities—a requirement that all transactions be put into writing, and a recordation requirement—can clarify the relationships ex ante so as to reduce the pressures on the enforcement system ex post without imposing any limitations on the substantive terms of the deal.

If a dispute does take place, a strong regime of freedom of contract reduces the pressure on courts to go beyond the standard rules of contractual interpretation, which include implied terms arising from the course of dealing between the parties as well as the industry standards that played such a large part in enriching the fabric of law in the 19th century.[55] But if we weaken the support for freedom of contract, it becomes more difficult to implement the rule of law. It is no small feat to orchestrate a series of contractual limitations based on the assumption that the inequality of bargaining power requires the state to intervene to alter the terms on some normative theory, including, as will become evident, under the Fair Labor Standards Act of 1938, which imposes extensive legal rules on minimum wages and overtime work.[56] By opening the door to government interference in the terms to which the parties voluntarily agreed, regimes that reject a strong conception of freedom of contract invariably produce situations in which the legal rights of contractual counterparties are vitiated.

Eminent Domain

The completeness of the common law system of entitlements embedded in the classical liberal system also carries over to the problem of dealing with eminent domain. Under the classical liberal position, all the incidents of property—dealing with possession, use, development, and disposition—receive equal protection because they carry equal weight in the basic scheme. Thus, the removal of any given right has to be justified by showing that doing so was needed to prevent some wrong against another person—the "police power" justifications—or was offset by some return benefit in kind, equal to or greater than the property right taken away.[57] Within these restrictions, the state always retains the option to take property, so long as it is then utilized for a public use. But the exercise of this option is subject to a price constraint: the state is required by the Fifth Amendment to pay for what it takes. In effect, the Fifth Amendment imposes a price constraint on the ability of the government to exercise its option to take private property. This constraint limits the ability of government to get something for nothing, which, in turn, forces it to take into account the estimated costs that its actions impose on others, as well as the claimed benefits for the world at large. And that constraint limits the government's discretion and thus reduces the likelihood that the government can favor in an ad hoc way some interests over others.

The moment when the discipline of this price constraint on eminent domain falters, it becomes possible for the state to use its powers to transfer huge amounts of wealth from one party to another.[58] Zoning and rent control, for example, dramatically enable the state to strip private property of its economic value without paying for the attendant private losses. In *Penn Central Transportation Co. v. City of New York*,[59] the Court adopted a low, or "rational basis," level of scrutiny for regulatory takings—that is, one that involves diminutions in the value of private property stemming specifically from the imposition of adverse government regulations. By using two different definitions of *private property*—one for private disputes and the other for government takings—the legal regime[60] has created doctrinal inconsistencies and contradictions that cannot withstand the slightest scrutiny. Thus, air rights are fully protected under New York law from private interference but can be taken without any compensation by either the state or the federal government, so long as doing so does not offend some undefined set of "investment-backed" expectations.[61] This inconsistency in definition is exactly the kind of abuse that Fuller laments. From this one unprincipled decision, the erosion of classical liberal eminent-domain protections has spread across the entire legal system and far beyond land-use cases, including to matters of financial regulation, such as artificial government measures designed to suck away the entire value held by the private shareholders of the two leading government-sponsored enterprises, Fannie Mae and Freddie Mac.[62]

The traditional classical liberal position of protecting private property from government taking increases the odds that various forms of government action will produce some net social benefit. But as it stands, it does not indicate when such a benefit arises, or how it ought to be distributed. The doctrine of unconstitutional conditions seeks to fill that void by stipulating that the gains in question should be divided pro rata among the parties to a particular scheme so as to prevent factional strife over gains from leading to their dissipation.[63]

This pro-rata limitation imposes a fixed and uniform division on both the gains and losses from any particular project. If the former comes to pass, the unconstitutional-conditions doctrine prevents the government from allocating all the gains of a positive-sum project to any particular parties, even if, after the dust has settled, the other parties are left with assets worth as much as those that they possessed before the government intervention. This pro-rata allocation of the potential surplus prevents factional activity by all parties seeking to garner a larger portion of the gain. Such strategic behavior is always a negative sum. It results in no increase in wealth and, in fact, always results in a dissipation of the anticipated surplus, owing to the costs of conflict over its division. The pro-rata requirement also works to mitigate project losses, since no one will seek to shrink the overall pie if his or her slice will be shrunk by virtue of that activity. But if the requirement is not imposed, well-situated players may maneuver to garner a larger share of a smaller pie, which means all the others are left with a smaller share.

The standard operation of the pro-rata requirement thus does not mandate the distribution of losses. Rather, the threat of that loss usually stops the factional activity in its tracks. So this requirement works like that of explicit compensation: certain transactions never take place because the cost of setting them up is too high, given that they are now borne by the parties who hope to obtain the gain. Once again, this property-rights definition works with the traditional system of eminent domain to cabin the level of discretion in public officials, and the reduction in this discretion makes it easier to administer a system of entitlements that comport with the rule of law.

Thus, taken as a whole, the major features of the classical liberal system are intended to leave government with the discretion needed to run a society while tamping down on its ability to deploy state powers for partisan advantage. In the pages that follow, I will apply the rule-of-law framework to evaluate the traditional and modern forms of the administrative state. I find that the former satisfies the framework's constraints in a way that the latter does not.

ENDNOTES

1. For my take, *see* Richard A. Epstein, How Progressives Rewrote the Constitution (Cato Inst., 2006) (detailing the major shifts in the expansion of federalism and the rejection of constitutional protection for economic liberties).

2. *Gundy v. United States,* 139 S. Ct. 2116 (2019).

3. I signed a brief urging the reversal of *Auer.* 588 U.S. __ (2019), Brief for the Cato Inst. et al. as Amici Curiae Supporting Petitioner, Kisor v. Wilkie, (No. 18-15), *available at* https://www.supremecourt.gov/DocketPDF/18/18-15/86530/20190131140447855_Kisor%20merits.pdf. Much of the brief was influenced by Jonathan H. Adler, *Auer Evasions,* 16 Geo. J.L. & Pub. Pol'y 1 (2018).

4. *Auer v. Robbins,* 519 U.S. 452 (1997).

5. *Bowles v. Seminole Rock & Sand Co.,* 325 U.S. 410 (1945).

6. *Chevron U.S.A. Inc. v. Nat'l Res. Def. Council,* 467 U.S. 837 (1984).

7. *Nat'l Cable & Telecomm. v. Brand X Internet Servs.,* 545 U.S. 967 (2005).

8. *Motor Vehicle Mfrs. Ass'n v. State Farm Mut. Auto. Ins. Co.,* 463 U.S. 29 (1983).

9. *Gutierrez-Brizuela v. Lynch,* 834 F.3d 1142, 1149 (10th Cir. 2016) (Gorsuch, J., concurring) (concurring in his own majority opinion with a more limited opinion critiquing current law).

10. Philip Hamburger, Is Administrative Law Unlawful? (U. of Chicago P., 2014). For a stern critique offering a resounding no, *see* Adrian Vermeule, *'No' Review of Philip Hamburger, 'Is Administrative Law Unlawful?',* 93 Tex. L. Rev. 1547 (2015).

11. Hamburger, *supra* note 10, at 6–7, as attacked by Gillian E. Metzger, *Foreword: 1930s Redux: The Administrative State Under Siege,* 131 Harv. L. Rev. 1, 34–35 (2017).

12. Peter Wallison, Judicial Fortitude: The Last Chance to Rein in the Administrative State (Encounter Books, 2018).

13. *Id.* at xii.

14. Richard A. Epstein, *The Role of Guidances in Modern Administrative Procedure: The Case for De Novo Review,* 8 J. Legal Analysis 47 (2016).

15. Richard A. Epstein, *Structural Protections for Individual Rights: The Indispensable Role of Independent Federal Courts in the Administrative State,* 26 Geo. Mason L. Rev. (forthcoming 2019). I use the phrase "independent tribunals" because in my view, the fixed terms of many Article I (legislative) courts work as well as, if not better than, the current life tenure given to judges in Article III courts.

16. *See generally* Metzger, *supra* note 11.

17. *Humphrey's Ex'r v. United States,* 295 U.S. 602 (1935).

18. *NLRB v. Jones & Laughlin Steel Corp.,* 301 U.S. 1 (1937) (upholding the National Labor Relations Act); *see also United States v. Darby,* 312 U.S. 100 (1941) (expanding the transformation by upholding the Fair Labor Standards Act of 1938 and overruling *Hammer v. Dagenhart,* 247 U.S. 251 (1918)); *Wickard v. Filburn,* 317 U.S. 111 (1942) (upholding acreage allocation provisions in the Agricultural Adjustment Act). I have attacked these and similar decisions in Epstein, *supra* note 1.

19. *W. Coast Hotel Co. v. Parrish,* 300 U.S. 379 (1937) (sustaining a minimum-wage law for women and overruling *Adkins v. Children's Hospital,* 261 U.S. 525 (1923)).

20. 5 U.S.C. § 551–559 (2018).

21. Cass R. Sunslein and Adrian Vermeule, *The Morality of Administrative Law,* 131 Harv. L. Rev. 1924 (2018)

22. Lon L.Fuller, The Morality of Law (2d ed. 1969)(Yale U. Press, 1964).

23. Jeffrey A. Pojanowski, *Neoclassical Administrative Law,* 133 Harv. L. Rev. (forthcoming 2019).

24. *Id.* (manuscript at 7–14). He also treats James Landis in this class, which, I think, oversimplifies the situation.

25. *Id.* (manuscript at 14).

26. *Id.* (manuscript at 14–15); *Skidmore v. Swift Co.,* 323 U.S. 134 (1944).

27. Pojanowski, *supra* note 23 (manuscript at 18).

28. Henry M. Hart, Jr. and Albert M. Sacks, The Legal Process: Basic Problems in the Making and Application of Law (William N. Eskridge Jr. et al. eds., Foundation Press, 1995). For instructive commentary, *see* William N. Eskridge, Jr. and Philip P. Frickey, *The Making of Legal Process,* 107 Harv. L. Rev. 2031 (1993).

29. *Norway Plains Co. v. Boston & Maine R.R.,* 67 Mass. (1 Gray) 263 (1854). Chief Justice Shaw's paean to the adaptive capacities of the common law covers all the relevant bases: "The effect of this expansive and comprehensive character of the common law is, that whilst it has its foundations in the principles of equity, natural justice, and that general convenience which is public policy; although these general considerations would be too vague and uncertain for practical purposes, in the various and complicated cases, of daily occurrence, in the business of an active community; yet the rules of the common law, so far as cases have arisen and practices actually grown up, are rendered, in a good degree, precise and certain, for practical purposes, by usage and judicial precedent." *Id.* at 267.

30. Eskridge and Frickey, *supra* note 28, at 2035.

31. *See infra* Part 2, at 48.

32. Pojanowski, *supra* note 23 (manuscript at 28).

33. For the initial use of this phrase, *see* Thomas W. Merrill and Kristin E. Hickman, Chevron's *Domain,* 89 Geo. L.J. 833, 836 (2001); for its further explication, see Cass R. Sunstein, Chevron *Step Zero,* 92 Va. L. Rev. 187 (2006).

34. *United States v. Mead Corp.,* 533 U.S. 218 (2001); *see generally* Thomas W. Merrill, *The* Mead *Doctrine: Of Rules and Standards, Meta-Rules and Meta-Standards,* 45 Admin. L. Rev. 807 (2002) (describing a rule-like approach to *Mead*); Thomas W. Merrill and Kathryn Tongue Watts, *Agency Rules with the Force of Law: The Original Convention,* 116 Harv. L. Rev. 467 (2002).

35. *Mead,* 533 U.S. at 221.

36. James M. Landis, The Administrative Process (Yale U. Press, 1974) (1938).

37. For a discussion of how Landis became disillusioned about the overlegalization of the process, *see* Charles H. Koch, Jr., *James Landis: The Administrative Process,* 48 Admin. L. Rev. 419, 433 (1996) ("The administrative process contemplated by Landis is not presently in operation. He reflected on a flexible concept that facilitates careful designs focusing on particular decision-making tasks. He worked from the foundational principle that government should be run as a business. . . . Today, we have too much law about the administrative process. The business of government, like others, needs serious deregulation").

38. For discussion, *see* Epstein, *supra* note 14, at 54–56, 58–60 (comparing administrative practices of notice contemporary with APA to later judicial innovations, and comparing APA sections 553(b) and 705).

39. *See generally* Epstein, *supra* note 15.

40. Fuller, *supra* note 22, at 153.

41. *Id.* at 38–39.

42. *Id.* at 53.

43. *Id.* at 209–10.

44. *Id.* at 53.

45. *Id.* at 211.

46. For discussion, *see* Richard A. Epstein, Takings: Private Property and the Power of Eminent Domain 210–13 (Harv. U. Press, 1985) (explaining how, when the people from whom wealth is taken are not in the same group as those to whom it is given, takings "can be transformed into a mass mode of exploitation").

47. John Locke, Second Treatise of Government §124, Peter Laslett ed. (Cambridge U. Press, 1988) (1689).

48. *Id.*

49. *Id.* at § 125 (emphasis added).

50. Friedrich A. Hayek, The Road to Serfdom (Routledge, 1944).

51. For a more detailed discussion, *see* Richard A. Epstein, Design for Liberty: Private Property, Public Administration, and the Rule of Law (Harv. U. Press, 2011).

52. *Lambert v. California,* 355 U.S. 225 (1957); *Gundy v. United States,* 139 S. Ct. 2116 (2019).

53. Harold Demsetz, *Toward a Theory of Property Rights,* 57 Am. Econ. Rev. 347 (1967).

54. For discussion, *see Swetland v. Curtiss Airports Corp.,* 41 F.2d 929 (N.D. Ohio 1930), *rev'd,* 55 F.2d 201 (6th Cir. 1932).

55. *See, e.g., Ghen v. Rich,* 8 F. 159 (D. Mass. 1881) (importing long-standing, well-known industry customs of first possession into formal law).

56. Fair Labor Standards Act of 1938, 29 U.S.C. §§201–219 (2017). For some of the law's endless variations dealing with waiting time, on-call time, rest and meal periods, sleeping times, and more, *see* U.S. Dep't of Labor, Wage and Hour Division, Fact Sheet #22, Hours Worked Under the Fair Labor Standards Act (FLSA) (July 2008), *available at* https://www.dol.gov/whd/regs/compliance/whdfs22.pdf.

57. *See generally* Epstein, *supra* note 46.

58. Sadly, the public-use requirement is not rigorously enforced under modern jurisprudence. *See Kelo v. City of New London,* 545 U.S. 469 (2005) (holding that "public use" includes a transfer to a private developer).

59. *Penn Cent. Transp. Co. v. City of New York,* 438 U.S. 104 (1978).

60. For the origins of this doctrine, *see United States v. Willow River Power Co.,* 324 U.S. 499 (1945), which I critique in Richard A. Epstein, *Playing by Different Rules? Property Rights in Land and Water* in Property in Land and Other Resources 317 (Daniel H. Cole et al. eds., Lincoln Institute of Land Policy, 2012).

61. *Penn Cent.,* 438 U.S. at 124.

62. *See, e.g., Perry Capital LLC v. Mnuchin,* 864 F.3d 591 (D.C. Cir. 2017), which I critique

in Richard A. Epstein, *D.C. Circuit Refuses to See Limits to Government Power and Inexcusably Upholds the Net Worth Sweep,* FORBES (Mar. 3, 2017), *available at* https://www.forbes.com/sites/richardepstein/2017/03/03/d-c-circuit-refuses-to-see-limits-to-government-power-and-inexcusably-upholds-the-net-worth-sweep/#5c9c4fa74167. The "net worth sweep" refers to the government's decision in August 2012 to require the distribution of all net profits of Fannie and Freddie to be paid over to the United States, without limitation, rendering the shares worthless even after the recovery of the housing market.

63. Richard A. Epstein, BARGAINING WITH THE STATE 98–103 (Princeton U. Press, 1993).

PART 2

THE TRADITIONAL APPROACH TO ADMINISTRATIVE LAW

The Founding Period

So long as there is government, there will always be an administrative state. There is no workable theory of the state—let alone one consistent with the American constitutional order—so minimalist that it refuses to allow the government to impose taxes, borrow money, hire employees, maintain a military, deal with the regulation of commerce, and provide some structure to patent and copyright laws, or, in other words, exercise all the enumerated powers of Congress under Article I, Section 8, of the United States Constitution.

The Constitution provides for separate departments of the federal government: the legislative, executive, and judicial. Ideally, each department is charged with different tasks delegated to different persons. The Appointments Clause,[1] which was at issue in recent litigation,[2] welcomes such delegation by designating three classes of employees, some of whom require Senate confirmation; some of whom may be appointed by the president, the courts of law, or the department heads, if Congress so chooses; and some who are mere employees appointable in the ordinary course of government business. No matter where the lines are drawn among these classes, downward delegation is a necessity of any sound administrative system. It is naive to think that the United States could ever have been run by the president and his key advisers acting alone.

The question is how the requirements of the rule of law apply to authority that Congress delegates to an administrative agency. Delegation is a necessary part of the tool kit of any complex organization. The ordinary corporation divides power between its board of directors and its executive team. In some cases, and increasingly more often, the chairman of the board is distinct from the chief executive officer; in other cases, a single person sits in both chairs, showing how hard it is to maintain complete separation. Yet with either structure, there is nothing more common than for a board to lay out a general plan that allows—or indeed, requires—that management enjoys a good deal of discretion in the mode of its implementation. The attention span of any legislative body for a given task is limited, and its ability to fine-tune any scheme of legislation is cabined by its hazy information about the complications likely to arise down the road and the difficulties of staffing up for the administrative chores of sustained action. Some delegation is needed, no matter how limited the government.

It is, of course, always uncomfortable to think of delegation in such loose terms as "necessary or appropriate" action. But lest one condemn those terms out of hand, it is important to note that the Constitution uses similar terms in defining the scope of the powers that it delegates to the legislature. Here are a few examples. First, the "necessary and proper" clause should not be read as an open door through which any executive or administrative scheme may proceed.[3] Taken in sequence, its two requirements are that the law be first necessary and then proper,[4] which is a narrower reading than the broader interpretation given by Chief Justice John Marshall in *McCulloch v. Maryland*, when he wrote: "Let the end be legitimate, let it be within the scope of the constitution, and all means which are appropriate, which are plainly adapted to that end, which are not prohibited, but consist with the letter and spirit of the constitution, are constitutional."[5] A still-broader granting of power is found in each of the Reconstruction amendments, dealing, respectively, with the existence of slavery and involuntary servitude, the privileges or immunities of citizenship, due process and equal protection, and the right to vote. Congress is then entitled to enforce all these broad substantive guarantees "by appropriate legislation."[6]

There is no textual litmus test that allows for Congress or the courts to determine whether the means chosen in a particular case are sufficiently tied to a legitimate end so as to meet that standard. The test is essentially one of tightness of fit between the ends sought and the means selected for their achievement. But even this test is not infinitely pliable, given that it is "necessary to prevent the Fourteenth Amendment from obliterating the Framers' carefully created balance of power between the States and the National Government."[7] None of these constitutional provisions can be rejected on the grounds that they are unconstitutionally vague. The same conclusion applies to statutes that contain similar language authorizing delegation to some administrative body. In both cases, the semantic and structural issues relating to vagueness are the same. Accordingly, the attacks on most of these statutory provisions cannot be facial—that is, based on the text of the statute alone. Instead, they must be made on an as-applied basis.

Even within this broad framework, one set of limitations remains powerful. Congress cannot use delegation to evade Fuller's rule-of-law constraints that bind its own exercise of legislative power. Each of the constraints that addresses bias, the right to be heard, consistency, retroactivity, notice, and the like apply with equal force to actions taken pursuant to delegated authority as to direct congressional actions. The principle at work here is nothing more than an application of the well-established maxim of private law that an agent that receives delegated authority enjoys the powers available to the principal, and no more. Any other rule makes delegation a royal road to the evasion of constitutional and statutory constraints. Hence, on this view, the only real dispute is whether an administrative delegatee should be subject to *greater* scrutiny by courts than Congress, given that the political constraints on agencies are usually weaker than those faced by their principal.

Within this framework, the hard question in all these situations is how to draw the line between legislation and administration. The basic challenge is set out in Article I, Section 1, of the Constitution: "All legislative Powers herein granted shall be vested in a Congress of the United States, which shall consist of a Senate and House of Representatives."[8] The use of the term "all" suggests that Congress shall have a monopoly over all legislative activities, which necessarily excludes the two other branches of government—the executive and judiciary—from exercising that power. The use of the phrase "herein granted" is yet another illustration of the constitutional passive, in which the identity of the grantor, either the people or the state legislatures—it is not quite clear which—gives the power to Congress. Either way, Congress does not have unconstrained power and is subject to the limitations that attach to the grant, whether those conditions be express or implied.

The use of the term "vested" brings back images of vested rights in the law of property; that is, rights that are fully clothed and protected, which means, at the very least, that they cannot be undone by ordinary legislative action but remain fixed in the absence of some constitutional amendment. From these basic textual provisions, it follows that the legislative power cannot be delegated to any other party, including a different branch of government, an administrative agency, a state government, or any private party.

The lack of any explicit prohibition against delegation does not undercut this conclusion. The Constitution is, on many particulars, an incomplete document, and therefore the normal principles of implication used to resolve unsettled issues in private law apply with equal force in a public law setting. That process works because there is a well-formed theory of government that fills in the gaps for constitutions as it does for private charters,[9] all of which involve the basic notion that a public office is a public trust that necessarily imposes limits on what all officials can do. As in so many areas, a uniform set of common law principles imposes on all private actors who receive delegated authority the standard duties of loyalty and care expected of all agents in all contexts. Those limits on the power of delegation exist under the familiar principle *Delegata potestas non potest delegare* ("It is not possible for a delegated power to be further delegated"), or in its alternative formulation, *Delegatus non posse delegare* ("A delegatee cannot delegate"). The Latin formulation shows that the principle long antedates the adoption of the United States Constitution.

That proposition is treated as a self-evident truth of natural law. But as with so many propositions of this sort, it has powerful utilitarian foundations, which can be retrofitted onto doctrines of private and public law that were not known or formalized at the time.[10] Elected bodies of all sorts have complex compositions of competing interests. Delegation involves two moving parts: what Congress does by way of legislation; and what Congress does when it delegates power to some subordinate body. Both these interfaces become more difficult to manage as the level of discretion involved in the delegation increases. That one insight explains why the earlier periods were generally successful because of, as will become apparent, the close constraints on the nature of the delegation process that were easier to respect in the earlier period because of the more limited ambitions of legislation.

Thus, as to the first problem regarding how Congress acts through legislation, Judge Neomi Rao has introduced the useful notion of the "collective Congress."[11] Her basic point is that when Congress is forced to exercise its decision collectively, it is necessary to engage in discussion and compromise. Congress's oversight function, however, is not done collectively but by individual members of Congress or committees. The argument for this kind of delegation is expertise. But with that supposed expertise comes the risk of a clubby, close relationship between individual members of Congress and the administrative agencies they oversee, which can easily push the substantive agenda in their favored direction. As these agents gain greater power, they will tend to resist any corrective legislation that Congress imposes.

No one can be sure of how the complex political dynamic will play out in various contexts. It is all too common that particular outcomes can shift widely, depending on the initial constellation of political forces, all of whom necessarily make probabilistic judgments. Hence the outcome of any individual case and the overall patterns of delegation are notoriously difficult to predict. Nonetheless, these political vagaries certainly cannot be ignored, because the phenomena that Rao identifies is yet another application of the general principle that weak systems of property rights induce political intrigue—the classic rent-seeking—that leads to antisocial behavior.

That same risk is at work on the other side of the equation, wholly apart from any residual oversight by members of Congress and committees. Thus, delegation poses the risk that the party to whom the powers are delegated, if left free of supervision, may deviate sharply from the original statutory plan. This slippage in control means that the delegated parties are likely to move the legislative mandate in either direction: make it too narrow; or, as they do more often, make it extend far beyond its original purpose, which happens all the time today when various agencies issue guidances and letter rulings that go far beyond original sentiments.[12]

In addition, the delegation makes it that much harder to hold any determinate political body accountable for the misdeeds of its subordinates, given that the original body can always claim that it made its delegation in good faith, so that the fault lies with the delegated body that is conveniently insulated from direct control by citizens (in the case of public bodies) or shareholders (in the case of private ones). It is therefore possible to say that the Constitution incorporates all these principles by reference.

This conventional wisdom has been powerfully challenged by Eric Posner and Adrian Vermeule, who give a far narrower account of the nondelegation principle in their well-known article "Interring the Nondelegation Doctrine."[13] The gist of their position is that the nondelegation doctrine imposes this minimum constraint only on congressional action. Congress is the only body that can exercise its legislative powers. In their view, whenever the president enforces any law, he is "simply executing the statute according to its terms, and in obedience to the constitutional obligation to 'take Care that the laws be faithfully executed.' "[14] But this text is better read to presuppose that the law has been created elsewhere—namely, by Congress—and the president is then under a constitutional duty to execute it. Taken to its limits, the Posner-Vermeule position could not object to the following proposition: the president may adopt any code of substantive and procedural law that he likes, consistent with the binding constraints of the Bill of Rights. The same could be said about the powers to regulate foreign or interstate commerce, to develop a patent and copyright system, or, indeed, anything else over which Congress is prepared to cede its powers.

One way to test the validity of their position is to ask how the matter was perceived in the Founding period by parties who had to deal with these questions. The traditional form of this doctrine is to say that informed practice helps fill in the gaps of constitutional interpretation.[15] More recently, the same principle has been advanced under the term "liquidated," whereby the meaning of an unclear provision of the Constitution is "fixed" by the early practices associated with its use.[16] The two principles of implication operate everywhere in the Constitution. They include the entire development of the doctrine of unconstitutional conditions and police power, both of which are developed solely by implication from established text.[17] The nondelegation doctrine falls into the same class.

I have put forward the added notion elsewhere, drawn from private law comparisons dealing with easements, of a prescriptive constitution, which goes one step beyond the use of customary practices to fill constitutional gaps. Thus, in many situations, it is appropriate to stick with an embedded constitutional practice even after it is widely acknowledged to have been inconsistent with the constitutional text when first laid down.[18] These historical reversals are difficult to accommodate within traditional constitutional theory. It is painful for judges and scholars to make an explicit home for any prescriptive rights, the constitutional text takes an interpretive beating, and we come to speak with confidence about such constitutional oxymorons as Article I courts whose judges necessarily lack the limitations on life tenure applicable for Article III judges[19] and with the constitutionality of state inheritance taxes.[20] Surely, the long-standing practice of delegation is a response to any claim that all delegations are unconstitutional, even if it does not, of itself, sort out those that are permissible from those that are not.

At one level, the proposition that delegation is permissible seems counterintuitive, given the stress on the separation of powers found in perhaps the most influential preconstitutional work, John Locke's *Second Treatise of Government*:

> The legislative cannot transfer the power of making laws to any other hands; for it being but a delegated power from the people, they who have it cannot pass it over to others. The people alone can appoint the form of the commonwealth, which is by constituting the legislative, and appointing in whose hands that shall be. And when the people have said we will submit to rules, and be governed by laws made by such men, and in such forms, nobody else can say other men shall make laws for them; nor can the people be bound by any laws but such as are enacted by those whom they have chosen and authorised to make laws for them.[21]

This passage surely shows a general disposition, but it by no means solves all problems because it does not offer any account of what counts as a legislative or administrative activity. To be sure, the enforcement of particular laws against particular individuals counts as the executive function. But what about the mass of administrative rules that were as much a part of governance in England in Locke's time as they are in the United States today? It is necessary to push a bit further to see how these principles play out in the American context, whose constitutional structure bears only limited resemblance to that in historical England. It is therefore especially instructive that a strong version of the Lockean vision was very much present during the House of Representatives' extensive dialogue regarding a delegation question that seems simple to us today but was regarded as a fundamental concern toward the end of the 18th century, when one of the major functions of the nascent American Constitution dealt with the postal authority.[22] Indeed, one of the four original cabinet positions was the postmaster general. The applicable constitutional provision that governs this power reads: "[Congress shall have the power] to establish Post Offices and Post Roads."[23] That simple provision was the subject of a spirited debate in 1791 between Congress and the president before the House of Representatives over the distribution of authority.[24] The initial legislation before Congress contained a list of post roads that were to be constructed under the supervision and authority of the president.

It is difficult to think of any constitutional statute that contemplates this division of power between Congress and the president. But in the House, Representative Sedgwick moved to take out the listed roads and to substitute in their place the phrase "By such route as the President of the United States shall, from time to time, cause to be established."[25] That amendment marked a powerful shift of power to the president. The lines of debate were between those who thought that the executive's greater knowledge should be used to create an efficient system of post roads and those who agreed with Representative Livermore when he said that "he did not think they could with priority delegate that power, which they were themselves appointed to exercise."[26]

The House then constituted itself as a committee of the whole, where debate would continue at length on both textual and pragmatic grounds and where claims would be made suggesting two positions in deep tension with each other: that the Congress and the president each had claims to superior abilities to locate these new post offices. That basic choice is largely indeterminate. Individual representatives may have superior knowledge about the ideal location of post offices within their own districts. But post roads are a network industry, and the president or his delegate is more likely to understand the necessary interconnections across districts than the individual members of Congress, acting alone. For the purposes at hand, the key point is that in their blanket dismissal of any nondelegation doctrine, Posner and Vermeule do not discuss the post-road debate at all. Moreover, the House refused to adopt Sedgwick's amendment, which is an early and powerful indication—a constitutional liquidation, if you choose—of early practice that contemplates a robust role for the basic nondelegation norm.

The harder question is whether that decision is correct as a matter of principle. Here, it is possible to make the case that it was more defensible on constitutional grounds in 1791 than it is today. This variation of the "living constitution" has nothing to do with changes in societal values as to the proper role of government, which arises when classical liberalism is put into opposition with modern progressive positions. Delivering the mail is still a proper government function today, even if a large number of private parties—FedEx and UPS, to name only two of the most prominent—are able to perform that function as well as, or better than, the federal government. Rather, the key element that drives the distinction is the question of scale. It is one thing for a small Congress to have undertaken the designation of post roads in 1791, and quite another for Congress to do that today, when the size of the nation and the population governed has increased exponentially.

One way to approach the problem is to ask about the distribution of powers that takes place in a private corporation, organized by voluntary consent, between the board of directors and the CEO. The larger the corporation, the more day-to-day decisions have to be delegated to the CEO, for without that delegation, the indisputable functions of the board of directors—to set general policy, to develop strategic plans, to oversee mergers and acquisitions, to appoint and monitor the CEO, and so on—will be swamped by a huge number of low- and mid-level administrative decisions. Any board could try to delegate its functions to some staff functionaries, but how a complex body exercises its oversight decisions is anyone's guess. Hence the size of the executive branch, as well as the amount of business controlled by it, necessarily grows with the complexity of the organization.

The same principle that applies to public bodies applies to private ones, so that today it is virtually inconceivable that it would be an impermissible delegation to the executive branch to farm out a route system for delivering the mail. This point is of great importance because it indicates that the power of the nondelegation problem must necessarily erode with time, as administrative necessity starts to overtake the pristine view that an abstract principle of separation of powers will necessarily supply a unique answer to this riddle and will continue to work well over time.

Today, there is little doubt that a heroic Congress could try to designate the locations of all post roads and post offices, and indeed, it could probably specify which contractors the president or his delegates must hire to finish the job. Remember that Article II, Section 3, of the Constitution requires the president to "take care that the Laws be faithfully executed," where the word "be" necessarily contemplates that the president is allowed to—indeed, must—delegate his constitutional powers to the various "departments" under his supervision. The nondelegation doctrine thus has firm constitutional underpinnings, even if, by necessity, it leaves a large gray area in its application. But beware of what Representative Page observed in the post-road debate: "If this House can, with propriety, leave the business of the post office to the President, it may leave to him any other business of legislation; and I may move to adjourn and leave all the objects of legislation to his sole consideration and direction."[27] The central challenge to the nondelegation doctrine is to avoid this reductio ad absurdum and to find ways to allow delegation of post-road designation without letting Congress turn over all legislative business to the president by a single statute.

The 19th and Early 20th Centuries

The difficulties of trying to find that intermediate position became evident in the evolution of administrative law over the course of the 19th and early 20th centuries—that is, before the constitutional revolution that culminated in the October 1936 Supreme Court term. During this period, few cases, if any, presented a major challenge to the principle of nondelegation, because the relatively modest conception of government rule dictated the kinds of cases that were brought before the Court prior to the New Deal. During the 19th century, the United States government dealt with four core functions. First, it had to set up sensible rules to deal with contracts made with civil service employees and military personnel. At a minimum, these contracts needed to set out the terms of service; grounds for dismissal or demotion; and provision for termination, retirement, and pension benefits. Second, the United States had to develop rules for the orderly disposition of public lands, whether by sale or lease, to all sorts of parties—including individuals, railroads, and other corporations. Third, it faced the related problem of granting individual applicants patents and copyrights. And fourth, it had to administer taxes and tariffs, which, in an age prior to the income tax, required an extensive system of control to oversee the activities of widely dispersed customhouses.

The discharge of these tasks created a large and impressive body of administrative law over a period of many years, going back to the first days of the Washington administration.[28] Professor Metzger has acknowledged this point, though she fails to understand the enormous gulf between the early administrative state and its modern incarnation. The first two of the four problems handled by the federal government during the 19th century were largely contractual, and the sign of a good body of administrative law is that it recognizes those deep contractual roots. As a general proposition, any system of contracts works best when a large number of small, related transactions allows the parties to develop a rich set of customary practices to deal with the situations at hand.[29]

In easier cases, the parties operate behind a veil of ignorance because they occupy symmetrical roles in relationship to each other. For example, that is the case with business partners in relational contracts, where the duties of good faith and reasonable care are reciprocal between them. In other relations, such as employment, where the parties do not occupy symmetrical roles, customary law emerges more slowly because it is harder to establish the general efficiency of a rule that tends on its face to favor one side or another. In the administrative context, the presence of a third party may ease the problem of bias, which is why a reputation for impartiality is so critical in dealing with routine disputes involving employment relations, both for civilian and military

43

personnel, as well as in land transfers.

Over time, a cadre of impartial government officials can make small adjustments to develop a systematic set of practices that create parity between persons in like positions through the choice of an efficient set of rules. Indeed, after reading many of these early cases, this model of independent professionalism seems to have gained some real traction, reflected in the careful way in which the Supreme Court decided matters of 19th-century administrative law with an eye to long-standing practices.

Metzger misses all these dynamics when she seeks to force these earlier cases into a modern mold that champions judicial deference to administrative action. To advance her cause, she attributes the misleading proposition of Professor Bamzai[30] that "describing sources asser[t] historical support for such deference,"[31] without once noting that the reasons for supporting deference in the early cases are wholly different from the reasons supporting deference in today's legal disputes. In Bamzai's words, "Under the traditional [i.e., 19th century] interpretive approach, American courts 'respected' longstanding and contemporaneous *executive* interpretations of law as part of a practice of deferring to longstanding and contemporaneous interpretation *generally*."[32]

Bamzai's article does not closely examine the underlying factual patterns showing how this process was operationalized.[33] But their common thread refers to "contemporaneous construction," often by persons who helped design or implement the basic scheme in its formative period.[34] The closest analogies to these practices are the rules that govern the "practical construction" of ordinary business contracts.[35] Historically, the government pension office has always treated warrant officers, including boatswains, as commissioned officers. In light of that consistent history, the Court refused to let a single claimant upset that uniform practice. Thus, in *Brown v. United States*,[36] the plaintiff sought to recover certain retirement benefits on behalf of the decedent at a rate higher than that allowed by the relevant commission. On this matter, administrative custom controlled:

> [I]t had been the uniform practice of the president to place warrant officers on the retired list, and large numbers of these officers had been so retired. No protest or objection was made

44

by Brown during his life-time, either to his retirement or rate of pay. The accounting officers of the treasury had uniformly held that longevity pay to retired officers was not authorized by [statute].[37]

The accumulated weight of past practice was thus decisive, so that the connections between standard principles of contractual interpretation and administrative law remained tight, all in sharp contrast to modern practice.

The Court took the same approach in interpreting grants of public lands. In *United States v. Alabama Great Southern Railway*,[38] the Court considered a dispute over how to measure the size of a rebate that a railroad, which had received a government land grant, owed to its customers. The judicial response was emphatic:

[I]n case of ambiguity the judicial department will lean in favor of a construction given to a statute by the department charged with the execution of such statute, and, if such construction be acted upon for a number of years, will look with disfavor upon any sudden change, whereby parties who have contracted with the government upon the faith of such construction may be prejudiced.[39]

The Court, accordingly, tied the size of the rebate to the fraction of the railroad line that had received a government subsidy rather than to the entire line, which avoided incongruities in the system of requiring rebates as a quid pro quo for subsidies. The emphasis here is on proportionality as a way to cabin discretion, which is completely at odds with the modern administrative law culture of deference.

The same basic approach was applied to various taxation issues. Two illustrations help tell the full story. In *Murray's Lessee v. Hoboken Land & Improvement Co.*,[40] the question was whether the government had to bring suit in an Article III court—in which the Constitution vests "the judicial power" of the United States[41]—to recover from a customs agent the taxes collected in the ordinary course of business, or whether a specialized non–Article III court could adjudicate the dispute. The case arose out of the epic misdoings of one Samuel Swartwout, a customs officer who had fled to England after embezzling enormous sums from the federal government, which then sought to recover some of those losses by seizing Swartwout's lands in the United States.[42] The use of administrative courts to resolve these types of issues had evolved slowly from the kinds of internal administrative reviews that were first adopted in those cases. By 1855, that administrative practice had been well established for 35 years, without signs of serious distress, and the Supreme Court, as Professor Jerry Mashaw notes, was loath to strike down a customary system that had worked well for so long.[43]

Yet the doctrinal challenge remained: How could the Court reach that result without undermining the constitutional framework, which located the entire judicial power in Article III courts, where judges served with lifetime tenure? The innovative judicial answer was to create a "public rights" exception to the Article III judicial power. The Supreme Court looked to "settled usages and modes of proceeding existing in the common and statute law of England" and determined that Congress could not withdraw from the judiciary matters that are "the subject of a suit at the common law, or in equity, or admiralty," but that it could reallocate public rights matters.[44] Accordingly, under *Murray's Lessee*, the best account of this principle covers only those cases in which one of the parties to the dispute is a government agency charged with the administration of a program that involves either grants or taxes, but not ordinary disputes between private persons.[45]

The most important follow-up decisions to *Murray's Lessee* both involve the application of the tariff laws. As a matter of basic administration, tariff laws present the ideal target for a delegation of responsibilities. The government assesses tariffs on a huge number of products from a large number of different countries. The judgments in each case often depend on a precise constellation of facts that it is hard to pigeonhole in any precise matter. In addition, it often happens that relations between the United States and other countries will evolve during the period that the legislation is in effect. When Congress is out of session, there must be someone on the ground who is capable of making the needed adjustments. By process of elimination, that someone must be the president or some applicable official in the executive branch. Hence, so long as the tariff enterprise is regarded as legitimate, delegation to administrative agencies will be a sheer necessity, which the case law recognizes.

The point at issue in *Field v. Clark*[46] involved the application of the

Tariff Act of 1890 to various dresses, apparel, fabrics, and laces imported into the United States by Marshall Field & Co. and other notable retailers. The tariffs levied on these goods were approved by an administrative body, the Board of General Appraisers, and affirmed by circuit courts. One charge raised in the case was that the actions of the customs board were set out beyond the permissible scope of delegation. What was at issue, more precisely, was a provision that sought to secure "reciprocal trade with countries" selling the same general lines of goods.[47]

A key provision in the act required the president to identify those tariffs imposed by other nations that "he may deem to be reciprocally unequal and unreasonable." Once those are identified, the president then has the power to suspend the exemption from the tariffs of goods from these countries so identified coming into the United States, to the dismay of their importers. The discharge of that duty necessarily required that the president account for changed conditions on the ground, which Congress could not do at the time of passage. After an exhaustive review of the relevant precedents,[48] Justice John Marshall Harlan penned this sentence: "That Congress cannot delegate legislative power to the president is a principle universally recognized as vital to the integrity and maintenance of the system of government ordained by the Constitution."[49] Posner and Vermeule treat this passage as "dictum,"[50] which misses the entire point. The confident way in which the passage is stated clearly indicates that it is essential to the basic decision and not merely a casual observation. Justice Harlan instead treated the proposition as the encapsulation of a uniform tradition dating back to the founding of the Republic, if not before. The key issue in the case therefore was not the validity of the principle but its application to the particular case, where Justice Harlan was at pains to note the extensive rules and regulations that cabin presidential power. He thus explained:

> Congress prescribed the levies to be imposed, and then provided that the President would examine the commercial regulations of other countries producing and exporting sugar, molasses, coffee, tea and hides, and form a judgment as to whether they were reciprocally equal and reasonable, or the contrary, in their effect upon American products. But when he ascertained the fact that duties and exactions, reciprocally unequal and unreasonable, were imposed [on these various

goods], it became his duty to issue a proclamation declaring the suspension, as to that country, which Congress had determined should occur. He had no discretion in the premises except in respect to the duration of the suspension so ordered.[51]

It is hard to think of a more sensible distribution of powers than the one adopted in that case, which dispels the view that presidential power was not sufficiently constrained in order to sustain the regulation.

A similar analysis applies to the 1928 case *J. W. Hampton, Jr. & Co. v. United States*,[52] where the Court sustained the use of a long-standing Article I tribunal—the Tariff Commission—to administer tariffs (the substantive merits of which were beyond the scope of the case). The statutory scheme imposed tariffs on foreign goods such that "the duties not only secure revenue, but at the same time enable domestic producers to compete on terms of equality with foreign producers in the markets of the United States."[53] The statutory command is a variation on the reciprocity theme in *Field*. Chief Justice William Howard Taft wrote: "It may be that it is difficult to fix with exactness this difference, but the difference which is sought in the statute is perfectly clear and perfectly intelligible."[54] Note the twofold use of "perfectly."

In dealing with the case, Sunstein treats *Hampton* as if it upheld a broad delegation that was not different in kind from the delegations required under New Deal legislation,[55] without examining the provision in any degree of detail. But Taft was surely correct when he stressed the circumscribed nature of the delegation. The range of the tariff addition at issue was from four to six cents per unit. The implementation of this mechanical task did not amount to an impermissible delegation precisely because of the clear directive to which the overall system had to conform. Hence, the Article I court could set the tariff, which could then be approved or disapproved by the president. The issue involved in this case does not, of course, involve any private right, and hence Chief Justice Taft did not discuss *Murray's Lessee*. By the same token, the precision of the delegation in *J. W. Hampton* eliminated the possibility of a runaway administrative agency using its vast discretion in defiance of Congress.

The scope of the public rights doctrine under *Murray's Lessee* was limited. In *Crowell v. Benson*,[56] decided in 1932, the Court, for the first time, permitted an administrative agency, rather than an Article III court, to adjudicate a private rights dispute. The case dealt with a controversy concerning a version of workers' compensation laws applicable to longshoremen and harbor workers.[57] Chief Justice Charles Evans Hughes made it very clear that the case did not fall within the public rights exception: workmen's compensation was a "private right, that is, of the liability of one individual to another under the law as defined."[58] But even as the Court permitted the agency adjudication of a private right, it noted that it would require a de novo review in federal court of any question before the tribunal that raises a jurisdictional issue. In *Crowell*, the statutory pronouncement altered the common law rule. But at no point did anyone think that Congress could obliterate the distinction between Article I and Article III courts by simply adding the words, "This case involves a public right because Congress says so."

The strict limitations on administrative action evident in *J. W. Hampton* carried over to the area of retroactive rate-making, which was met with a frosty reception in the pre–New Deal era. Thus, in another 1932 case, *Arizona Grocery v. Topeka, Atchison, & Santa Fe Railway*,[59] the Court invoked the retroactivity principle in refusing to allow the Interstate Commerce Commission to lower the rates that it had ordered a railroad to use for shipping various goods through adjudication. The principle of retroactivity figured centrally in the opinion's rationale.[60] The Court first noted that when by "[statutory] mandate the Commission declares a specific rate to be the reasonable and lawful rate for the future, it speaks as the legislature, and its pronouncement has the force of a statute."[61] Accordingly, the commission, in its exercise of "a delegated power legislative in character," would not be free to alter the rate up or down during adjudication:[62]

> Where, as in this case, the Commission has made an order having a dual aspect, it may not in a subsequent proceeding, acting, in its quasi-judicial capacity, ignore its own pronouncement promulgated in its quasi-legislative capacity and retroactively repeal its own enactment as to the reasonableness of the rate it has prescribed.[63]

Sunstein and Vermeule rightly cite this case as strong support for Fuller's conception of the rule of law.[64] Its survival in the modern era, however, is another question, for all the modern cases have systematically undermined this prohibition.[65]

Efforts of this sort are also evident in the rate-making decisions from this period, which worked hard to ensure that the administrative effort to cut down on monopoly profits did not lead to a systematic confiscation of wealth. So in *Board of Public Utility Commissioners v. New York Telephone Co.*,[66] the Court stressed the integrity of the annual accounting period and held that the New York Telephone Company was not permitted to use its reserve for depreciation to offset a shortfall in revenue for any particular year. The discipline of the calendar year is an important constraint against temporal cross-subsidies, which, in turn, can lead to confiscation. It is all too easy to tolerate a loss in a given year on the facile assumption that higher rates the next year could make up for it. But the political forces that allow this tactic to be used on one occasion pave the way for its repetitive use, so that at the end of the process, no rate increase can possibly make up for the accumulated shortfalls. Higher rates may be allowed, in theory, but could not be imposed in practice because they would be more than any unregulated monopolist would charge in the same market. The decision in *Board of Public Utility Commissioners* thus presents a commendable vindication of rule-of-law virtues. There are no viable cross-subsidies in a competitive market, and no such system should be imposed de facto by the manipulation of temporal accounting across years.

A similar decision from that period showing the same tendency toward discipline is found in *Railroad Retirement Board v. Alton Railroad Co.*,[67] in which the Court resoundingly rejected statutory provisions that sought to retroactively extend the liability of railroads far beyond their original contractual obligations. The language of Justice Owen Roberts is unforgiving:

> The statute would take from the railroads' future earnings amounts to be paid for services fully compensated when rendered in accordance with contract, with no thought on the part of either employer or employee that further sums must be provided by the carrier. The provision is not only retroactive in that it resurrects for new burdens transactions long since past and closed; but as to some of the railroad companies it constitutes a naked appropriation of private property

upon the basis of transactions with which the owners of the property were never connected.[68]

The 1935 Turning Point

At this point, we come to the two transitional cases in which the Court did apply the nondelegation doctrine to strike down the first generation of New Deal legislation. The timing of these cases is critical, for both were decided the same year as *Alton Railroad*; yet neither of them bears any relationship on its facts to the earlier line of cases. Sunstein made this famous quip about the nondelegation doctrine in 2000: "It is more accurate, speaking purely descriptively, to see 1935 as the real anomaly. We might say that the conventional doctrine has had one good year, and 211 bad ones (and counting)."[69] But this quip is based on the typical fact-free analysis of administrative law, which moves to such a high level of abstraction on the statutory scheme that it misses the fundamental transformation that takes place on the ground. Sunstein, in his article on nondelegation canons, misses the essential point because he fails to identify a single case in which relatively narrow circumscribed opinions violated any sensible conception of the nondelegation doctrine. Indeed, at no point does he even mention the word "tariff" in dealing with *Field* or *Hampton*.

It is critical to understand that administrative law principles cannot be understood in a vast substantive void. Once the cases are reviewed, the correct evaluation takes a very different form from the Sunstein quip. Indeed, the conventional nondelegation doctrine had 148 good years before the New Deal. Put otherwise, a better way to read the situation is to note that the doctrine exerted such a powerful effect on legislatures—think again of the post-road debates—that they conformed to the standard without the need for judicial compulsion. But by 1935, the first wave of New Deal legislation came before the courts and required a very different kind of response, given the breadth of the new progressive agenda for overriding market decisions in such key areas as labor and agriculture. The level of ambition in these schemes made it difficult for Congress to specify, for example, the thousands of codes needed in order to regulate economic activity at the granular level envisioned by the New Deal. It is easy to forget the enormous scope of this enterprise under the National Industrial Recovery Act of 1933 (NIRA), which the Court eventually struck down for excessive delegation in the 1935 decision *A.L.A. Schechter Poultry Corp. v. United States.*[70] One brief account shows the scope of the effort:

> In the course of its short life from August 1933 to February 1935, NRA formulated and approved 546 codes and 185 supplemental codes filling 18 volumes and 13,000 pages; and 685 amendments and modifications. It issued over 11,000 orders interpreting, granting exemptions from, and establishing classifications under the provisions of individual codes.[71]

The objects of these regulations included wage and overtime provisions; price controls of various sorts; and detailed rules governing rebates, discounts, advertisements, and the like. The sole statutory authority for putting these rules into place was that they constituted codes of fair competition and in no way sought "to promote monopolies or to eliminate or oppress small enterprises," or discriminate against them.[72]

One might ask why Congress was so eager to transfer its authority without strings attached, for which the best answer is that NIRA was couched as "emergency legislation" that would last, at most, for two years, and even less if the president or a joint resolution of Congress declared that the emergency "has ended."[73] At the time, it was understood that Congress had greater regulatory powers in emergencies than at other times—most notably, in connection with the rent-control regulation sustained in the aftermath of World War I[74] and the mortgage moratoriums upheld in *Home Building and Loan Association v. Blaisdell.*[75] Justice Benjamin N. Cardozo in his concurrence in *Schechter* condemned this system as "delegation running riot."[76] But the key control against such wayward power was the short length of the mandate—two years. For that short fuse meant that this enormous power would not fall into the hands of a Republican president after a possible defeat in the 1936 election, when the new president would surely have different ideas of how to implement the task.

The main act in *Schechter* was not the period of delegation but its breadth of mandate to deal with "unfair competition." Chief Justice Hughes captured the difference between the old and new legal regimes by looking at the two alternative readings of the phrase "unfair competition." The hard question for these purposes is whether the new statutory definition meets the intelligible-principle standard of *Hampton*. There is a split verdict. The answer is yes if the common law definitions are used; but no, if they are not. One reason that the modern regime fails is that the vastness of its scheme does not comport well with Lon Fuller's conditions for the rule of law. Again, the result is a split verdict. Use the narrower definitions, and all is fine. Use the broad definitions, and the inconsistency, turgidity, and unpredictable nature of the system remain at a high level, whether the standard is applied by the courts or by administrative agencies.

Here is the key passage of the Hughes opinion in *Schechter*, which deftly sets out the relationship between two conceptions of unfair competition that are, in fact, worlds apart:

> The Act does not define "fair competition." "Unfair competition," as known to the common law, is a limited concept. Primarily, and strictly, it relates to the palming off of one's goods as those of a rival trader. In recent years, its scope has been extended. It has been held to apply to misappropriation as well as misrepresentation, to the selling of another's goods as one's own—to misappropriation of what equitably belongs to a competitor. [*Int'l News Serv. v. Associated Press* 248 U.S. 215, 241, 242 (1918).] Unfairness in competition has been predicated of acts which lie outside the ordinary course of business and are tainted by fraud, or coercion, or conduct otherwise prohibited by law. *Id.*, p. 258. But it is evident that, in its widest range, "unfair competition," as it has been understood in the law, does not reach the objectives of the codes which are authorized by the National Industrial Recovery Act. The codes may, indeed, cover conduct which existing law condemns, but they are not limited to conduct of that sort. The Government does not contend that the Act contemplates such a limitation. It would be opposed both to the declared purposes of the Act and to its administrative construction.
>
> The Federal Trade Commission Act (§ 5) introduced the expression "unfair methods of competition," which were declared to be unlawful. That was an expression new in the

law. Debate apparently convinced the sponsors of the legislation that the words "unfair competition," in the light of their meaning at common law, were too narrow. We have said that the substituted phrase has a broader meaning, that it does not admit of precise definition, its scope being left to judicial determination as controversies arise. What are "unfair methods of competition" are thus to be determined in particular instances, upon evidence, in the light of particular competitive conditions and of what is found to be a specific and substantial public interest. [*Fed. Trade Comm'n v. Beech-Nut Packing Co.*, 257 U.S. 441, 453 (1922); *Fed. Trade Comm'n v. Keppel & Bro.*, 291 U.S. 304, 310–312 (1934); *Fed. Trade Comm'n v. Algoma Lumber Co.*, 291 U.S. 67, 73 (1934).] To make this possible, Congress set up a special procedure. A Commission, a quasi-judicial body, was created. Provision was made for formal complaint, for notice and hearing, for appropriate findings of fact supported by adequate evidence, and for judicial review to give assurance that the action of the Commission is taken within its statutory authority.[77]

This passage gives some hint of the enormous gulf between the classical liberal conception of unfair competition that stresses force and fraud and the progressive conception that purports to find market failure in the inequality of bargaining power that it claims exists even in competitive markets. The progressive conception has to be wrong because it ignores the simple proposition that no seller or employer has any control over market price in a competitive market. The full text of Section 5 of the Federal Trade Commission Act (FTCA) covers both deception and unfair competition. The former term links itself closely to notions of fraudulent behavior that fit within the standard libertarian prohibitions. The tort of misappropriation articulated by Justice Mahlon R. Pitney in *International News Service v. Associated Press*[78] goes beyond those twin conceptions, but when it is limited to misappropriation by direct competitors, it in fact improves the overall production and dissemination of information by stopping dangerous forms of free riding, without preventing the dissemination of that information by the general public upon publication and by rival newspapers after a single day.[79]

Equally striking in this passage is the switch in the second paragraph where Hughes argues that the creation of the Federal Trade Commission cures the difficulty of definition by interposing an administrative agency to fill the gaps related to that statute. When he wrote this opinion, his claim was justified because all the cases he cited dealt with various antitrust issues, including those dealing with retail price maintenance, which were also covered by the Sherman Act. In one key case, *Dr. Miles Medical Company v. John D. Park & Sons Co.*,[80] written by none other than then-Justice Hughes in 1911 during his first tour of duty on the Supreme Court, Hughes announced that retail price maintenance was a per se antitrust violation, and the follow-up cases all dealt with variations on the common theme. His reading of the cases up through 1935 supports his position. Nonetheless, the post-1935 cases tell a more mixed story.

To see why, let's start with the dangers that arose from Section 5 of the Federal Trade Commission Act once it was unmoored from both the law of misrepresentation and the law of antitrust. The text of the act did not prevent that migration because it declares only that "unfair or deceptive acts or practices" are unlawful.[81] The discussion of "deceptive acts" ties back into common law notions of misrepresentation, and thus its application posed no serious challenge to sound principles of delegation to administrative agencies. But the reference to "unfair" created an open intellectual wound, ripe for abuse. As the list of market imperfections expands under the progressive mind-set, the list of unfair trade practices (like the list of unfair labor practices) expands with it. Thus in *E. I. Du Pont de Nemours & Co. v. FTC*,[82] the Second Circuit had to convey this Federal Trade Commission (FTC) order:

> The FTC held that Du Pont, Ethyl and two other antiknock compound manufacturers, PPG Industries, Inc. ("PPG") and Nalco Chemical Company ("Nalco"), had engaged in unfair methods of competition in violation of § 5(a)(1) when each firm independently and unilaterally adopted at different times some or all of three business practices that were neither restrictive, predatory, nor adopted for the purpose of restraining competition.[83]

It should be clear from this formulation that the class of potential antitrust-like violations that restrain competition is an empty set, once restrictive and predatory practices are put aside. Indeed, Judge Walter R. Mansfield made exactly that point about the abusive potential of FTC. He began by noting the legitimate sphere of activity that applies when dealing with classical antitrust violations, and then, in what was a virtual rerun of Hughes's opinion in *Schechter*, explored the implications of letting FTC, in which Hughes had placed much faith, determine the scope of the antitrust laws. Hughes then writes in *Schechter*:

> The Commission here asks us to go further and to hold that the "unfair methods of competition" provision of § 5 can be violated by non-collusive, non-predatory and independent conduct of a non-artificial nature, at least when it results in a substantial lessening of competition. We recognize that § 5 invests the Commission with broad powers designed to enable it to cope with new threats to competition as they arise.
>
> However ... appropriate standards must be adopted and applied to protect a respondent against abuse of power. As the Commission moves away from attacking conduct that is either a violation of the antitrust laws or collusive, coercive, predatory, restrictive or deceitful, and seeks to break new ground by enjoining otherwise legitimate practices, the closer must be our scrutiny upon judicial review. A test based solely upon restraint of competition, even if qualified by the requirement that the conduct be "analogous" to an antitrust violation, is so vague as to permit arbitrary or undue government interference with the reasonable freedom of action that has marked our country's competitive system.
>
> The term "unfair" is an elusive concept, often dependent upon the eye of the beholder. ... A line must therefore be drawn between conduct that is anticompetitive and legitimate conduct that has an impact on competition. Lessening of competition is not the substantial equivalent of "unfair methods" of competition. Section 5 is aimed at conduct, not at the result of such conduct, even though the latter is usually a relevant factor in determining whether the challenged conduct is "un-

fair."… Similarly, if anticompetitive impact were the sole test, the admittedly lawful unilateral closing of a plant or refusal to expand capacity could be found to be "unfair." The holder of a valid product patent could be prevented from exercising its lawful monopoly to charge whatever the traffic would bear, even though "a monopolist, as long as he has no purpose to restrain competition or to enhance or expand his monopoly, and does not act coercively, retains [the right to trade with whom he wishes]."[84]

In essence, *Du Pont* at the administrative law level respects the same kind of constraints that Hughes had applied through the nondelegation doctrine in *Schechter*. What is most instructive about *Du Pont* is the massive misinterpretation that it received in what is surely the most important patent and antitrust case in recent years, *Federal Trade Commission v. Qualcomm Inc.*,[85] in which District Court Judge Lucy Koh held that Qualcomm's entire long-term worldwide business model was illegal because of the company's unfair and illegal business practices under Section 5 of FTCA. Her opinion quotes selectively from *Du Pont*:

> When a business practice is challenged by the [FTC], even though, as here, it does not violate the antitrust or other laws and is not collusive, coercive, predatory or exclusionary in character, standards for determining whether it is "unfair" within the meaning of § 5 must be formulated to discriminate between normally acceptable business behavior and conduct that is unreasonable or unacceptable.[86]

But at no point did Judge Koh quote the last sentence of *Du Pont* that gives to a patentee the right to charge whatever price it wants for its patented technology, which was one of the central issues in *Qualcomm*. This omission is no small matter. Patent law is especially solicitous of "pioneer patents," which open up new areas.[87] The financial reward is an inducement to enter the space, and the ability for new entrants to compete with rival technologies—also emphasized in *Du Pont*—applies an effective market limitation to the process. A detailed examination of Judge Koh's opinion reveals that she made many other mistakes as well.[88] The overall lesson is that once structural errors are built from the ground floor, bad consequences necessarily follow. More concretely, Hughes's argument that administrative agencies will buffer the broad use of statutory language is highly contingent, and often wrong. All too often, ambitious administrators will stretch that authority to the breaking point. Those errors will rarely, if ever, run in the opposite direction. Judges like Mansfield, with a classical liberal orientation, do not have to stretch language to counteract excessively broad statutes. But progressive judges like to use a far broader definition of market failure, which, in the end, is wholly at odds with the pro-competitive purposes of the antitrust laws. It is perhaps no surprise that the Ninth Circuit issued a sharp rebuke to Judge Koh when it ordered a stay of her decision, pending review, on the ground that her decision went far beyond the existing law in finding supposedly competitive injury in unilateral pricing actions.[88a] The results are not pretty, as will become apparent by looking at the modern administrative state.

Up to now, the discussion here has been to identify the key parameters of traditional administrative law. Generally, administrative bodies systematically applied the standard rules of contractual interpretation and routinely incorporated background practices from industry and agencies. These historical norms are far removed from *Chevron* and *Brand X*.[89] Traditionally, any statutory delegation was tightly tethered to a limited scope. The cost-adjustment formulas used in *J. W. Hampton*, for example, were a relatively simple form of price adjustment, ideally suited for administrative resolution under the public rights exception. Likewise, the opposition to retroactive laws was categorical and worked as a constraint on the power of Congress and of administrative agencies. In sum, no one who raises rule-of-law concerns regarding the operations of the modern administrative state would have had any qualms about traditional forms of administrative practice.

THE FRAMEWORK APPLIED IN MODERN TIMES

The early administrative state was a blend of modest regulation and government contracts in such areas as land and patent transfers, as well as personnel and retirement obligations. All these issues persist in the modern administrative state, but they do not define it. Instead, the watershed moment came with the vast increase in government aspirations through the New Deal, which followed the simultaneous collapse of all the traditional constitutional constraints. Federalism no longer left a protected space for state action. The separation of powers was under constant challenge, with the rise of independent administrative agencies. And constitutional protection of property and contract rights ebbed. All these developments combined to create a large space for administrative action. The general question is how this new combination played out. The more specific question—relevant to some, but not all, of these issues—is how Fuller's framework applied to the new regime—an issue that receives little to no attention in *The Morality of Law*.

Bias and the Right to Be Heard

Although bias is missing from Fuller's framework, it always is fair to ask how it applies to this new environment. Here, the first constraint of the rule of law is the right to have a case adjudicated by a neutral judge under rules that guarantee a right to be heard. The rule against bias is implemented within the judicial system in many different ways. It is common for courts to exercise general jurisdiction such that they hear a broad class of cases, reducing the probability that a judge in any individual case will have formed strong preconceptions that shape the matter's outcome. In modern technical areas such as patents, taxation, and bankruptcy, this advantage is offset by the absence of field-specific knowledge required for accurate adjudication. In these areas, specialized courts may—and the issue is rightly contested—have some kind of institutional advantage. But even in such cases, other structural protections have to be put into place to ensure that these Article I courts—specialized tribunals whose judges do not have lifetime terms—are free from any form of institutional bias. One such protection against bias that these courts use are systems of rotating panel composition that ensure that the same judges do not sit together on the same cases over time.

These protections are lacking in an administrative agency that unites three functions under the same roof: the ability to engage in rulemaking, the ability to prosecute individual cases, and the ability to adjudicate the case in question. The ostensible justification for the development of three-in-one enforcement models is to reduce the time needed to bring cases to conclusion and thus to advance the efficiency of the administrative state. But these short-term benefits are only part of the larger picture, and they tend to ignore the structural losses that take place under such an arrangement.

The basic doctrine of separation of powers at the constitutional level is a recognition of the dangers that short-term efficiency advantages pose to the long-term legitimacy of the overall system. Aggregating legislative, executive, and judicial authority in a single person gives administrators too much power to pick and choose favorites and is often combined with truncated processes lacking the protections of cross-examination, discovery, and ordinary burdens of proof, especially in quasi-criminal matters that can involve potential job suspensions and hefty fines. This results in higher error costs that can, in turn, lead to greater levels of social demoralization that undercut the legitimacy of the state as a whole.

For these purposes, the intertwining of rulemaking and enforcement power is not necessarily of concern because the melding of legislative and executive functions seems, in some sense, largely unavoidable within complex administrative schemes. But the same cannot be said of the judicial function, which is often also lodged within the agency itself. Although Fuller does not deal with the issue of bias, it is hard to think that he would disagree with the analysis that follows.

At the most general level, the problem starts as one of appearances. Administrative agencies are run by single leaders or by commissions. In the former, power is concentrated in the hands of a single person, for whom, in acting alone, it would be untenable to appoint the judges who will decide particular cases.[90] The situation is scarcely better when a commission or board has the power to decide cases itself, or to appoint the individuals who will make those decisions. By statute or practice, it is common today for such commissions to have an odd number of members, usually five, to which the president gets to appoint a chairman from his own party, with the other members evenly split.[91] The usual rationale of administrative agencies stresses the subject-matter expertise of the agency's members. But the explicit and self-conscious partisan division of leadership makes it crystal-clear that key policy decisions turn on far more than agency expertise, and this reality plays out in the frequent reversals of policy as the presidency changes parties and board membership shifts by one. Indeed, the frequent necessity of some broad delegations affords a strong reason for rigorously observing the aforementioned rule-of-law constraints when it comes to board composition. I would go so far as to say that the current board and commission authority is a violation of the standard protections of procedural due process, such that the creation of independent, specialized Article I courts is required.

The issue here, however, is not merely one of appearances; it is also one of reality. Two recent Supreme Court decisions demonstrate the risk of excessive bias within the administrative law system.

In *Oil States Energy Services, LLC v. Greene's Energy Group, LLC*,[92] the Court considered whether the *inter partes* review system created by the America Invents Act of 2011 violated the requirements of separation of powers. It held—wrongly, in my view—that the public rights doctrine meant that the Patent Trial and Appeals Board (PTAB) may take cases away from Article III (or, by implication, any new Article I) courts.[93] For these purposes, the objectionable administrative law practice is the explicit ability of the head of PTAB to stack the panels with individually selected judges who favor his or her point of view in order to "secure and maintain uniformity of the Board's decisions."[94] That power means that the initial selection of judges is done with an eye to the outcome of the litigation.

Even worse, until some long-overdue administrative corrections were made within PTAB in 2018,[95] the board's practice allowed its head to add more judges to a panel to secure the desired outcome. No Article III or Article I court would ever tolerate such a stacking of the deck. It would have made perfectly good sense for the Court to issue a per se judgment that the requirements of procedural due process are necessarily violated by this kind of overt bias. It is also worth noting that once these cases are tried before PTAB, the various procedures used need not be the same as those used in district court,[96] which raises the obvious question of whether like cases will be treated alike. It follows that the jury right that applies under the Seventh Amendment to a common law action is also lost. Having two distinct procedures for the same cause of action always raises difficult questions of perception and creates opportunities for strategic behavior. Needless to say, all these issues would disappear if all post-issuance patent reviews were conducted in Article

III or Article I courts.

A similar pattern of abuse was evident in *Lucia v. Securities and Exchange Commission*,[97] which involved provisions of the Dodd-Frank Act that allowed for administrative law judges (ALJs) appointed by the Securities and Exchange Commission (SEC) to try cases involving violations of the various securities laws. In *Lucia*, the appointed ALJ was Cameron Elliot, who had an unbroken record of imposing heavy fines on the parties brought before him, as well as banning them from participating in the industry. Just those sanctions were imposed on Raymond Lucia and his corporation for a set of actions that did not involve any loss to any individual, had been commonly performed by others, and was even vetted previously by both the SEC and a private industry group. As might be expected, standard procedural protections in the case were skirted at various key points.[98]

The initial judgment by the ALJ was reviewed by the full commission, which affirmed it on a strictly party-line vote. The outcome was reversed by the Supreme Court on the ground that Elliot had been improperly appointed. Even though Elliot's decision was not considered final, his extensive powers over the case meant that, as an inferior officer, he would have had to be appointed by a head of department, which had not been done.[99] But the Appointments Clause argument works for this case and this case only. After the decision, SEC announced that it would make proper appointments; the gaping bias issue was left unresolved.[100] The ultimate solution requires that these cases be tried before some independent tribunal, whether in an Article I or Article III court. Intra-agency appointments will not do the job.

A far better appreciation of the role of custom and history in administrative law is found in *Ortiz v. United States*,[101] decided in the same term as *Oil States* and *Lucia*. Justice Elena Kagan rightly rejected a strong amicus plea by Professor Bamzai, who argued that it was improper for the Supreme Court to review any decisions made by the Court of Appeals for the Armed Services (CAAF) because it was an executive branch agency and hence not an Article III court.[102] Justice Kagan did not worry that CAAF is formally in the executive branch because its location could be changed by statute under current constitutional doctrine. To her, the key constitutional safeguard lay in the fact that CAAF judges could not be dismissed at will but served on good behavior for a limited 15-year term. The military tribunals over which CAAF presided also follow all standard rules of procedure for judicial events, and their judgments have the same effect as any other court, such as res judicata.[103]

The decisive factor for Justice Kagan was the long and unbroken historical practice of exempting military courts from Article III requirements, which dates back to the earliest courts-martial and persisted through the various reforms of military justice initiated after World War II. The question of original pedigree therefore yielded, as it should, to an unbroken historical practice, to the contrary of what happened in *Oil States* (in which Justice Kagan was in the majority).[104]

Military courts fall within the Supreme Court's appellate jurisdiction, even though they do not operate in the same fashion as Article III courts, because the unified military command structure means that the ordinary protections of separation of powers, once removed, have to be replaced by other procedures, including greater judicial assistance for the accused, than are found in ordinary civilian proceedings.[105] Nonetheless, these important procedural differences do not upset the general social understanding of the role of courts because military courts still decide cases within the general understanding of the rule of law that is the subject of this discussion.

In a deep sense, the issue is not dissimilar to that raised in *Murray's Lessee*. When there is a mature legal system that has operated without a hitch since the founding of the nation, it is just too late in the day to undo that institution by noting that it does not have all the attributes of an Article III court. Indeed, the *Oil States* case would have been far more palatable if the *inter partes* review involved a stable court that followed the usual rules of impartiality and rotation of judges, but it did not.

Guidances

A second distinctive issue in modern administrative law involves the uses of administrative "guidances" as a way around the requirements of a full-blooded notice and comment procedure normally prescribed for announcing administrative rules.[106] This issue is, again, one that arose in practice only during the mid-1990s,[107] so that it could not have been addressed by Fuller. Somewhat more puzzlingly, the topic of guidances is not addressed at all by Sunstein and Vermeule and receives only passing attention from Metzger.[108] Nonetheless, the issue has been at the forefront of much modern litigation and deserves close attention here.

In principle, no one can object to the use of guidances on routine housekeeping chores that are part and parcel of every administrative agency. No regulated party wants to slip up by improperly formatting documents or sending exhibits to the wrong office. But the issue takes on a decidedly different coloration when an administrative agency, without any public comment or external review, uses the guidance technique to stake out aggressive substantive positions by simply saying that its guidances are not final decisions and therefore not formally binding on private parties.

In fact, such documents guide any and all activities undertaken within the agency. Guidance documents dare regulated parties to deviate from the quasi-rules of which they can be said to have notice, and thereby run the risk of severe sanctions and fines imposed under the agency's broad discretion. That result comes from the fact that these guidances are treated as nonevents in judicial proceedings. It is commonly said that no individual party has standing to challenge a guidance on its face because the administrative applicant has not, as of yet, suffered some discrete pocketbook injury that is normally the entry card into federal court.

The Court's 1997 decision in *Bennett v. Spear*[109] sets out two requirements for judicial review of agency actions. First, the action must mark the "consummation" of the agency's decision-making process—it must not be of a merely tentative or interlocutory nature. And second, the action must be one by which "rights or obligations have been determined," or from which "legal consequences will flow."[110] The typical guidance does not meet the second requirement, and hence is not treated as a final agency action subject to immediate appeal under Section 704 of APA.[111] Faced with potential sanctions imposed under the agency's own views of its discretionary power, any party, however sophisticated, is left in limbo. These rules have a de facto final effect, but at the same time, no court or other independent body can review the determination in question. In some cases, a regulated party could be bold (or foolish) enough to risk invoking agency wrath by refusing to comply with the guidance's every detail and challenging eventual enforcement decisions in court.

Private parties face the all-too-credible threat of litigation by a government party that has no real financial constraints in individual cases. The government is a repeat player, which enables it to establish a creditable threat position. It is for good reason that private parties decide to back off from a full-scale confrontation, even when their case is sound. The surrender is often prudent for individual defendants in a particular litigation. But its long-term ripple effects are corrosive of all rule-of-law protections.

The appropriate response in these situations is to ensure that people have the ability to seek de novo review if their conduct is covered by these guidance statements.[112] There is no reason to think that anyone would ever press an agency when the information that it supplies is informative. But there is every reason to think that the appropriate rules in question are those enacted by Congress or, in the alternative, through regulations that themselves offer sufficient procedural protections to insulate government actors from undue political pressure during promulgation. Without such safeguards, open-ended statutes are subject to gloss by agencies that all too often have powerful incentives to expand their own jurisdiction. The diffuse nature of this injury is not a reason to deny standing. What it points out, and clearly so, is that many people have found guidance to be a powerful chill on their behavior, for which they cannot seek review unless they run the serious risk of disobedience followed by penalty and ex-post challenge. There is little reason in these cases to worry that many parties would bring ex-ante challenges if allowed. Indeed, the same techniques that are used to deal with review of notice and comment rulemaking can be invoked here. It is possible to consolidate some actions and stay others so that there is an orderly resolution of the claims in question.

One powerful illustration of the abusive nature of guidance is the (in)famous 2011 "Dear Colleague" letter issued by the Obama administration,[113] which outlined appropriate procedures for colleges and universities to apply in handling sexual harassment claims, which was later withdrawn by the Trump administration.[114] Title IX of the Education Amendments of 1972[115] forbids all educational institutions, including universities and colleges that receive federal funds, from discriminating on the grounds of sex. The statute contains only a substantive standard; it does not set out any procedures that covered institutions must use in order to deal with this issue. The most straightforward interpretation of this provision is that the government can examine individual complaints to see if any violation of the substantive norm has taken place. The 2011 guidance, however, laid out an elaborate set of procedures that universities and colleges must use in adjudicating allegations of sexual assault involving their students. It was issued to avoid scrutiny and the potential loss of federal funds, not only for the particular unit that is found out of compliance but also for any other separate units in these large and complex institutions.

The standards set by the 2011 guidance, moreover, flirt with major violations of the rudimentary norms of procedural fairness. The withdrawn guidance letter required a preponderance-of-the-evidence standard in decisions made by tribunals set up within universities, notwithstanding that the quasi-criminal nature of the offense—which carries the threat of expulsion coupled with massive and irreversible reputational damage—seems to call for a higher standard of proof.

The "Dear Colleague" standard departed from the practices adopted in most universities, which had previously used a clear-and-convincing-evidence standard for their internal purposes. In addition, the proposed procedures limited the role of attorneys and called for the anonymity of the accuser in many cases, denying any option for cross-examination, no matter how serious the charges.

These practices leave the accused in some systems with few, if any, procedural protections. The guidance allowed for internal review panels with handpicked members to increase sanctions and impose or reverse a finding of innocence on their own motion without remand for further evidence. It is worth noting that no individual university was prepared to buck these guidelines, given the possible sanctions—which would entail the loss of all government funding for the university, often amounting to hundreds of millions of dollars of grants for activities like medical research. Of even greater concern, many universities, when rid of the external compulsion, have opted to keep these new norms as their own rather than undertake another revision. Thus, Stanford provost Persis Drell affirmed that Stanford "has no intention of retreating, in any way, on the subjects of sexual assault and harassment."[116]

Given that administrative relief was not possible, the only way to challenge these sanctions was through individual lawsuits brought by aggrieved students. That litigation shows how the use of these dubious guidance provisions invites systematic bias, truncation of the right to be heard, and other affronts to standard due-process protections of the sort stoutly defended by Fuller and routinely incorporated into the criminal-justice system. To take but one example, in *Doe v. Alger*,[117] John Doe was suspended from James Madison University on charges of rape. The complainant, Jane Roe, brought charges against him four months after the pair had sex. The initial hearing, at which both testified, resulted in a decision for Doe. But that decision was subsequently reversed by an ad hoc board, which considered new evidence submitted by Roe without giving Doe the opportunity to appear and present new evidence on the other side. The sanction was a suspension of five and a half years for Doe that was affirmed first by the vice president of student affairs and then by the university president. His right to be heard was needlessly truncated, and the internal reversal of the prior acquittal without a new trial violates the most rudimentary norms of procedural due process. Upon hearing the case, the federal court found a loss of property rights from the suspension but refused to acknowledge a so-called liberty interest in harm to reputation, though publicity resulting from the university's proceedings has made it difficult for Doe to gain admission to any other institution. These proceedings—culminating in severe sanctions—unfortunately appear to satisfy all the requirements of the Obama administration's "Dear Colleague" letter, showing the direct connection between the use of guidances and fundamental affronts to due process.

Nondelegation

The basic challenge here is whether the modern application of the nondelegation doctrine is consistent with sound constitutional and administrative law provisions. With the demise of the National Industrial Recovery Act in *Schechter*, Congress quite consciously sought to separate out discrete problems, which were then addressed in separate pieces of legislation such as the Fair Labor Standards Act of 1938 (FLSA) and some version of the National Labor Relations Act of 1935 (NLRA),[118] given that the codes called for recognition of the system of collective bargaining. It is hard to resist the conclusion that this massive legislation transferred huge control downward throughout the system. Yet what happens after *Schechter*, when this type of delegated statutory authority becomes permanent? Now the nondelegation claim is a still-closer question, as key language from NIRA was imported wholesale into NLRA, where it received a much fuller definitional and institutional treatment. The clear sense is that under modern case law, this delegation would be constitutional, at which point the only remaining constraint against the abuse of power is political. From my point of view, the nondelegation doctrine is best understood as a last-ditch effort to derail a statute that should have been struck down on different grounds, also articulated in *Schechter*, for impermissibly regulating local commerce—that is, the shipment of goods after they are loaded onto local delivery trucks—and as an interference with liberty of contract under the two well-known but widely rejected decisions in *Adair v. United States*[119] and *Coppage v. Kansas*.[120] Once the federal government is entrusted with these vast powers under the Commerce Clause, it is hard to see how the nondelegation doctrine could function as an effective third line of defense.

Thus, in subsequent cases, the delegation was upheld by the Supreme Court. One of these cases is *Yakus v. United States*,[121] which arose out of a criminal conviction for selling the best cuts of beef at a price above the maximum levels allowed under the Emergency Price Control Act, imposed at the beginning of World War II. The delegation was done in the broadest of terms. It allowed the price administrator to set prices that "in his judgment will be generally fair and equitable."[122] But it would be a mistake to assume that this is the sole constraint on the operation of the section. Of perhaps greater importance is the subrule that stated that "the Administrator shall ascertain and give due consideration for the prices prevailing between October 1 and October 15, 1941."[123] Given the huge number of products on the market between those dates and the great difficulties involved in setting prices for them individually, it was a virtual certainty that the prevailing price standard would necessarily dominate in most cases, given its administrative ease. But, as with all price-fixing systems, it cannot work, for example, with agricultural commodities, where "abnormal or seasonal market conditions" could require some further adjustments in particular cases.[124]

In dealing with the delegation question, it is critical to first note that the law was an emergency law operative in time of war, at which time the general willingness of the courts to intervene is at its low ebb.[125] Second, the rule in question was temporary in nature. The initial act called for it to be terminated on June 30, 1943, but it was later extended until June 30, 1944. Unlike the situation with rent-control statutes,[126] it was quite clear that the duration of this law would collapse under its own weight. Third, the challenge in this case worked itself up through a criminal proceeding, so that the ultimate decision on the validity of the act took place on March 27, 1944, just as the statute was about to terminate. It is an open question as to whether the same result would have happened if there was a facial challenge to the law, but even that could not have been completed in the short time between the announcement and the implementation of the statute. In dealing with *Yakus*, the common view is to stress the "fair and equitable" language. But on balance, the choice is clear. If there is to be a system of price controls in wartime, it must be put into place by administrative means.

The case therefore looks quite different from *Schechter*, from which it was explicitly distinguished on the grounds that NIRA "prescribed no method of attaining [its statutory] end save by the establishment of codes of fair competition, the nature of whose permissible provisions was left undefined."[127] *Yakus* was a 6–3 decision, and there is much to be said on the other side. But questions of delegation do give rise to real issues of scale and degree, and the dissent of Justice Roberts offers no guidance on how any price-control system should be implemented. On balance, I think that *Yakus* was right, for even before the New Deal, governments exercised many emergency powers in time of war, not always with the best results.

The second major delegation case after *Yakus* is *Mistretta v. United States*,[128] in which the delegation question is harder to resolve. As a general proposition, the law is always better at identifying fundamental principles of right and wrong than it is at assessing the remedy for the wrong, once identified. That proposition applies to criminal, as well as civil, law, as there is no unique formula that indicates which cases of murder deserve the death penalty, which deserve life imprisonment, and which deserve some lesser punishment. It is always possible for people to have some loose sense of which factors inculpate and which exculpate. But even if there were perfect agreement on which factors belong on which list, two sorts of residual uncertainty would remain, for which informed discourse would not produce a consensus. First, how much weight should be given to each of the factors? Second, how should each factor be evaluated in the context of each individual case? At the same time, it is easy to find odd disparities in the treatment of different cases, across different judges, and even in the decision of a given judge. There are too many permutations for all cases to fall into a wholly consistent order. There is, of course, a common belief that like cases should be treated alike. But that principle does not make it easy to determine which cases fall into which classes.

The Sentencing Reform Act of 1984[129] sought to fill this gap, and *Mistretta* held that the *mandatory* guidelines issued pursuant to the statute were valid, by an appeal to the "intelligible principle" doctrine of *Hampton*. The tariff correction rules in *Hampton* represent a modest, semi-mathematical exercise. The command in *Mistretta* envisions a comprehensive administrative reform of the entire federal criminal code. But, in the end, the rationale for the decision was simply that if Congress wanted guidelines, there was only one way for it to get them: by the formation of a commission. It is not possible to have Congress delegate the enormous task of first promulgating and then continuously updating the guidelines to some committee.

In defense of his decision, Justice Harry Blackmun wrote: "Applying this 'intelligible principle' test to congressional delegations, our jurisprudence has been driven by a practical understanding that in our increasingly complex society, replete with ever changing and more technical problems, Congress simply cannot do its job absent an ability to delegate power under broad general directives."[130] To push matters along, Congress developed its own guidelines system, which included "sentencing ranges" applicable "for each category of offense involving each category of defendant."[131] It added further guidelines for drug offenses, crimes of violence, recidivists, kingpins, and the like.[132] The strongest argument for the delegation is that it is not possible to think of any more specific guidelines that could provide greater precision while still maintaining a sufficient level of generality.

Even with these qualifications, *Mistretta* is far removed from *Hampton*, in which precise mathematical tests were capable of precise application. But the choice was stark: do it this way, or don't do it at all. So why do it? The best explanation is that it is hard to envision any major substantive changes in the criminal law through the revision of sentencing guidelines that come close to the huge transformation involved in *Schechter* with the rival definitions of "unfair competition." It is also difficult to infer any illicit purpose in the entire effort to rationalize the overall system, given that standardization is a way to control discretion, which is wholly consistent with classical liberal principles.

By the same token, it is easy to see why individual judges protest the limitations on their discretion—usually doing so for reasons that reflect their view that the mandatory guidelines are an impermissible stranglehold on judicial independence. By no stretch of the imagination do sentencing guidelines have to be enforced for all cases that involve sentencing. This is in sharp contrast to *Yakus*, where the system of price controls has to be uniform if it is to work at all. And it is no surprise that over time, the guidelines ceased to be mandatory, even though it is doubtful how much change there was in practice.[133]

It seems quite clear that the difficulties of scale and complexity weighed heavily in both *Yakus* and *Mistretta*. It is equally clear that the uneasiness of both cases has led to continuous turmoil over the modern application of the doctrine, which came to a head in *Gundy v. United States*.[134] This case—reduced to its simplest level—looked at whether, in the Sex Offender Registration and Notification Act (SORNA),[135] Congress could permissibly delegate to the attorney general the decision to apply a new registration requirement to sex offenders whose convictions predate the passage of the statute. In a rare left–right coalition, none of the amici curiae briefs supported the federal government. But that is where the agreement ended. At the one end, the New Civil Liberties Alliance (organized by Philip Hamburger) took the position that Congress could not divest itself of any of the lawmaking power conferred on it by Article I of the Constitution—an approach that could ban all delegation of any sort.[136] On the other side, the American Civil Liberties Union sought to preserve the tradition of broad delegation in economic affairs while condemning the use of broad delegation in criminal contexts.[137]

In the end, *Gundy* did nothing to resolve the disarray concerning the nondelegation doctrine. The most unusual feature of the case was not its 5–3 vote to uphold the statute. That outcome arose because Justice Brett Kavanaugh had not yet taken his seat on the Court when *Gundy* was argued and thus did not participate in the vote. A 4–4 decision would have resulted in affirmance without an opinion. Perhaps the case could, and should, have been set for reargument. But that was not done, so to allow the battle royal between the four liberals led by Justice Kagan and the three conservatives led by Justice Gorsuch, Justice Samuel Alito issued a short and puzzling opinion, in which he announced: "To reconsider the approach [to nondelegation] we have taken for the past 84 years, I would support that effort [to revisit the nondelegation doctrine]. But because a majority is not willing to do that it would be freakish to single out the provision at issue here for special treatment."[138] Clearly, the matter is put to rest, so who has the better of the current argument?

Let's start with the basic provision of "Initial registration of sex offenders unable to comply with subsection":

> The Attorney General shall have the authority to specify the applicability of the requirements of this subchapter to sex offenders convicted before the enactment of this chapter or its implementation in a particular jurisdiction, and to prescribe rules for the registration of any such sex offenders and for other categories of sex offenders who are unable to comply with subsection (b)[dealing with initial registration].[139]

Pursuant to this section, the attorney general first issued an interim rule in February 2007, which held that SORNA applied in full to all sex offenders. That rule was made permanent in December 2010, almost four years later. There was no evidence that any detailed inquiry was made into an intermediate position that might have been taken. As Justice Gorsuch complained in his long and powerful dissent, there is nothing within this provision that indicates whether all, some, or none of the defendants, let alone which ones, should be subject to the rule, or why. In addition, the twice-made decision to apply SORNA across the board makes it clear that subtle distinctions on individual equities or enforcement difficulties played no role in articulating the rule. In her majority opinion, Justice Kagan sought to deflect this concern by reading the provision "in context." But the supposed context was just a generalized statement that Congress wanted to address the applicability of SORNA to offenders as soon as compliance was possible.[140] Yet her argument is weak because it ignores the possibility, such as that developed in *Mistretta*, of the preparation of a set of congressional guidelines that might have indicated how to undertake the inquiry.

In light of this discussion, perhaps the most sensible resolution of *Gundy*'s challenge is to understand the gulf that separates it from the successful arguments raised in *Yakus* and *Mistretta*. The basic position is that extensive delegations may be appropriate when it is certain that the final choices will require complex adjustments to deal with novel cases and imprecise comparisons. But in *Gundy*, we only have a yes/no decision that Congress could make as well as, or better than, the attorney general acting on his own. In this case, point delegation becomes an evasion of responsibility and should be struck down. The principle clearly applies in criminal cases, but I see no reason why it should not extend to civil cases as well. There is nothing about the advent of the administrative state, or the vast expansion of congressional powers, that always requires delegation for successful implementation. Start small, by noting that Congress, too, can make once-and-for-all determinations.

The Delegation of Benefit Distributions

One of the major features of the revolution that came with the New Deal is that it greatly expanded the role of government, not just in enforcing criminal and civil sanctions but also in distributing benefits of great value to private individuals through the administrative process. A question arises about the extent to which rule-of-law constraints should limit the power of government to give away valuable licenses to private parties. In dealing with this issue, Fuller was profoundly uneasy because he did not see how his rule-of-law provisions applied in cases where the government granted rewards to private firms or individuals,[141] particularly in connection with the award of valuable routes by the Civil Aeronautics Board and the award of valuable spectrum by the Federal Communications Commission (FCC). Fuller devotes a grand total of four pages to these two agencies.[142] At no point, however, does he address whether the modern administrative state has the tools that allow it to make grants of public property to private parties by administrative means alone. Sunstein and Vermeule express similar uneasiness, noting: "Fuller's view of the inherent unsuitability of economic allocation to legal (as opposed to managerial) resolution, would exclude a substantial chunk of what agencies do from the domain of administrative law's morality."[143]

There is good reason to join in their skepticism, but this bald conclusion does not get to the root of the governance problem. When ordinary individuals make gifts of their own assets, they can choose the persons to whom they wish to make the gift and the terms and conditions on which the gift is made. They are typically absolute owners of the property in question and therefore need satisfy no one but themselves. In those cases, they can either sell or give as they see fit. But fiduciaries lay under much sterner obligations, at least in the absence of explicit authorization to engage in certain types of transactions. Normally, they may never give away trust property and can sell it only for the maximum rate of return. Where the dealings take place at arm's length, the trustees are given some slack under the business judgment rule. But where there is self-dealing, there must be an independent "fair value" appraisal to show that the transaction was not a disguised gift.

The situation changes radically when someone is put in control of public assets, which are appropriately described as being held in public trust, thus placing on government agencies all the standard duties of trustees in managing and dealing with the property. One of those duties is to ensure that the property in question is devoted to public use, which means that it can never be given away to this or that private party, without receiving something in return. I have elsewhere described this situation as the inverse of the Takings

Clause: public property shall not be transferred for private use without compensation, just as a corporation is not permitted to make a gift of corporate assets to any person if it cuts against the interest of the shareholders.[144] The correct solution for distributing these valuable assets, therefore, is always to conduct some form of auction, so that the government avoids any charge of favoritism and gets the highest return for its investment. It is a matter of business judgment whether the frequencies should be leased or sold to private parties. It was just that solution that was most prominently proposed by Ronald Coase in his classic 1959 article "The Federal Communications Commission,"[145] to which neither Fuller in 1964 nor Sunstein and Vermeule in 2018 refer.

Nor was the auction approach seriously considered in the formative years of FCC. Instead, the allocation system was one of administrative fiat, and here, as with *Schechter*, the delegation had to be broad enough to allow FCC to set up some nonmarket solution for the allocation of the spectrum. The applicable words of its enabling statute called for FCC to make allocations in accordance with the "public interest, convenience, and necessity,"[146] which is no standard at all. But when he upheld this delegation in *National Broadcasting Co. v. United States*,[147] Justice Frankfurter did not offer any guidance on how FCC should complete its task. Instead, he took the extra precaution of creating property rights in the spectrum that could then be auctioned off to private parties:

> [W]e are asked to regard the Commission as a kind of traffic officer, policing the wave lengths to prevent stations from interfering with each other. But the Act does not restrict the Commission merely to supervision of the traffic. It puts upon the Commission the burden of determining the composition of that traffic. The facilities of radio are not large enough to accommodate all who wish to use them. Methods must be devised for choosing from among the many who apply. And since Congress itself could not do this, it committed the task to the Commission.[148]

Justice Frankfurter's observation about the condition of scarcity is the reason to have an auction, not to avoid one. But once it set off down the wrong path, FCC could never make good on the task delegated to it under the statute. Political jockeying dominated the question in search of free goods,[149] which is one reason that, after modern reforms, broadband spectrum today is routinely auctioned off to the highest bidder.

The great conceit of administrative law in this area is that the agency has some way to discharge its management task, once the delegation is made. This is not always the case. Hence the question is whether any government gift program should be allowed at all. To reach a conclusion, we have to come to grips with a common issue raised in connection with corporations' giving charitable gifts: either they give them to help build goodwill for the firm, or they make transactions only that a vast majority of the shareholders prefer.[150] Governments are not normally in the business of improving goodwill, nor are they likely to mirror the preferences of a diverse citizenry. It is far too late for it to be wise to challenge the huge system of wealth transfers that happen through Social Security, Medicare, and the like. But none of those programs has ever addressed the disposition of productive assets, which is the implicit constraint that is operative in the spectrum cases.

ENDNOTES

1. U.S. Const. art. II, § 2, cl. 2. ("[The president] shall nominate, and by and with the Advice and Consent of the Senate, shall appoint Ambassadors, other public Ministers and Consuls, Judges of the Supreme Court, and all other Officers of the United States, whose Appointments are not herein otherwise provided for, and which shall be established by Law: but the Congress may by Law vest the Appointment of such inferior Officers, as they think proper, in the President alone, in the Courts of Law, or in the Heads of Departments.")

2. *See, e.g., Lucia v. Sec. & Exch. Comm'n,* 138 S. Ct. 2044 (2018) *(rev'g Raymond J. Lucia Cos., Inc. v. Sec. & Exch. Comm'n,* 832 F.3d 277 (D.C. Cir. 2016)). For further discussion, *see* Richard A. Epstein, *Structural Protections for Individual Rights: The Indispensable Role of Independent Federal Courts in the Administrative State,* 26 Geo. Mason L. Rev. (forthcoming 2019).

3. U.S. Const. art. I, § 8, cl. 18 ("The Congress shall have Power . . . [t]o make all Laws which shall be necessary and proper for carrying into Execution the foregoing Powers, and all other Powers vested by this Constitution in the Government of the United States, or in any Department or Officer thereof").

4. Gary Lawson and Patricia B. Granger, *The "Proper" Scope of Federal Power: A Jurisdictional Interpretation of the Sweeping Clause,* 43 Duke L. J. 267 (1993).

5. *McCulloch v. Maryland* 17 U.S. 316, 421 (1819). The chief justice did not quite explain why it was necessary to have a federal bank when credit for the United States was freely available elsewhere. Nor did he explain why it was proper, given the risk of monopoly.

6. *See* U.S. Const. amend. XIII, § 2; amend. XIV, § 5; amend. XV, § 2.

7. *United States v. Morrison,* 529 U.S. 598, 620 (2000) (striking down part of the Violence Against Women Act of 1994).

8. U.S. Const. art I, § 1.

9. Gary Lawson et al., The Origins of the Necessary and Proper Clause (Cambridge U. Press, 2010). *See also* Max Schanzenbach and Nadav Shoked, *Reclaiming Fiduciary Law for the City,* 70 Stan. L. Rev. 565 (2018) (insisting that city officials owe fiduciary duties, "as supported—indeed, necessitated—by U.S. law's history, structure, and normative logic").

10. Richard A. Epstein, *The Utilitarian Foundations of Natural Law,* 12 Harv. J. L. & Pub. Pol'y 712 (1989) (applying consequentialist logic to many private law doctrines of property contract and tort).

11. Neomi Rao, *Administrative Collusion: How Delegation Diminishes the Collective Congress,* 60 N.Y.U. L. Rev. 1463 (2015).

12. Richard A. Epstein, *Foreword: Just Do It! Title IX as a Threat to University Autonomy,* 101 Mich. L. Rev. 1365 (2003) (showing how the mandate of Title IX of the Civil Rights Act has been expanded by administrative decisions and letter rulings to impose an entire legal regime on intercollegiate sports).

13. Eric A. Posner and Adrian Vermeule, *Interring the Nondelegation Doctrine,* 69 U. Chi. L. Rev. 1721 (2002).

14. *Id.* at 1725.

15. Curtis A. Bradley and Trevor W. Morrison, *Historical Gloss and the Separation of Powers,* 126 Harv. L. Rev. 411 (2012). One application of this principle is found in *Zivotofsky v. Kerry,* 135 S. Ct. 2076 (2015), where constitutional practice was held to vest in the president the right to recognize foreign nations, an example of a "federative power" that the Constitution does not assign to any particular branch of government.

16. William Baude, *Constitutional Liquidation,* 71 STAN. L. REV. 1, at 1, 8–21 (2019) (presenting Madison's view of the subject).

17. Richard A. Epstein, *Our Implied Constitution,* 53 WILLAMETTE L. REV. 295 (2017).

18. Richard A. Epstein, THE CLASSICAL LIBERAL CONSTITUTION: THE UNCERTAIN QUEST FOR LIMITED GOVERNMENT 68–71, 97–100 (Harv. U. Press, 2014).

19. *Murray's Lessee v. Hoboken Land & Improvement Co.,* 59 U.S. 272 (1855) discussed *infra* Part 2, at 45–46.

20. *Magoun v. Illinois Tr. & Sav. Bank,* 170 U.S. 283, 287 (1898) ("Legacy and inheritance taxes are not new in our laws. They have existed in Pennsylvania for over sixty years and have been enacted in other States. They are not new in the laws of other countries").

21. John Locke, SECOND TREATISE ON GOVERNMENT, Peter Laslett ed. (Cambridge U. Press, 1988) (1689)

22. Richard R. John, SPREADING THE NEWS: THE AMERICAN POSTAL SYSTEM FROM FRANKLIN TO MORSE 1–24 (Harv. U. Press, 1998).

23. U.S. CONST. art. I, § 8, cl. 7.

24. 3 ANNALS OF CONG. 229–41 (1791).

25. *Id.* at 229 (emphasis removed).

26. *Id.*

27. *Id.* at 233.

28. Jerry L. Mashaw, CREATING THE ADMINISTRATIVE CONSTITUTION: THE LOST ONE HUNDRED YEARS OF AMERICAN ADMINISTRATIVE LAW (Yale U. Press, 2012); *see also* Richard R. John, SPREADING THE NEWS: THE AMERICAN POSTAL SYSTEM FROM FRANKLIN TO MORSE 1–24 (Harv. U. Press, 1998).

29. For a discussion of the rate of customary contract formation, *see* Richard A. Epstein, *The Path to the T. J. Hooper: The Theory and History of Custom in the Law of Tort,* 21 J. LEGAL STUD. 1 (1992).

30. Aditya Bamzai, *The Origins of Judicial Deference to Executive Interpretation,* 126 YALE L. J. 908, 912–13, 912, n.5 (2017).

31. Gillian E. Metzger, *1930s Redux: The Administrative State Under Siege,* 131 HARV. L. REV. 141, n.245 (2017).

32. Bamzai, *supra* note 30, at 916 (italics in original).

33. For a discussion of this process, *see* Epstein, *Structural Protections for Individual Rights: The Indispensable Role of Independent Federal Courts in the Administrative State,* 26 GEO. MASON L. REV. at 21–26 (forthcoming 2019).

34. *See, e.g., Edward's Lessee v. Darby,* 25 U.S. 206, 210 (1827).

35. For the applicable rules, *see* U.C.C. §§ 1–303 (AM. LAW INST. & UNIF. LAW COMM'N 2003) (dealing with the course of performance, the course of dealing, and trade usage. The first applies to a particular transaction; the second to a pattern of transactions between the same parties; and the last to an industry practice. The more individuated the evidence, the more powerful).

36. *Brown v. United States,* 113 U.S. 568 (1885).

37. *Id.* at 569.

38. *United States v. Alabama Great S. Ry.,* 142 U.S. 615 (1892).

39. *Id.* at 621.

40. *Murray's Lessee v. Hoboken Land & Improv. Co.,* 59 U.S. 272 (1856).

41. U.S. Const. art. III, § 1 ("The judicial Power of the United States, shall be vested in one supreme Court, and in such inferior Courts as the Congress may from time to time ordain and establish").

42. For a fuller account, *see* Mashaw, *supra* note 28, at 217–18.

43. *Id.*

44. *Murray's Lessee,* 59 U.S. at 277, 284. For my detailed discussion of these matters, *see* Richard A. Epstein, *The Supreme Court Tackles Patent Reform: Why the Supreme Court Should End Inter Partes Review in Oil States,* 19 Federalist Soc. Rev. 116 (2017).

45. *See* Caleb Nelson, *Adjudication in the Political Branches,* 107 Colum. L. Rev. 559 (2007). For the perspective that the public rights exception covers cases only in which life, liberty, and property are not at issue, *see* William Baude, *Adjudication Outside Article III,* 133 Harv. L. Rev. (forthcoming 2019), *available at* https://papers.ssrn.com/sol3/papers.cfm?abstract_id=3194945. The point seems odd because all cases typically involve one of the three, and this interpretation does not take into account the public status of the defendant in these cases. Neither article stresses the customary evolution under which these Article I courts were up and running for decades before they were subject to a systematic constitutional challenge.

46. *Field v. Clark,* 143 U.S. 649 (1892).

47. Tariff Act of October 1, 1890, 26 stat. 573, c. 1244, § 3.

48. *Field,* 143 U.S. at 682–92, citing *The Aurora v. United States* ("The Brig *Aurora*"), 11 U.S. 382 (1813), and referring thereafter to an unbroken line of Supreme Court precedents.

49. *Id.* at 692.

50. Posner and Vermeule, *supra* note 13, at 1739.

51. *Field v. Clark,* 143 U.S. at 692–93.

52. *J. W. Hampton, Jr. & Co. v. United States,* 276 U.S. 394 (1928).

53. *Id.* at 404.

54. *Id.*

55. Cass R. Sunstein, *Nondelegation Canons,* 67 U. Chi. L. Rev. 315 (2000).

56. *Crowell v. Benson,* 285 U.S. 22 (1932).

57. Longshoremen's and Harbor Workers' Compensation Act, 33 U.S.C. §§ 901–950 (1946).

58. *Crowell,* 285 U.S. at 51.

59. *Arizona Grocery v. Topeka, Atchison, & Santa Fe Ry.,* 284 U.S. 370 (1932).

60. *Id.* at 386.

61. *Id.*

62. *Id.* at 387.

63. *Id.* at 389.

64. Cass R. Sunstein and Adrian Vemeule, *The Morality of Administrative Law,* 131 Harv. L. Rev. at 1956–609 (2018).

65. *See infra* Part 4, at 161–174.

66. *Bd. of Pub. Util. Comm'rs v. New York Tel. Co.,* 271 U.S. 23 (1926).

67. *R.R. Bd. v. Alton R.R. Co.,* 295 U.S. 330 (1935).

68. *Id.* at 349–50.

69. Sunstein, *supra* note 55, at 322.

70. *A.L.A. Schechter Poultry Corp. v. United States,* 295 U.S. 495 (1935). *See also Panama Ref. Co. v. Ryan,* 293 U.S. 388, 413 (1935). I put aside the second successful nondelegation challenge in *Panama Refining* because it involved an administrative glitch that resulted in the noninclusion of key provisions in the statute.

71. Louis L. Jaffe, *An Essay on Delegation of Legislative Power: II,* 47 COLUM. L. REV. 561, 570 (1947).

72. National Industrial Recovery Act of 1933, Pub. L. No. 73-67, § 3(a)(2), 48 Stat. 195, 196 (1933).

73. *Id.* § 2(c), 48 Stat. at 196.

74. *See Block v. Hirsh,* 256 U.S. 135 (1921).

75. *Home Bldg. & Loan Ass'n v. Blaisdell,* 290 U.S. 398 (1934).

76. *Id.* 295 U.S. at 563 (Cardozo, J., concurring).

77. *Schechter,* 295 U.S. at 531–32.

78. *Int'l News Serv. v. Associated Press,* 248 U.S. 215 (1918).

79. For my defense of this result, see Richard A. Epstein, *The Basic Structure of Intellectual Property Law* in OXFORD HANDBOOK OF INTELLECTUAL PROPERTY LAW 25, 43–45 (Rochelle C. Dreyfuss et al. eds., Oxford U. Press, 2018); Richard A. Epstein, *International News Service v. Associated Press: Custom and Law as Sources of Property Rights in News,* 78 VA. L. REV. 85 (1992).

80. *Dr. Miles Med. Co. v. John D. Park & Sons Co.,* 220 U.S. 373 (1911).

81. 15 U.S.C. § 45(a)1 (2017).

82. *E .I. Du Pont de Nemours & Co. v. FTC,* 729 F.2d 128 (2d Cir. 1984).

83. *Id.* at 130.

84. *Id.* at 138.

85. *Fed. Trade Commn. v. Qualcomm Inc.,* Case No. 17-CV-00220-LHK, 2019 WL 2206013 (N.D. Cal. May 21, 2019).

86. *Id.* at 11.

87. For the standard account, *see* the USLegal definition of *pioneer patent law:* "Pioneer patent refers to a patent that covers a function or a major technological advance never before performed. . . . Under the U.S. law, the claims relating to a pioneer patent are entitled to broader interpretation and therefore, should be given a broader range of equivalents." *Pioneer Patent Law and Legal Definition,* USLEGAL, *available at* https://definitions.uslegal.com/p/pioneer-patent/ (last visited Aug. 10, 2019). That last phrase refers to the doctrine of equivalents that allows a patentee to sue for infringement of a device that is not explicitly covered by the patent. For discussion, *see Warner-Jenkinson Co., Inc. v. Hilton Davis Chem. Co.,* 520 U.S. 17 (1997).

88. *See* Richard A. Epstein, *Judge Koh's Monopolization Mania: Her Novel Assault Against Qualcomm Is an Abuse of Antitrust Theory,* NEB. L. REV. (forthcoming 2019). Here is an especially pointed criticism from a current FTC commissioner who disavows her own agency:

    Here, the judge concluded that Qualcomm had a duty to license its intellectual property to chip-making rivals, even though Qualcomm did not have a pre-existing, voluntary and profitable course of dealing with them. So she expanded the scope of *Aspen Skiing [v. Aspen Highlands Skiing,* 472 U.S. 585 (1985)] [dealing with duties to deal with former customers]. Peering into the distant past, she found that in 1999

Qualcomm said it was licensing some patents to some chip makers. Although it has long since stopped, and presumably those patents have long since expired, she reasoned that "Qualcomm itself has licensed its [patents] to rival" chip makers, and therefore had a duty under *Aspen Skiing* to "continue" doing so.

Never mind that the judge's reference point involved licensing different patents, to different competitors, in a different century. By this logic, *Aspen Skiing* now means that if a company ever sells any product to any competitor, it then could have a perpetual antitrust obligation to sell every product to every competitor.

See Christine Wilson, *A Court's Dangerous Antitrust Overreach: Qualcomm Licensed Some of Its Chips 20 Years Ago. A Judge Says That Obliges It to License All of Them Now,* WALL ST. J. (MAY 28, 2019), *available at* https://www.wsj.com/articles/a-courts-dangerous-antitrust-overreach-11559085055. For the weaknesses of the Supreme Court's opinion in *Aspen Skiing, see* Dennis W. Carlton, *A General Analysis of Exclusionary Conduct and Refusal to Deal—Why Aspen and Kodak Are Misguided,* National Bureau of Economic Research Working Paper No. 8105 (Feb. 2001), *available at* https://www.nber.org/papers/w8105.

88a. *Federal Trade Commission v. Qualcomm, Inc.,* 935 F. 3d 752 (9th Cir. 2019).

89. *Nat'l Cable & Telecomm. v. Brand X Internet Servs.,* 545 U.S. 967 (2005).

90. *PHH Corp. v. Consumer Fin. Prot. Bureau,* 839 F.3d 1 (D.C. Cir. 2016) (Kavanaugh, J.), *rev'd en banc,* 881 F.3d 75 (D.C. Cir. 2018) (Pillard, J.). For my defense of the Kavanaugh position, *see* Richard A. Epstein, *Regulatory Enforcement Under New York's Martin Act: From Financial Fraud to Global Warming,* 154 N.Y.U. J.L. & BUS. 805, 810–13 (2018).

91. For the structure of the FCC, *see* Nat'l Telecomms. & Info. Admin., *The Federal Communications Commission (FCC), available at* https://www.ntia.doc.gov/book-page/federal-communications-commission-fcc (last visited Aug. 10, 2019). For information on the National Labor Relations Board, *see* The Board, NAT'L LAB. REL. BOARD, *available at* https://www.nlrb.gov/about-nlrb/who-we-are/board (last visited Aug. 10, 2019).

92. *Oil States Energy Servs., LLC v. Greene's Energy Grp., LLC,* 138 S. Ct. 1365 (2018).

93. Epstein, *The Supreme Court Tackles Patent Reform, supra* note 44.

94. *Nidec Motor Co. v. Zhongshan Broad Ocean Motor Co.,* 868 F.3d 1013, 1020 (Fed. Cir. 2017). The Court in *Nidec* was troubled by these due-process concerns but did not rule on them because the case was decided on other grounds.

95. Gene Quinn, *USPTO Begins Process for Finding New Leadership at the PTAB,* IPWATCHDOG.COM (Sept. 5, 2018), *available at* http://www.ipwatchdog.com/2018/09/05/uspto-finding-new-leadership-ptab/id=100995.

96. For discussion, *see* Brief for Petitioner, *Oil States Energy Services, LLC v. Greene's Energy Group, LLC,* 138 S. Ct. 1365 (2018)(No. 16-172), *available at* http://www.scotusblog.com/wp-content/uploads/2017/08/16-712-ts.pdf.

97. *Lucia v. SEC,* 138 S. Ct. 2044 (2018).

98. *See, e.g.,* Brief of the New Civil Liberties Alliance as Amicus Curiae Supporting Petitioners, *Lucia v. SEC,* 138 S. Ct. 2044 (No. 17-130), *available at* https://www.supremecourt.gov/DocketPDF/17/17-130/37036/20180228145918749_17-130%20Lucia%20Amicus%20Brief.pdf.

99. *Freytag v. Commissioner,* 501 U.S. 868 (1991) (holding that "special trial judges" in the tax court are inferior officials even though they do not have the final say in the cases over which they preside).

100. Mark Schoeff, Jr., *SEC Orders New Enforcement Hearings as a Result of Supreme Court Ruling,* Inv. News (Aug. 28, 2018), *available at* https://www.investmentnews.com/article/20180828/FREE/180829920/sec-orders-new-enforcement-hearings-as-a-result-of-supreme-court.

101. *Ortiz v. United States,* 138 S. Ct. 2165 (2018).

102. Brief (2018) of Aditya Bamzai as Amicus Curiae Supporting Neither Party, *Ortiz v. United States,* 138 S. Ct. 2165 (No. 16-0671). The Supreme Court paid Bamzai the extraordinary compliment of allowing him to participate in oral argument, given the evident excellence and sophistication of his brief.

103. *Ortiz,* 138 S. Ct. at 2174.

104. *Id.* at 2174–78.

105. Uniform Code of Military Justice (UCMJ), art. 27, 10 U.S.C. § 827 (2016). Congress imbued the UCMJ with procedural protections, including mandatory appointed counsel for all serious courts-martial. *See United States v. Steele,* 53 M.J. 274 (C.A.A.F. 2000); the stringent rules forbidding unlawful command influence in trials in UCMJ, art. 37, 10 U.S.C. § 837 (1968); and *United States v. Baldwin,* 54 M.J. 308 (C.A.A.F. 2001). The Court has a long history of recognizing the distinct but fundamentally sound nature of this non–Article III adjudicatory system. *See, e.g., Middendorf v. Henry,* 425 U.S. 25 (1973); *Solorio v. United States,* 483 U.S. 435 (1987).

106. For my more detailed account of the issue, *see* Epstein, *supra* Part I, note 15.

107. Todd Rakoff, *The Choices Between Formal and Informal Modes of Administrative Regulation,* 52 Admin. L. Rev. 159, 159 (2000).

108. Metzger, *supra* note 31, 10–11, 19, 25–26, 78.

109. *Bennett v. Spear,* 520 U.S. 154 (1997).

110. *Id.* at 178–79 (internal citations omitted).

111. *See Abbott Labs. v. Gardner,* 387 U.S. 136, 150–51 (1967) (reviewing APA's finality requirement).

112. For my extended critique, *see* Richard A. Epstein, *The Role of Guidances in Modern Administration Procedure: The Case for* DeNovo *Review,* 8 J. Legal Analysis 47 (2016).

113. Russlynn Ali, Assistant Secretary for Civ. Rts., Office for Civ. Rts., U.S. Dep't of Educ., "Dear Colleague" Letter (Apr. 4, 2011), *available at* https://www2.ed.gov/about/offices/list/ocr/letters/colleague-201104.pdf.

114. Candice Jackson, Acting Assistant Secretary for Civ. Rts., Office for Civ. Rts., U.S. Dep't of Educ., "Dear Colleague" Letter at 1 nn.1–2 (Sept. 22, 2017), *available at* https://www2.ed.gov/about/offices/list/ocr/letters/colleague-title-ix-201709.pdf.

115. Title IX of the Education Amendments of 1972, 20 U.S.C. §§ 1681–1688 (2017) and its implementing regulations, 34 C.F.R. §§ 106.1–106.9 (2006).

116. Persis Drell, quoted in Adesuwa Agbonile, *New Federal Assault Regulations Will Roll Back Protections for Victims. How Might This Impact Stanford's Campus?,* Stan. Daily (Sept. 4, 2018), *available at* https://www.stanforddaily.com/2018/09/04/new-federal-sexual-assault-regulations-will-roll-back-protections-for-victims-how-might-this-impact-stanfords-campus.

117. *Doe v. Alger,* 175 F. Supp. 3d 646 (W.D. Va. 2016).

118. National Labor Relations Act of 1935, 29 U.S.C. §§ 151–169 (1935).

119. *Adair v. United States,* 208 U.S. 161 (1908) (striking down federal collective-bargaining statutes).

120. *Coppage v. Kansas,* 236 U.S. 1 (1915) (striking down a Kansas collective-bargaining statute).

121. *Yakus v. United States,* 321 U.S. 414 (1944).

122. *Id.* at 420.

123. *Id.* at 421.

124. *Id.*

125. *See* the *Selective Draft Law Cases,* 245 U.S. 366 (1918). The same principle was carried forward, more dubiously, in dealing with a moratorium on the enforcement of home mortgages in *Home Building & Loan Association v. Blaisdell,* 290 U.S. 398 (1934).

126. *See Block,* 256 U.S. at 257.

127. *Yakus,* 321 U.S. at 424.

128. *Mistretta v. United States,* 488 U.S. 361 (1989).

129. 18 U.S.C. §§ 3551–3559 (1982 ed., Supp. IV); 28 U.S.C. §§ 991–998 (1982 ed., Supp. IV).

130. *Mistretta,* 488 U.S. at 372.

131. *Id.* at 374 (quoting 28 U.S.C. § 994(b)(1982, Supp IV)).

132. *Id.* at 378.

133. *United States v. Booker,* 543 U.S. 220 (2005).

134. *Gundy v. United States,* 139 S. Ct. 2116 (2019).

135. Sex Offender Registration and Notification Act, 34 U.S.C. § 20913 (2006).

136. Brief of the New Civil Liberties Alliance as Amicus Curiae Supporting Petitioner at 5-16, *Gundy v. United States, available at* https://perma.cc/5F67-NCA5.

137. Brief of the American Civil Liberties Union as Amicus Curiae Supporting Petitioner at 5-16, *Gundy* (No. 17-6086) (U.S. June 1, 2018), *available at* https://perma.cc/8UAJ-37ES.

138. *Gundy,* 139 U.S. at 2131.

139. 34 U.S. § 20913(d)(2006).

140. *Gundy,* 139 S. Ct. at 2123.

141. Lon L. Fuller, THE MORALITY OF LAW (2d ed., 1969)(Yale U. Press, 1964).

142. *Id.* at 170–75.

143. Sunstein and Vermeule, *supra* note 64, at 1969–70.

144. *See* Richard A. Epstein, *The Public Trust Doctrine,* 7 CATO J. 411, 417 (1987).

145. R. H. Coase, *The Federal Communications Commission,* 2 J.L. & ECON. 1 (1959).

146. Section 303 of the Communications Act of 1934 states: "Except as otherwise provided in this Act, the Commission from time to time, as public convenience, interest, or necessity requires, shall—(a) Classify radio stations; (b) Prescribe the nature of the service to be rendered by each class of licensed stations and each station within any class; [etc.]." Communications Act of 1934, Pub. L. No. 73-416, 48 Stat. 1064, 1082, codified as amended at 47 U.S.C. § 303(2017).

147. *Nat'l Broad. Co. v. United States,* 319 U.S. 190 (1943).

148. *Id.* at 215–16.

149. *See* Thomas W. Hazlett, *The Rationality of U.S. Regulation of the Broadcast Spectrum,* 33 J.L. & Econ. 133 (1990).

150. M. Todd Henderson and Anup Malani, *Corporate Philanthropy and the Market for Altruism,* 109 COLUM. L. REV. 571 (2009).

PART 3

THE *CHEVRON* SYNTHESIS

SECTION 706(A) OF THE ADMINISTRATIVE PROCEDURE ACT

The two most contentious issues in modern administrative law arise under Section 706(a) of the Administrative Procedure Act (APA). This provision addresses questions of both law and fact, and the major debate in administrative law circles centers on the extent of deference that should be afforded to an administrative agency on each. The untidy state of American administrative law prior to the Supreme Court's landmark 1984 *Chevron* decision is well summarized by Professor Thomas Merrill:

> That law had been something of a hodge-podge, but the conventional wisdom was that it required courts to assess agency interpretations against multiple contextual factors, such as whether the agency interpretation was longstanding, consistently held, contemporaneous with the enactment of the statute, thoroughly considered, or involved a technical subject as to which the agency had expertise.[1]

It should be evident that this account of administrative law dovetails nicely with the description of 19th-century administrative law offered by Professor Aditya Bamzai,[2] but that deep connection is uniformly ignored or rejected by defenders of the modern administrative state. Thus, Professor Gillian Metzger laments that rehabilitating these older views "may serve to undercut the legitimacy of national administrative governance"[3] as it exists today. In a similar vein, Professors Cass Sunstein and Adrian Vermeule laud the *Chevron*[4] doctrine in part because they think that any more rigorous restraint would run the risk of making it harder for experts to update the agency's position in the face of new knowledge and changing circumstances. Political accountability even suggests that a preference for consistency is an affirmatively bad idea. The whole point of political accountability is to allow new policy directions as presidential administrations come and go.[5]

I regard both these justifications for *Chevron* as unsound, as a matter of public policy and constitutional law, because they fly in the face of the rule-of-law constraints championed by Fuller. Metzger is incorrect to afford administrative law an unearned presumption of legitimacy, which it deserves only when it operates subject to proper institutional constraints. Sunstein and Vermeule's rejection of the value of consistency conflicts with Fuller's strong defense of that virtue.

The updating of prior assumptions on the strength of new information is important, but any change does not represent an impermissible inconsistency if the switch is demonstrably justified by the collection of new evidence. It is just this form of customary incrementalism that characterized 19th-century administrative law. But radical changes in position and direction, especially on questions of law (as *Chevron* permits), impose a high social cost on the system. The added discretion given to an agency imposes heavy costs of uncertainty on private parties who are trying to organize their long-term investments and business strategies. Ten-year business plans should never be held hostage by two-, three-, or five-year changes in administrative policy preferences that turn settled statutory interpretations upside-down. One might as well say that the law of contract and tort—which also inevitably needs updating to take into account new innovations in technology and social practice—should be subject to the same degree of uncertainty, even though the same set of basic expectations for ordinary business interactions has been remarkably stable since Roman times.[6]

On a less philosophical level, it is also clear that modern administrative law represents a marked deviation from the strictures of APA itself. In defense of *Chevron*'s status quo, Metzger notes approvingly that "there are few judicial calls to pull back on these doctrines as nontextually supported incursions into agencies' rightful discretion."[7] Similarly, Sunstein and Vermeule do not directly address *Chevron*'s lack of fidelity to the text of APA. To see why this is a real problem, it is critical to reproduce key portions of Section 706(a), titled "Scope of Review," which lays out the original ground rules as follows:

> To the extent necessary to decision and when presented, the reviewing court shall decide all relevant questions of law, interpret constitutional and statutory provisions, and determine the meaning or applicability of the terms of an agency action. The reviewing court shall—
>
> (1) compel agency action unlawfully withheld or unreasonably delayed; and
>
> (2) hold unlawful and set aside agency action, findings, and conclusions found to be—
>
> (A) arbitrary, capricious, an abuse of discretion, or otherwise not in accordance with law;
>
> (B) contrary to constitutional right, power, privilege, or immunity;
>
> (C) in excess of statutory jurisdiction, authority, or limitations, or short of statutory right;
>
> (D) without observance of procedure required by law;
>
> (E) unsupported by substantial evidence in a case subject to sections 556 and 557 of this title or otherwise reviewed on the record of an agency hearing provided by statute; or
>
> (F) unwarranted by the facts to the extent that the facts are subject to trial de novo by the reviewing court.
>
> In making the foregoing determinations, the court shall review the whole record or those parts of it cited by a party, and due account shall be taken of the rule of prejudicial error.[8]

This statutory provision does not once use the word "deference" but instead sets out a list of explicit controls that reviewing courts should routinely exercise over administrative actions. The difficulties in modern administrative law start with the astonishing observation that *Chevron* at no point refers to Section 706, even though its announced rule is a radical departure from the text—one that fuels the strong separation-of-powers objection to the modern administrative state.[9] Section 706's initial principal command requires that the reviewing court, "[t]o the extent necessary to decision and when presented . . . shall decide all relevant questions of law, interpret constitutional and statutory provisions, and determine the meaning or applicability of the terms of an agency action."[10] The text goes on to note that a softer standard of oversight is applied to hold "unlawful and set aside agency action, findings, and conclusions found to be—arbitrary, capricious, an abuse of discretion, or otherwise not in accordance with law."[11]

In his latest article on the subject, Sunstein makes the strong claim that Congress has the broad power to require courts to defer to agency interpretations of statutes and exercised said power when enacting APA.[12] That view does not comport well with Section 706's "[t]o the extent necessary to decision," language covering any case in which a matter is brought for judicial review. That review was "necessary" in *Chevron* itself; and to decide means to decide de novo, just as it does in any other case outside the administrative law context where appellate courts are called on to decide questions of law. In no other context does that notion imply deference to a decision of the district court or other initial decider. The same implications come with the phrase "when presented," which means that de novo review applies when the issue is fairly put before the appellate court. Lower standards of review (e.g., arbitrary and capricious review) apply in those cases that do not present questions of law in this fashion.

The interpretive choices also have constitutional significance, for as Justices Gorsuch and Kavanaugh insist, *Chevron* is flatly inconsistent with the principle of separation of powers, which prohibits Congress or the president (even with judicial acquiescence) from stripping Article III courts of their basic judicial function. It would thus never be acceptable for Congress to enact a general statute saying that, in all cases, the appellate courts must defer to an agency decision on a matter of law. Nonetheless, Sunstein goes on to conclude that courts should keep *Chevron* in place even if it had been wrongly decided at the outset in order to avoid the confusion of transition.[13] But that argument makes sense only if *Chevron* can be defended on its own terms, which is not the case. The basic distribution of powers set out under Section 706(a) is sound as a matter of principle. Indeed, it follows the logic used to demarcate the relative functions of trial and appellate courts in an effort to minimize error in dealing with questions of law and fact, which takes into account the differential competences at the two stages of litigation. To see how this works out, I first address questions of law and then turn to questions of fact.

The *Chevron* Two-Step

Perhaps the most fatal words in the history of American administrative law are found in the famous two-part analysis of Section 706(a) review offered in *Chevron*:

> First, always, is the question whether Congress has directly spoken to the precise question at issue. If the intent of Congress is clear, that is the end of the matter; for the court, as well as the agency, must give effect to the unambiguously expressed intent of Congress. If, however, the court determines Congress has not directly addressed the precise question at issue, the court does not simply impose its own construction on the statute . . . Rather, if the statute is silent or ambiguous with respect to the specific issue, the question for the court is whether the agency's answer is based on a permissible construction of the statute.[14]

It is not possible to mount a principled objection to the first stage of this test. It would be clearly lawless to reject any reading of a statute that is "clear" from the face of the text. But there is an enormous controversy over *Chevron*'s second step, which requires a court to defer to the interpretation of the agency whenever the statute is found to be either silent or ambiguous on the question presented.

The first objection to this maneuver is that no one can identify the pivot point between Step One and Step Two. Theories of statutory interpretation are plentiful and highly contested, as judges and scholars work hard to reconcile theories of plain meaning, context, structure, and purpose into a coherent whole. It takes little ingenuity to invoke a particular theory of statutory interpretation that finds silence or ambiguity in a given statutory text in order to increase the scope of judicial deference on a given issue. There can, of course, be no uniformity in the application of these tests, so that for those judges who favor the large administrative state, *Chevron* offers a painless and effective way to allow agencies to expand the scope of their activities. The temptations here are too great. The thesis of this part of the book is that *Chevron* Step Two should be resoundingly rejected. Of course, there are statutory gaps and ambiguities, but the proper response in all cases is for judges to give the most plausible interpretation that they can glean from all available sources. Then the artificial line between Step One and Step Two would disappear, and cases would instead lie on a continuous spectrum from hard to easy, just as they do in other contexts.

To put the point in perspective, why is it that the insertion of an administrative agency requires a fundamental revision of responsibility on key questions of statutory construction? It is widely settled that on questions of law, judges engage in de novo review outside the administrative law context. Their comparative advantage in working through statutory materials relating to some combination of text, structure, history, and purpose remains even in administrative law cases. Statutory interpretation is what judges, both generalist and specialist, are trained to do. Of course, some cases will be close, given the imperfections of statutory drafting on the one side and the occurrence of novel conditions on the other. But that state of affairs is common for all statutes, with or without agency administration. There is no reason to think that administrative agencies do better on the interpretive legal questions that fall well within the judicial wheelhouse.

This point, moreover, seems doubly clear on matters pertaining to an agency's jurisdiction, given the obvious risk of aggrandizement of regulatory authority. This is why Section 706(2)(F) appears to give courts of law the last word—without deference to agencies—on jurisdictional matters, a position that the Supreme Court nevertheless rejected in *City of Arlington v. FCC*.[15] True to the modern preference for an administrative law that is disconnected from APA, *City of Arlington* never bothers to cite or quote the relevant statutory provision enacted by the sitting Congress, relying instead on a palpable evasion that claims to follow the will of an imaginary Congress: "We do not ignore that command when we afford an agency's statutory interpretation *Chev-*

ron deference; we respect it. We give binding deference to permissible agency interpretations of statutory ambiguities *because* Congress has delegated to the agency the authority to interpret those ambiguities 'with the force of law.' "[16] *City of Arlington* followed *Mead Corp.*, which determined that *Chevron* deference was accorded to agency actions with the force of law, a quality inferred "from the agency's generally conferred authority and other statutory circumstances."[17] In effect, an unsupported implication of legislative intent is said, incorrectly, to work an end run around the explicit command of Section 706. One does not have to be a hard-core legal formalist to reject this ad hoc form of interpretation. Virtually all statutes require some degree of qualification and elaboration by implication, but not in ways that contradict (without reason) the explicit textual command.[18]

The use of deference gives rise to this set of subordinate questions only because modern administrative law refuses to be guided by the foundational principle that statutory texts should be given their ordinary meaning unless there is something in their local context that points in the opposite direction. The ordinary meaning test, moreover, is not just a matter of administrative law. The best illustration of this comes from constitutional law, specifically from the pen of Chief Justice Marshall in *Gibbons v. Ogden*,[19] which rejected a narrow interpretation of the Commerce Clause that would have allowed the federal government to run inspection points only at state lines but not to follow navigation into the interior of a state: "In regulating commerce with foreign nations, the power of Congress does not stop at the jurisdictional lines of the several States. It would be a very useless power, if it could not pass those lines."[20] Earlier, Justice Marshall explained how he reached that conclusion:

> As men, whose intentions require no concealment, generally employ the words which most directly and aptly express the ideas they intend to convey, the enlightened patriots who framed our constitution, and the people who adopted it, must be understood to have employed words in their natural sense, and to have intended what they have said. If, from the imperfection of human language, there should be serious doubts respecting the extent of any given power, it is a well settled rule, that the objects for which it was given, especially

91

when those objects are expressed in the instrument itself, should have great influence in the construction.[21]

The test of natural meaning is, to some, a sign of linguistic naiveté or an undue attachment to textualism, when in fact it is the precise opposite. In connection with *Gibbons*, ordinary meaning allowed for the regulation of all "intercourse" among the several states without allowing the federal government to trespass on the "purely internal commerce of each state,"[22] a formula that set out clear lines separating state power from federal power. This is a model of clarity compared with the modern affectation that talks about activities that "substantially affect interstate commerce," which affectation, in essence, overwhelms the initial constitutional division and thus allows the federal government to regulate in support of labor and agricultural cartels.[23]

Under the natural meaning test, all administrative actions are judged by the same standard, so that there is no need to establish a cottage industry to decide what levels of deference are needed for different kinds of legal materials. Is it really necessary to have one rule of interpretation for notice and comment proceedings—and another, say, for classifications of various import tariffs issued by the United States Customs Service,[24] and still another for a letter ruling by the secretary of labor?[25]

Under the unified approach, the entire classification question, which covers dozens of agencies doing hundreds of different tasks, disappears. If it turns out that an agency has great sophistication in dealing with some set of tasks, it does not need the bonus of deference to make its views known to, and persuasive upon, the courts. It can present its arguments and win on the strength of its position, or lose if it turns out that its purported interpretation cannot meet the test of ordinary or natural meaning. There is, therefore, no need to invent a "Step Zero" to decide whether to apply the two-part *Chevron* test to begin with.[26] Indeed, that two-part test is itself unstable when it commands that if the statute is clear, follow the text; if it is not, follow the agency, so long as its interpretation is reasonable.[27] The obvious difficulty with this formulation is that it is often unclear whether a statute is ambiguous, so that the relative scope of the two parts of *Chevron* is a perpetual weak link in the analysis.[28]

The wisdom of this ordinary meaning rule is made clear by observing how the Supreme Court adopted its *Chevron* rule in the context of the underlying dispute.[29] The case revolved around interpreting the term "stationary source" as it appeared in the Clean Air Act.[30] At stake was how that term applied to an industrial plant that contained many smokestacks. The Reagan administration championed the use of a "bubble concept" whereby all the smokestacks within the plant would be treated as a single unit, so that the company could make whatever internal adaptations it wanted within the plant, so long as the total level of emissions from the facility did not increase. The administrative ease of this position was such that, without new permitting, each change would increase total productive output or reduce total pollution, or both.

But there was a fly in the ointment. At the time, environmental groups opposed the bubble concept, fearing that it would lead to an endless cycle of modest improvements that would allow the firm to escape the ever-tougher standards for new emissions that they hoped to impose industry-wide.[31] That objection makes no sense in principle. A steady stream of incremental improvements avoids the epic all-or-nothing disputes that could put all improvements on hold for years. Any effort to impose high standards on new facilities results in keeping older, less efficient facilities in use long past their productive lives, as firms will patch up their old equipment to avoid the costs and delay of installing new equipment. In the long run, some firms may take the leap, but many will not. In the short term, there will be systematic social losses for which there will be few offsetting long-term gains down the road.

Justice Stevens knew of the sharp policy disagreement between the Carter and Reagan administrations on this issue, which led to a shift in definitions when Reagan took office.[32] Instead of accepting at face value the Reagan administration's interpretation and giving the statute its natural meaning in light of its general purposes, Justice Stevens concluded that the statutory term was unclear and deferred to the agency, with the implicit subtext that if the narrower interpretation had been adopted, that, too, would have been the law. In his most recent defense of *Chevron*, Sunstein claims that deference is really inescapable because the usual tools of statutory interpretation that look to some combination of text and purpose come up empty once an appeal to agency deference is rejected.[33]

But his conclusion falters on two grounds. First, taking into account Chief Justice Marshall's injunction against "useless" powers, why read a statute so narrowly that the exception on which the bubble concept relied can be invoked only rarely, if at all? Why not conclude that the broader interpretation is superior because the added flexibility will allow, in the short and long runs, a higher level of useful output at a lower level of emission, consistent with the statute's overall structure?

To be sure, the argument in favor of the extended bubble rests in part on the notion that technology can rapidly improve in this area. But that looks to be a safe and accurate assumption, given that there has never been a period in which technological improvements have been at a standstill. The hard-line environmentalist approach, summarized by Merrill, that assumes that advances will be made only under judicial compulsion, appears to be a real mistake. This argument against *Chevron*'s methodology does not rest on the assumption that courts are better able than agencies to figure out which technical improvements are needed. It assumes only that even in the absence of legal compulsion, firms will find it in their interest to make the needed adjustments, which is exactly what will happen if a firm can internalize all the gains from technological improvements so long as pollution levels remain within capped limits. It makes little sense to tie up matters with dangerous equipment modifications, which themselves will generate yet another round of legal and factual disputes.[34]

Yet suppose that *Chevron* was a true toss-up case. It hardly does any good to have the law switch from one administration to another, given the long lead times for the completion of any power generation facility. And it hardly follows that deep ambiguity in one statute means that all statutes will labor under that same disability. Indeed, in most cases, some combination of text and purpose works quite well, which affords an added reason that this form of discretion is ill-advised.

Second, in more recent writings, Sunstein joins forces with Professor Lawrence Solum to advance yet another linguistic move to save *Chevron* from its critics.[35] The proposal in this instance works off Solum's long-term insistence that one key to a sound understanding of language rests on "an old distinction in American legal theory between 'interpretation,' which calls for discerning the meaning of a statute, and 'construction,' which calls for determining the legal effect of the statute, through implementation rules, specifications, and other devices."[36] In their view, the notion of construction involves the creation of some safe space when a term is vague or open-textured.

But it is far from clear why the redefinition of a traditional problem with a new distinction answers the question of why courts should not use their best efforts to get at the correct meaning when there is some lack of clarity in these cases. Nor does the distinction they identify give the most sensible use of "interpretation." Another way to look at the problem is to note that the interpretation of any written legal document involves answering two questions. The first deals with the meaning of the established terms to understand the content and scope of the prescription. The second is whether some exception to that prescription may be implied on the basis of how it fits into the larger context of the contract, statute, regulation, or constitution of which it is a part. This question of implication is not a search for semantic meaning of the disputed term. It is, rather, an effort to show that a given command is subject to some principled exceptions. It is a question of construction, while the effort to find the meaning of the stated terms is one of interpretation.

Here is how this question of interpretation works.[37] The First Amendment requires that Congress pass no law abridging the freedom of speech. One key semantic element in the First Amendment is whether the term "speech" covers written text and forms of acting that do not involve speech. There seems to be no intelligible reason that anyone would want to protect the spoken word without also protecting the written (or typed) word or human gestures. Whether the purpose of protecting speech is for efficient government, self-realization, or voluntary cooperation, the protection runs across the entire field. Hence it becomes inexorable that the word "speech" be transformed into "expression," so as to bring analogous cases into the protected zone.[38]

A sensible interpretive strategy would never adopt a sterile literalism to defeat that approach. Similarly, in dealing with private property under the Fifth Amendment's Takings Clause, one would be hard-pressed to think of any reason that land should be protected to the exclusion of animals, chattels, corporate shares, or intellectual property. It hardly matters whether the protection of private property is intended to stem government abuse, promote individual self-sufficiency, or be the handmaiden to the market economy. All forms of property seem to fall within the larger term, which cannot be truncated to cover just real estate. Again, we have a question of interpretation, where the scope of the coverage is read broadly.

On this view, the matter of construction deals with a different question: whether there are excuses or justifications that limit the exercise of the particular guarantee. Excuses and justifications are part of law, just as they are part of ordinary speech and moral discourse. So even though the term "police power" appears nowhere in the Constitution, the phrase has to be read into it to avoid the absurd conclusion that freedom of speech (or expression) must also protect fraud, defamation, intimidation, and assault because words or other forms of expression are involved.[39] Likewise, the police-power exception has to be read into the Takings Clause, or else property owners may use their guns to kill or their lands to pollute public and private waters with impunity.

Once police power is recognized, it becomes necessary to develop a normative theory to decide what counts as a justification for the use of government force. The strongest theory says that the government, which is intended to preserve order, may use force, albeit in a bounded way, to prevent private use of force (including nuisance) and fraud (including defamation) that will injure others. But by the same point, the government cannot use police power to suppress legitimate economic competition, to prevent the construction of any ordinary property, or to silence speech that is intended to persuade politically or to induce an ordinary commercial transaction. Modern constitutional law tends to hew closely to this line in First Amendment cases and to deviate from it broadly in cases under the Takings Clause.

The point here is not to develop a full-bore theory of interpretation that covers all cases. Rather, it is to note that the meaning that should attach to the term "stationary source" is a straight question of interpretation because it does not involve any claim for an exception to the basic statutory command. This interpretive move, if properly understood, helps explain the lack of congruence between a theory of originalism and one of textualism, for the former always involves issues of both coverage and circumvention, on the one hand, and excuses and justifications, on the other. The key to understanding the combined mission of interpretation and construction is that the same devices needed to deal with private law disputes also work for legislative and administrative actions as well as constitutional theory.

Notwithstanding the major difficulties with *Chevron*, the Supreme Court, speaking through Justice Clarence Thomas, and over a spirited dissent by Justice Scalia, doubled down on that decision in *National Cable & Telecommunications Ass'n v. Brand X Internet Services*.[40] In so doing, the Court upended the 19th-century practice in which judicial deference was afforded only to a long line of low-level decisions on such vital matters as contract interpretation and grant construction, both of which were a far larger part of the administrative docket then than they are now. *Brand X* is also in manifest tension with Fuller's general insistence that the requirement of consistency over time is a minimum prerequisite of the rule of law.

The precise issue in *Brand X* was whether FCC could reclassify, without any real explanation, broadband cable Internet services from their status as a provider of "telecommunications services" to the alternative status as "information-service providers." As suppliers of telecommunications services, carriers are subject to the traditional requirements that they charge their customers, under the traditional formula, only reasonable and nondiscriminatory rates.[41] They are further required to build systems that allow for interconnection with other common carriers.[42] And they must make contributions to a federal universal service fund that provides subsidies to certain designated parties.[43] Providers of information services are largely freed of these regulatory burdens. The exact line between these two classifications, in turn, depends on the distinction between basic services, which involve simple transmissions of information over a network with minimum steps to convert ordinary language messages into code and back again, and enhanced services, which involve more complex operations, including voice mail and other data services. FCC did the appropriate study and reclassified broadband cable Internet service as an enhanced or information service.[44]

As a matter of first principle, I am strongly in favor of a view that removes the traditional shackles of rate-of-return regulation from the modern telecommunications industry. But that policy position is wholly irrelevant to the statutory question in the case, for the issue of an agency's about-face in regulatory position should, as an administrative law matter, come out the same way, even if some reclassification sought to increase the regulatory burden by reclassifying enhanced services as basic ones. As usual, administrative law is intended to implement legislative decisions, not to overturn them, so Justice Thomas's decision to address FCC's move to deregulate resolves the rule-of-law questions in a manner in which Fuller would not approve.

A first-best interpretation that treated this entire issue as a matter of law subject to de novo review would obviate the debate. But the simplest reading of APA's Section 706(a) is blocked by *Chevron*. Thus the issue in *Brand X* was whether that decision, which allows the administrative agency to chart its initial course, also allows it to change course without serious explanation. Justice Thomas had no hesitation in applying the basic *Chevron* framework to conclude, in a most non-Fullerian way, that "agency inconsistency is not a basis for declining to analyze the agency's interpretation under the *Chevron* framework. Unexplained inconsistency is, at most, a reason for holding an interpretation to be an arbitrary and capricious change from agency practice under the Administrative Procedure Act."[45] Justice Thomas then had to address why the arbitrary and capricious standard should be displaced because there was a reasoned appellate decision on the statutory question at issue, *AT&T Corp. v. City of Portland*,[46] which held that the statute meant the opposite of FCC's new asserted position.

One sensible way to approach this problem is to hold that an agency can now benefit from an authoritative judicial interpretation so that it does not have to craft its own rules. But Justice Thomas took the opposite tack and held that, since agencies are better able than courts to make difficult policy choices, the sequence of decisions does not matter. It is only if the initial interpretation is beyond reproach as unambiguous under *Chevron* Step One that the agency ruling will not be displaced, even if that agency ruling overturns an earlier judicial decision. It does not even appear that the agency is under a duty to consider the prior judicial opinion when it makes its own decision. The result is that *Chevron* was taken a step further, and with it the dangers of agency flip-flops and bias are further insulated from judicial review. The narrower the reach of *Chevron* Step One, the greater an agency's discretion.

Navigable Waters

It is important to note the high stakes that arise when judicial decisions are subordinated in the fashion previously described. One illustration of the transformative power of deference comes from the description of the term "navigable waters" in the Clean Water Act (CWA) as "the waters of the United States, including the territorial seas," which determines the scope of the jurisdiction of the Army Corps of Engineers.[47] The initial expansion of this definition occurred through a collusive 1975 settlement between the secretary of the army and the Natural Resources Defense Council recorded in *Natural Resources Defense Council, Inc. v. Callaway*,[48] in which the declaration and order of final judgment contained the following paragraph:

> Congress by defining the term "navigable waters" in Section 502(7) of the Federal Water Pollution Control Act Amendments of 1972, 86 Stat. 816, 33 U.S.C. § 1251 et seq. (the "Water Act") to mean "the waters of the United States, including the territorial seas," asserted federal jurisdiction over the nation's waters to the maximum extent permissible under the Commerce Clause of the Constitution. Accordingly, as used in the Water Act, the term is not limited to the traditional tests of navigability.[49]

Not a syllable of defense was offered to explain why the traditional tests of navigability, which asked whether a waterway could be used for some form of navigation, even floating logs down a river, should be jettisoned in favor of a far broader test involving indirect effects, driven by the New Deal expansion of Congress's commerce power, as previously noted.[50] Yet without the benefit of any reasoned judicial evaluation, the next move was for the Army Corps of Engineers to enter into the fray to transform the underlying situation. CWA forbids the discharge of dredged or fill material into "navigable waters," which are defined as the "waters of the United States," unless the party in question receives a permit from the Army Corps of Engineers.[51] As the Supreme Court wrote in *United States v. Riverside Bayview Homes, Inc.*,[52] this provision received a "redefinition" in the wake of *Callaway*:

> After initially construing the Act to cover only waters navigable in fact, in 1975 the Corps issued interim final regulations redefining "the waters of the United States" to include not only actually navigable waters but also tributaries of such waters, interstate waters and their tributaries, and nonnavigable intrastate waters whose use or misuse could affect interstate commerce.[53]

As the Court noted, the new regulation allowed the permit requirement to cover all wetlands that were situated adjacent to navigable waters and their tributaries. The work required to obtain these permits often takes months or years to prepare, both by the private party who submitted the permit application and by the Army Corps in its review. The broad definition of the "waters of the United States" to include "wetlands" only drives these costs upward by including lands that were "inundated or *saturated* by surface *or ground water* at a frequency and duration sufficient to support, and that under normal circumstances do support, a prevalence of vegetation typically adapted for life in saturated soil conditions."[54]

This regulation was promulgated after the judicial endorsement of the two major deferential doctrines, rational basis review and *Chevron*, both of which spurred the expansion of the modern administrative state. The first step in Justice Byron White's analysis in *Riverside Bayview* was to sidestep the landowner's effort to invoke the canon of constitutional avoidance to interpret the statute to minimize infringement of property rights. Instead, the Court denied that the slowdown in land-use approvals required under the permit system could amount to a regulatory taking under *Penn Central Transportation Co. v. City of New York*.[55] The possibility of a remote ex-post remedy for denied permits was sufficient to preclude earlier relief for permit slowdowns because "after all, the very existence of a permit system implies that permission may be granted."[56] But that proposition is wrong both ways. First, if the permit is not granted, normally no relief of any sort is available for losses incurred while waiting; and second, if, for some reason, the permit is granted, the interim losses will typically be noncompensable no matter how long the approval process is dragged out.[57]

Justice White then concluded that since the possibility of compensation under *Penn Central* was eliminated, the regulation in question need not be read narrowly to avoid some "spurious" challenge under the Takings Clause. The path was thus cleared to invoke *Chevron* deference by noting the difficulties in drawing a hard line between navigable waters and dry land. Accordingly, the new definition of "navigable waters" can cover wet places where navigation is impossible if an agency deems it so; *Chevron* now justifies a series of giant interpretative leaps in manifest conflict with the basic statute. The novel administrative scheme thus inverts the usual common law rule of construction of the term navigable waters.

Previously, ordinary activities could go forward unless there was some imminent or grave threat to traditional navigable waters, which is the direct opposite of a regime that puts all the emphasis on examining low-probability events prior to their occurrence. That last shift cannot be blamed on Congress because the entire transformation did not occur through legislation but through a combination of collusive litigation and administration regulation. The current process cannot be commended on its merits because it forces an exhaustive review of a thousand possible contingencies, most of which will never occur—and are known almost never to occur.[58] I have never encountered a systematic defense of this process. However, this entire nasty system is passed in silence by Sunstein and Vermeule, Metzger, and Pojanowski.

It was only a matter of time before individual administrative actions pushed the definition of navigable waters still further. The initial requirement of adjacency was dropped in *Solid Waste Agency of Northern Cook County v. Army Corps of Engineers*,[59] in which the Supreme Court held that the permit requirement attached to an abandoned sand and gravel pit that was "seasonably ponded," even though it formed no part of any system of navigable waters.[60] Thereafter, in *Rapanos v. United States*,[61] a hopelessly divided Court could not agree on whether a 54-acre parcel of land located some 11–20 miles from the nearest navigable waters was covered by the act. Four justices—John Roberts, Antonin Scalia, Clarence Thomas, and Samuel Alito—thought that the regulations did not go that far, and four—John Paul Stevens, David Souter, Ruth Bader Ginsburg, and Stephen Breyer—held that they clearly did. In the end, it was Justice Anthony Kennedy who, in Delphic words, concluded that "the Corps must establish a significant nexus on a case-by-case basis when it seeks to regulate wetlands based on adjacency to nonnavigable tributaries."[62] Good luck with that.

The dizzying procession continued with *Sackett v. EPA*,[63] in which the Army Corps insisted that its jurisdiction extended far enough to cover dry land that was separated from navigable waters by several lots that included permanent structures. When the lot owners started to fill in their land with dirt and rock, they received a compliance order from EPA to cease and desist from "causing such fill material to enter waters of the United States"[64] and warning that they could be subject to fines of $37,500 per day unless they obtained a permit. The Supreme Court allowed Sackett to bring an action under APA to challenge that determination without facing the cascade of fines. But at no point did the Court engage with the huge administrative apparatus that framed the debate.

A similar tale of woe occurred in *Army Corps of Engineers v. Hawkes Co.*,[65] where the Army Corps insisted that a landowner needed a permit to remove peat from wetland because the wetland had "a significant nexus" to the Red River of the North, located some 120 miles away. The Supreme Court held that the determination of the Army Corps was reviewable under APA, even though the Army Corps had insisted that its interim order was not a final judgment subject to judicial review.[66]

It should come as no surprise, therefore, that the cycle of revision continued apace. The Obama administration in June 2015 promulgated a very broad definition of "navigable waters of the United States" in the Waters of the United States Rule (WOTUS Rule), which was promptly subjected to a preliminary injunction on the grounds that the proposed definition "allow[ed] EPA regulation of waters that do not bear any effect on the 'chemical, physical, and biological integrity' of any navigable-in-fact water."[67] This quoted language matters because the Clean Water Act presupposes that its relevant "effluent limitations" include "any restriction established by a state or the [EPA] on quantities, rates, and concentrations of chemical, physical, biological, and other constituents which are discharged from point sources into navigable waters."[68] Absent that connection, there is no threat of pollution, and hence an effort to expand the jurisdiction of the Army Corps is undue.

Rapid change in the underlying political environment was made evident in February 2017, when the newly inaugurated Trump administration issued an executive order calling for a review of the Obama-era WOTUS Rule with an eye toward narrowing the definition of "navigable waters."[69] Thereafter, the Trump administration sought to suspend the operation of the rule for two years in order to better evaluate the overall situation. That effort was slapped down by a nationwide injunction issued by the federal court in the District of South Carolina, which took the sensible position that "the agencies' refusal to consider or receive public comments on the substance of the WOTUS rule or the 1980s regulation did not provide a 'meaningful opportunity for comment.' "[70]

There is no sign that these various procedural maneuverings will end anytime soon. The lesson that should be drawn from this line of cases is that subjecting matters of statutory interpretation to notice and comment rulemaking is the wrong way to produce clarity. At issue are pure questions of law on which any agency is entitled to have its own view, but a single authoritative judicial interpretation cuts through all the equivocation and thus leads to a more reliable outcome at a lower cost. By that standard, the convoluted definitions of "waters of the United States" have no place.

The federal government and the states both have strong traditional remedies to enjoin public nuisances if and when they occur. They are available to use against any party who commits such a tort, regardless of whether the conduct occurs in navigable waters, marshes, lowlands, or uplands. The great tragedy of modern administrative law on this issue is that it locks the legal system into a set of anticipatory remedies that come far too early in the process, which, in turn, generate excessive regulation that only benefits the opponents of development without offering any serious positive environmental payoff.[71]

Weyerhaeuser v. U.S. Fish & Wildlife Service

This same uneasy combination of weak protections for property rights and *Chevron* deference played out in the recent case *Weyerhaeuser v. U.S. Fish & Wildlife Service*.[72] At issue in the case was an interpretation of a phrase in the Endangered Species Act of 1973 (ESA).[73] Before the Supreme Court was the question of whether the U.S. Fish and Wildlife Service exceeded its statutory authority by designating as critical habitat some 1,544 acres of privately owned lands in Louisiana for use by the dusky gopher frog on the grounds that the land contained "those physical or biological features . . . essential to the conservation of the species."[74]

The designation was no haphazard affair. As the Fifth Circuit's majority opinion noted prior to the Supreme Court's review, the case involved an exhaustive "economic analysis, two rounds of notice and comment, a scientific peer-review process including responses from six experts, and a public hearing."[75] The inquiry was undertaken because the Fish and Wildlife Service thought that the frog's current habitat was too fragile to guarantee the animal's long-term survival. But the designated area also suffered from numerous admitted limitations. First, it was not currently in use by the frog. Second, no frog had been sighted in the region for over 50 years. And third, the habitat could be made suitable for the frog only if subjected to major renovations, for which no funds had been appropriated. The term "essential" normally carries the connotation that the activity must be done now. If something may or may not be done at some indefinite time in the future, it is not essential, so the Fish and Wildlife Service's designation would be beyond its statutory mandate, unless some magical deference was able to tip the balances in the opposite way.

The real question is whether the Fish and Wildlife Service should have the discretion to make such a designation at all. Designation alone did not allow the service to enter the land, or to keep the owner off it. But many other privileges normally associated with property control were transferred by force to the government with such a designation. The immediate consequence of the agency's designation was that Weyerhaeuser lost all its management prerogatives with respect to the land. It could not cut timber, plant new materials, or engage in any activities unless it first obtained permission. The loss of those prerogatives did not come cheap; the best estimate put the loss of productive asset value at $34 million. But the Fish and Wildlife Service would pay nothing to obtain the designation if it could persuade the Supreme Court to adopt its extended definition of "critical habitat."

Something is deeply amiss with this situation, and fortunately, the Court unanimously rejected the agency's position. The Court held that the Fish and Wildlife Service went a step too far when it sought to "designate as *unoccupied* critical habitat a 1544 acre site,"[76] given the statutory requirement that a critical habitat be at the time of its designation a subset of the total habitat of the species.[77] The unoccupied nature of the site was thus fatal, regardless of whether the site was regarded as "essential" to the agency's overall project, and the Court reversed on that narrow ground alone.

In so doing, the Court again pushed off to one side the larger questions of how to think sensibly about habitat designation, for its holding leaves unresolved how courts should treat a proposal by the Fish and Wildlife Service to update at enormous cost, and after extensive delay, any site that currently supports a tiny number of these dusky gopher frogs. At this point, the problem of proportionality returns to center stage, along with the serious open question of what, if anything, can be done to guard against administrative overclaiming of private property to further environmental objectives.

This question is no longer one of statutory interpretation. Instead, the root problem that emerges is identical to what clouds the analysis in *Riverside Bayview*—the narrow conception of the Takings Clause means that the government need not pay compensation in order to gain control over land. That result is also a function of *Chevron* deference as applied in the earlier case of *Babbitt v. Sweet Home Chapter of Communities for a Greater Oregon*,[78] in which the Supreme Court addressed the scope of the coercive power of the Fish and Wildlife Service under ESA. It ruled that, according to the act, the operative offense is to "(B) take any such species within the United States or the territorial sea of the United States; [or] (C) take any such species upon the high seas."[79] The statutory definition of to "take" is to "harass, harm, pursue, hunt, shoot, wound, kill, trap, capture, or collect, or to attempt to engage in any such conduct."[80] In *Sweet Home,* Justice Stevens invoked *Chevron* deference at the government's urging to read the term "harm" to include the destruction of critical habitat. That expansive meaning is inconsistent with the items otherwise enumerated in the statutory definition. "Harm" should be reserved for focused actions that attack some protected species, including, for example, poisoning or throwing newborn birds out of their nests and causing death. Treating habitat destruction—no matter how extensive—as harm makes no sense on the high seas, where the statute applies but where the federal government lacks any enforcement power.

This broad definition of "habitat" also makes a hash of the basic statutory scheme, which gives the government an explicit option under Section 5 to acquire, by voluntary purchase or condemnation, "lands and waters, or interest therein"[81] that are suitable for habitat protection. It seems painfully clear that the government will not purchase land under Section 5 if it can secure the protection of habitats at no cost. Justice Stevens speculated that the secretary of the interior "may also find the § 5 authority useful for preventing modification of land that is not yet but may in the future become habitat for an endangered or threatened species."[82] *Weyerhaeuser* proves him to be a bad prophet, for the government again left the condemnation power to the side. If the government has no immediate use for some property, why pay a dime for its occupation today when it can obtain full control over the landowner through permitting power whenever a desired use arises?

Yet note how this case would come out if condemnation, with just compensation, were the only option available to the government. The Fish and Wildlife Service may well perform identical studies and conclude that the land is indeed the best candidate for dusky gopher frog preservation. But would that be good enough? It is highly unlikely that the government would be prepared to pay $34 million to acquire that property outright for such a purpose. And if it did, it would then immediately think of ways to sell off some rights over the land to recoup its initial cost. The question of whether the decision was arbitrary or capricious would drop out of the equation because, having received full compensation, the landowner could not challenge any land-use decision by the government after the land was transferred. The weak system of property protection reflected in cases like *Sweet Home* and *Weyerhaeuser* puts an unacceptable strain on the entire system of administrative discretion. The situation is, in fact, the mirror image of the problem that the Supreme Court answered incorrectly in *NBC v. United States*[83] when dealing with spectrum allocation. In that case, the indefinite property rights at issue were in government-owned property. In the environmental cases, the property was private, but the level of government discretion on whether to regulate its use was unbounded by any strong system of property rights. Fuller's basic objection that rule-of-law considerations fail to work for managerial-type decisions explains why the *Chevron* doctrine only exacerbates a problem that begins more fundamentally with the weak protection of property rights—a topic that receives no sustained treatment in any of the aforementioned articles defending the administrative state. There is not one word from Metzger or from Sunstein and Vermeule explaining why the expansions achieved through *Chevron* deference are a healthy application of sound administrative law principles. And it should be clear that this exercise of deference most clearly is not. The next question is whether the weaknesses of *Chevron* deference can be corrected by the so-called major question doctrine. The evidence is decidedly mixed.

THE MAJOR QUESTION DIVERSION

The major question doctrine holds that no government agency can seek to exploit a textual ambiguity in order to achieve through regulation a fundamental change in doctrine.[84] Where it applies, the doctrine happily displaces the applicability of *Chevron* deference. There would be no need for any such tool if *Chevron* had not deviated from the standard interpretive canon—one that Fuller readily embraced—whereby the terms in any statute should be given their ordinary meaning whenever possible. But once *Chevron* sets that presumption aside, it takes a second step (or, in the *Chevron* cottage industry, a Step Zero) to rectify the initial mistake. It would be unduly optimistic to think that these errors are canceled out by the major question doctrine because, sadly, history reveals that, like so many canons of administrative law, judicial ingenuity allows this concept to mean different things to different people and to be followed by some judges in some cases but ignored by other judges in other cases. Reflecting a common trend in administrative law, progressive judges who seek to enlarge the sphere of government action are less receptive to limiting doctrines than conservative judges who attach greater weight to administrative restraint. The following are highlights in the development of the major question doctrine.

MCI Telecommunications Corp. v. AT&T

The major question doctrine finds its origins in *MCI Telecommunications Corp. v. AT&T*.[85] In his notable majority opinion, Justice Scalia, who found himself on all sides of the deference question during his time on the bench, took a strong stand that the fixed meaning of technical language in the Communications Act of 1934 precluded the application of *Chevron*.[86]

The dispute arose over the act's requirement that all rates be filed with FCC before they are allowed to go into effect. As something of an offset, Section 203(b) of the act provides that FCC could "modify" any basic filing requirement, thereby building some discretion into the act without doing much to define or guide such discretion.[87] FCC had previously issued a regulation decreeing that all nondominant carriers should receive an unfettered option as to whether to file their rates in advance. The question was whether that regulation fell within the scope of FCC's authority under Section 203(b) to "modify" basic filing requirements. One possible answer is that modifications come in all shapes and sizes and that the authority includes dispensing with a requirement in its entirety.

However, ordinary language does not support the view that modification includes removal, as the two terms actually stand in opposition to each other. The heading of Section 203(b) of the statute—"Changes in Schedule; Discretion of Commission to Modify Requirements"—by its own terms, allows some modification of such points as the timing or required date of a filing. However, in the section's heading, "Changes in Schedule" comes before "Discretion of Commission to Modify Requirements." The former is a housekeeping arrangement, and that character should limit the understanding of the modifications that are permitted. In the corresponding description, the statute explicitly prohibits changes "in the charges, classifications, regulations or practice which have been so filed" without certain notice. Why would a statute place limitations on this series of changes but permit an unencumbered waiver of the basic filing requirement? Put otherwise, the context in which the operative statutory language appears reaffirms a more limited reading of FCC's authority. Justice Scalia was right to conclude:

> Petitioners argue that it gives the Commission authority to make even basic and fundamental changes in the scheme created by that section. We disagree. The word "modify"—like a number of other English words employing the root "mod-" (deriving from the Latin word for "measure"), such as "moderate," "modulate," "modest," and "modicum"—has a connotation of increment or limitation. Virtually every dictionary we are aware of says that "to modify" means to change moderately or in minor fashion.[88]

Justice Scalia went on to say that he would not find an ambiguity permitting application of *Chevron* deference just because one available dictionary cited in the case takes the opposite position, providing a broader definition of "modification." Even that lone dictionary's definition may not have been generous enough to permit the gutting of a basic filing obligation.[89] Who can say what would have happened if *Chevron* was given full sway, which is what Justice Stevens, *Chevron*'s author, argued in dissent, claiming that the "dynamic character" of the telecommunications industry requires an abandonment of the "rigid literalism" that marked Scalia's majority opinion?[90] Literalism, as will become evident, is a selective virtue.

FDA v. Brown & Williamson Tobacco Corp.

The next discordant case in the development of the major question doctrine is *FDA v. Brown & Williamson Tobacco Corp.*,[91] which presented the question of whether FDA could regulate tobacco as a drug. It is possible to invoke some version of the major question doctrine with respect to this question by noting the huge reversal in FDA's policy, as FDA had argued for years that it lacked that very authority. Justice Sandra Day O'Connor's majority opinion held that the historical pattern of regulation militated decisively against FDA's assertion of regulatory authority. However, the definition of "drug" contained in the Pure Food and Drug Act points the other way:

> The term "drug" means (A) articles recognized in the official

United States Pharmacopoeia, official Homoeopathic Pharmacopoeia of the United States, or official National Formulary, or any supplement to any of them; and (B) articles intended for use in the diagnosis, cure, mitigation, treatment, or prevention of disease in man or other animals; and (C) articles (other than food) intended to affect the structure or any function of the body of man or other animals.[92]

Parts A and B of this definition are relatively straightforward and cover the vast majority of cases, but Part C is decidedly not, given its potentially unlimited reach. In his dissenting effort to uphold the regulation, Justice Breyer, joined by Justices Stevens, Souter, and Ginsburg, abandoned the anti-literalist approach that Stevens had relied on in his dissent in *MCI Telecommunications*:

[T]obacco products (including cigarettes) fall within the scope of this statutory definition, read literally. Cigarettes achieve their mood stabilizing effects through the interaction of the chemical nicotine and the cells of the central nervous system. Both cigarette manufacturers and smokers alike know of, and desire, that chemically induced result. Hence, cigarettes are "intended to affect" the body's "structure" and "function," in the literal sense of these words.[93]

The difficulty with Breyer's position is that he wrote about this issue as if it had never been addressed. In truth, this interpretive question had arisen dozens of times under FDA, and there was a strongly established interpretive tradition requiring that for any compound to be considered a drug, it was necessary to identify the therapeutic claims that the manufacturer made or that a seller made on behalf of the manufacturer.[94] Under this interpretative gloss, tobacco would certainly be treated as a drug if its manufacturers claimed that it could cure cancer. Having made such a claim, the company would then be required to submit its so-called drug for a rigorous round of clinical trials to see if the assertion was accurate. But, of course, no such therapeutic claim was made with respect to tobacco at the time of this litigation.

Yet, surprisingly enough, though Justice O'Connor was well aware of the precedent stating that products become drugs only when "their manufacturer or vendor makes some express claim concerning the product's therapeutic benefits,"[95] she ignored this easy answer and instead held that even if a product could be considered a drug without having such a therapeutic claim, that broader definition does not include tobacco. But why reject the standard mode of interpretation, which affords the only sensible—that is, functional—reading of the statute? The picture that emerges is one of total intellectual disarray. In dealing with pollution, Justices Stevens and Breyer ignored the literal meaning in favor of a one-off interpretation that guts a statutory scheme when dealing with filed rates. But they turned literal to embrace an absurd statutory interpretation that had been rejected in the field from day one when dealing with tobacco. Again, the question is not whether tobacco is subject to regulation. Indeed, after *Brown & Williamson*, the problem of tobacco was not solved in the interstices of the Pure Food and Drug Act. Tobacco would later become the subject of explicit regulation under the Family Smoking Prevention and Tobacco Control Act of 2009.[96]

Whitman v. American Trucking Association

The major question doctrine again came into play the year after *Brown & Williamson* in *Whitman v. American Trucking Association*.[97] There, the American Trucking Association sought to enjoin EPA from implementing new tighter standards known as national ambient air quality standards (NAAQS), which govern the release of ozone and particulate matter. Section 109(b)(1) of the Clean Air Act[98] directs EPA to set the primary air-quality standards, "the attainment and maintenance of which . . . are requisite to protect the public health" with "an adequate margin of safety."[99] The association challenged NAAQS, claiming that EPA had failed to take into account the costs of compliance before promulgating them. That simple challenge set up a battle royal between two rival conceptions of environmental regulation. Virtually all complex schemes are constructed in a setting dominated by scarcity. Since resources are limited, it is not possible to drive the level of pollutants down to zero. The good news is that Section 109(b)(1) is cognizant of that reality in that it does not demand that pollution be completely eliminated but only that there be a reduction of pollution to levels "requisite to protect the public health."[100]

Calculating that level is difficult, though, because the statute reads like a categorical command and cannot easily be applied in practice. It is commonplace in reducing the risks of pollutants for additional investments to have a diminishing marginal rate of return. Typically, the dollar amount invested in initial protections yields high returns; less so for amounts invested in the later ones. As a social construct, the ideal approach is to set up the following equilibrium: invest in safety precautions to the point where costs and benefits are equated at the margin, such that marginal benefits equal marginal costs.

Unfortunately, this formula is far easier to state in theory than it is to apply in reality. Start with the benefit side. It is not easy to evaluate the potential harm that any given carcinogen, alone or in combination, causes to other people. The task has to take into account differences in location, age, sex, and race. Even if those direct calculations could be made, it would still be hard to know how any given pollutant interacts with the larger environment, through which it could have all sorts of indirect effects on human well-being. Remember that "public health" is given a broad definition under the statutes administered by EPA, which impose some kind of statutory duty to attack these problems. Nor is it easy to make the requisite calculations on the cost side. Some precautions may reduce one form of pollution while increasing another, whereas other precautions, like scrubbers, may have benefits in curbing multiple forms of pollution but to an extent nevertheless hard to quantify.

What should we do with this difficulty? It appears that the statutory text looks only to the net level of benefits requisite for public safety while ignoring costs. But how do we know what level is "requisite"? For example, suppose that the government can eliminate 90% of pollution of a given sort by spending $100 million, reduce pollution an additional 9% by spending another $100 million, and so on. Is the initial 90% requisite? Is 99%?

Now let's consider the alternative perspective. The determined environmentalist can, and perhaps should, support some per se rule, such as those found in the Clean Air Act; after all, it is easy for regulated firms to expand the basic inquiry under a cost-benefit analysis solely to increase the delay and reduce the stringency of any given regulation. The per se rule may offer a poor measurement of social welfare, but it might make up for that weakness with its greater ability to be administered. It is an age-old conundrum: more accurate theoretical measures are far less reliable in practical application. At this point, it seems clear that the choice of governance standards does not raise any constitutional challenges, since the end is legitimate, and which techniques should be used in different cases is a close call. The matter is really one of statutory interpretation; and on that point, Justice Scalia invoked the major question doctrine, citing his earlier decision in *MCI Telecommunications* with this well-known quip:

> Accordingly, to prevail in their present challenge, respondents must show a textual commitment of authority to the EPA to consider costs in setting NAAQS under § 109(b)(1). . . . Congress, we have held, does not alter the fundamental details of a regulatory scheme in vague terms or ancillary provisions—it does not, one might say, hide elephants in mouseholes.[101]

In his concurrence, Justice Breyer accepted the result but challenged Justice Scalia's methodological choice:

> In order better to achieve regulatory goals—for example, to allocate resources so that they save more lives or produce a cleaner environment—regulators must often take account of all of a proposed regulation's adverse effects, at least where those adverse effects clearly threaten serious and disproportionate public harm. Hence, I believe that, other things being equal, we should read silences or ambiguities in the language of regulatory statutes as permitting, not forbidding, this type of rational regulation.[102]

Massachusetts v. EPA

The clash between these two interpretive visions came to the forefront in *Massachusetts v. EPA*,[103] a case in which the Court refused to invoke the major question doctrine. Although this far-flung litigation raised many issues, the one relevant here is whether carbon dioxide counts as a pollutant that should be subject to regulation under the motor-vehicle provisions of the Clean Air Act. Section 202(a)(1) of the

Act reads:

> The [EPA] administrator shall by regulation prescribe (and
> from time to time revise) in accordance with the provisions
> of this section, standards applicable to the emission of any
> air pollutant from any class or classes of new motor vehicles
> or new motor vehicle engines, which in his judgment cause,
> or contribute to, air pollution which may reasonably be
> anticipated to endanger public health or welfare.[104]

The Act defines two key terms in this passage as follows: An "air pollutant" includes "any air pollution agent or combination of such agents,
including any physical, chemical, biological, radioactive . . . substance
or matter which is emitted into or otherwise enters the ambient air."[105]
For its part, "welfare" includes within its scope "effects on . . . weath-
er . . . and climate."[106]

The major question doctrine would certainly have applied to this
case if, during the George W. Bush administration, EPA had decided
to list carbon dioxide as a pollutant covered by the Clean Air Act. Such
expansion in coverage would have required very different techniques
from those used to address the five other greenhouse gases (GHGs)—
methane, nitrous oxide, hydrofluorocarbons, perfluorocarbons, and
sulfur hexafluoride. The socially optimal level of emissions for these other
GHGs is zero. The only constraint against reaching that desired level
for these other gases was the sober realization of cost. Overinvestment
may produce "adverse effects" that "clearly threaten serious and
disproportionate public harm," such as directing enforcement efforts
to minor threats when other larger threats are looming nearby.

The consideration with respect to carbon dioxide is quite
different. Carbon dioxide levels cannot be reduced to zero, since it
is necessary for life. Thus, the hard question to decide is not whether
carbon dioxide is a pollutant but at what level of concentration it
becomes a pollutant, and why.[107] The simple explanation offered by
Justice Stevens is that special attention is required because the *Reports of
the Intergovernmental Panel on Climate Change* (IPCC) classify carbon
dioxide as a greenhouse gas that traps heat inside the atmosphere,
thereby raising global temperatures.[108] But his explanation misses, at
the very least, the equally important point that carbon dioxide can be

beneficial because GHGs can also keep the sun's rays from reaching the earth's atmosphere. In addition, carbon dioxide is of critical importance for photosynthesis, and even marginally rising concentrations have led to about a 13% increase in biomass, a greening of a portion of the earth's surface approximately equal in size to North and South America combined.[109] Any thorough analysis needs to account for both the positive and negative effects of carbon dioxide.

This analysis is complicated by the fact that water vapor is also a GHG. The effects of water vapor are harder to model because, unlike carbon dioxide, it is not spread uniformly across the globe but instead varies in intensity and impact.[110] Water vapor is found in far higher concentrations than carbon dioxide and is a more powerful GHG. The effects of water vapor dwarf the effects of carbon dioxide by a ratio of about 75–1. This begs the question: What good is regulating a weaker GHG when there is a stronger GHG that eludes regulation? In addition, there is ample evidence that various key phenomena, such as hurricane frequency, are cyclical in nature, so it is hard to square the notion that increases in carbon dioxide levels lead monotonically to higher temperatures.[111] The same is true with regard to rising sea levels, which are cyclical in nature and have been more minimal than predicted in the usual doomsday scenarios.[112]

Nor is it clear that further regulation will do any good. The key provision of the Clean Air Act applies only to pollution from "new" sources of emissions. The provision does not touch old cars on the road. Any regulation would increase the costs of new cars, which, in turn, would delay the substitution of older, dirtier vehicles with new vehicles. The piecemeal nature of this regulation thus leads us further from a sensible form of taxation—one that addresses all emissions, regardless of whether they come from new or old sources. Under such regulations, the correct improvements and replacements for aging vehicles are more likely to be made. But even this ideal form of new regulation makes sense only if the net harm from carbon dioxide is what the detractors claim—a debate that cannot be resolved administratively.

These assorted observations are only a tiny subset of the huge amount of information that has come out about climate change and the proper responses to it. People can debate this information, but for the purposes of administrative law, such debate is neither here nor there. Application of the major question doctrine should prevent any administration from implementing such vast change by fiat. In fact, after *Massachusetts*, EPA did issue its Endangerment Order in December 2009.[113] Worth noting is that sloppy procedures lead to incorrect outcomes. Here is a brief list of objections. One is the constant popular complaint that the endangerment findings did not receive any formal public review.[114] Another is the attack on the common claim that 97% of climate scientists believe that the carbon dioxide produced from human activity is the source of global warming.[115] And most recently, a claim with potentially enormous implications has been advanced independently by Finnish and Japanese researchers, to the effect that natural forces, not the human production of carbon dioxide, are the major drivers of climate change. The key claim by Finnish researchers Jyrki Kauppinen and Pekka Malmi is: "During the last hundred years the temperature increased about 0.1°C because of carbon dioxide. *The human contribution was about* 0.01°C."[116] Their study, too, has been energetically attacked on a variety of grounds and may yet prove to be in need of serious qualification.[117]

For administrative law purposes, the strength of these research findings is not relevant. But what does matter for administrative law is that EPA never did, or could, use its limited authority under the Clean Air Act to put any kind of coherent program into place for the regulation of carbon dioxide. Clearly, the changes entailed are far greater than any decision to abandon the filed-rate requirement for nondominant players in the telecommunications industry, to subject tobacco to FDA regulation (which has now been done by statute), or even to introduce a cost-benefit analysis into Clean Air Act rulemaking.

In his majority opinion, Justice Stevens is cognizant of this difficulty, shown by his going out of his way to distinguish *Brown & Williamson*, where he was in the dissent. But his argument fails at every level. Justice Stevens first claims that the Court in *Brown & Williamson* thought it was "unlikely that Congress meant to ban tobacco products" as drugs. But this is a total non sequitur to his conclusion that "EPA jurisdiction would not lead to any such extreme measures. EPA would only *regulate* emissions, and even then, it would have to delay any action 'to permit the development and application of the requisite technology, giving appropriate consideration to the cost of compliance.' "[118] This is a wholly inadequate description of what is perhaps the most ambitious regulatory agenda (of which motor vehicles are only a part) ever attempted.

Next, Justice Stevens pointed to an "unbroken series of congressional enactments" that made it clear that Congress used other schemes to regulate and, in some cases, subsidize tobacco.[119] It is equally clear that no one ever thought to regulate carbon dioxide emissions with the passage of the Clean Air Act. Justice Stevens went on to insist that EPA was wrong to claim that it could not regulate GHGs because other agencies had direct responsibility for setting the appropriate gas-mileage targets for new vehicles. But that claim was inconsistent with what Justice O'Connor said in *Brown & Williamson* about the importance of other regulatory schemes governing tobacco, by noting: "Congress has directly addressed the problem of tobacco and health through legislation on six occasions since 1965."[120]

It is also the case that under the Clean Air Act, the permissible amount of emissions for standard pollutants is quite small. Ordinary human beings exhale two tons of carbon dioxide each year, which would qualify them as stationary sources subject to regulation under the Act. In *Brown & Williamson*, Justice O'Connor stressed that the coverage formula for tobacco did not fit into any regime designed to test drugs for safety and side effects. Yet here, EPA made all sorts of adjustments to the permissible levels of emissions in the stated statutory standard to lend some kind of coherence to the scheme. Justice Scalia, in his dissenting opinion, did not have to quote or rely on the major question doctrine because EPA did not seek to stray beyond its appropriate mission. For him, it was enough to note that, given the vast difficulties, application of *Chevron* deference would lead to the right result. And so it is that Justice Stevens's majority opinion represents a huge departure from his earlier decision, the merits of which become more questionable with each passing day.

King v. Burwell

Finally, let's consider *King v. Burwell*.[121] This case involved the tax credits available to individuals who purchased their required health-care insurance to avoid a tax penalty under the individual mandate of the Patient Protection and Affordable Care Act (ACA).[122] The tax credits were available on equal terms to those individuals who purchased their insurance on the federal exchange and those who purchased their insurance on state exchanges. As a matter of first principle, there is an obvious advantage to having a uniform standard that covers both groups: it gives each state an undistorted choice as to whether to adopt or reject the overall system. But it would be a mistake to assume that from a dynamic standpoint, this is the only viable approach. One key issue of concern is whether the federal government wants to take on the central managerial burden or prefers to have a decentralized system that can allow it to reduce its own costs. One way to do the latter is to incentivize states to construct their own exchanges at their own expense, with only limited federal support. These two ends are in obvious tension with each other, since an effort to subsidize state exchanges seeks to distort the choice between the two types of exchanges in order to induce states into action.

As a matter of administrative law, the choice of approaches should be a matter left to Congress in the design of the plan and should, if the major question doctrine is in full force, require the most accurate reading of the particular statute without any consideration of the choice to create ex-ante incentives or administrative structures ex post. The point is hardly novel, and before the Supreme Court handed down its decision in *King*, Jonathan Gruber, an MIT economics professor and one of the architects of ACA, answered a question by stating his preference for the ex-ante incentives:

> The federal government has been sort of slow in putting out its backstop, I think partly because they want to sort of squeeze the states to do it. I think what's important to remember politically about this, is if you're a state and you don't set up an Exchange, that means your citizens don't get their tax credits. But your citizens still pay the taxes that support this bill.[123]

None of this, however, made it into Chief Justice Roberts's opinion in *King*. The nub of the dispute is captured in this passage:

> The parties dispute whether Section 36B authorizes tax credits

for individuals who enroll in an insurance plan through a Federal Exchange. Petitioners argue that a Federal Exchange is not "an Exchange established by the State under [42 U.S.C. §18031]," and that the IRS Rule therefore contradicts Section 36B. The Government responds that the IRS Rule is lawful because the phrase "an Exchange established by the State under [42 U.S.C. §18031]" should be read to include Federal Exchanges.[124]

One key to a successful statutory construction is to read the provision without caring about the outcome that it generates. With this in mind, Section 18031 says what it means and means what it says. The use of extratextual evidence is not intended to undermine the statute's meaning but only to offer additional confirmation of that meaning. Statements like Gruber's are instructive because they only reinforce the plain meaning of the statutory language. Nonetheless, Chief Justice Roberts is intent on forcing an alien meaning of Gruber's words. Here is one example of his sleight of hand:

> If the State chooses not to do so, Section 18041 provides that the Secretary "shall . . . establish and operate *such Exchange* within the State." §18041(c)(1) [emphasis added]. . . . By using the phrase "such Exchange," Section 18041 instructs the Secretary to establish and operate the *same* Exchange that the State was directed to establish under Section 18031. See Black's Law Dictionary 1661 (10th ed., 2014), (defining "Such" as "That or those; having just been mentioned"). In other words, State Exchanges and Federal Exchanges are equivalent—they must meet the same requirements, perform the same functions, and serve the same purposes.[125]

The chief justice places far too much weight on the terms "such" and "same." The simple response here is that the statute orders the federal government to establish the *same type* of exchange to serve the same kind of functions. Functional parity is not perfect identity.

ACA cannot order the federal government to set up a state exchange because it is not a state, any more than it could order the states to set up a federal exchange. In this case, the verbal fireworks are cover for a different kind of institutional concern, given that Chief

Justice Roberts was far less concerned with the supposed ambiguity in the words "state exchange" and much more worried about the level of disruption that he thought would arise if the subsidies were removed from all persons who obtained insurance through the federal exchange. It is not clear whether he would have given the term its ordinary meaning if the program had not been put into effect. But what is sufficiently clear is that, as a textual matter, the relevant precedents are *Brown & Williamson* and *Whitman*, both of which support the proposition that major changes made through administrative action require clear congressional authorization, so that an ambiguity is not manufactured where none exists.

In this case, the chief justice held the precise opposite. As he writes, "we have held that Congress 'does not alter the fundamental details of a regulatory scheme in vague terms or ancillary provisions.' "[126] But there is nothing vague about the language in the command set out in Section 18041 of the Affordable Care Act. Nor is it remotely credible to claim that the entire text is ambiguous because the relevant provision is in a subsection. What matters is its importance and the purpose behind it, both of which cut against the chief justice.

Brown & Williamson is similarly transformed. The chief justice noted that *Chevron* rests on the (supposed) theory of an implied delegation by Congress to an agency to fill in ambiguous statutory gaps. *Brown & Williamson* is now said to stand for the proposition that Congress intended no such delegation because the matter was too important to be left to an agency like the IRS, which had no health-care expertise. As the chief justice explained in his opinion:

> Whether those credits are available on Federal Exchanges is thus a question of deep "economic and political significance" that is central to this statutory scheme; had Congress wished to assign that question to an agency, it surely would have done so expressly. It is especially unlikely that Congress would have delegated this decision to the IRS, which has no expertise in crafting health insurance policy of this sort. This is not a case for the IRS.[127]

But health-care expertise is not implicated in deciding whether payments made over federal exchanges should generate certain subsidies. That is a simple administrative matter that the IRS is equipped to decide. Nonetheless, this last passage seems to say that the availability of the tax credits to people who purchase them on the federal exchange is so critical that what was done by the Obama administration could not be undone by any subsequent administration. As such, it amounts to a rare reversal of *Chevron*. The chief justice concedes that the phrase " 'an Exchange established by the State under [42 U.S.C. §18031]' is properly viewed as ambiguous."[128] He then entrenches that provision against reversal by the next administration.

That bold move takes administrative law into uncharted waters. What is really going on here is that Chief Justice Roberts thought that the entire matter was so important that he would adopt a position clearly contrary to the statutory text on the grounds that it would lead to better substantive results. So we now have a kind of reverse major question doctrine that says that when an important departure is made based on established statutory text and the departure becomes sufficiently entrenched, it cannot be reversed by any subsequent administration.

The entire opinion is a mass of unpersuasive sophistry that stands for the proposition that the chief justice and his colleagues live in a parallel universe in which it is improper to "rewrite" the statute to exclude federal exchanges from the subsidy program. Politics then dominates language—as perhaps it always will when the stakes are high enough. In this instance, the author of the major question doctrine, Justice Scalia, could have completed his dissent after his first paragraph, which notes, quite acidly: "The Court holds that when the Patient Protection and Affordable Care Act says 'Exchange established by the State,' it means 'Exchange established by the State or the Federal Government.' That is, of course, quite absurd, and the Court's twenty-one pages of explanation make it no less so."[129] Any hope that the major question doctrine can rehabilitate the dubious morality of modern administrative law in America is, at best, an illusion, and likely to remain so, unless and until the canon of ordinary construction once again occupies the field.

ENDNOTES

1. Thomas W. Merrill, *The Story of Chevron: The Making of an Accidental Landmark,* 66 ADMIN. L. REV. 253, 255–56 (2014).

2. Aditya Bamzai, *The Origins of Judicial Deference to Executive Interpretation,* 126 YALE L. J. 908 (2017).

3. Gillian Metzger, *1093s Redux: The Administrative State Under Siege,* 131 HARV. L. REVIEW, at 49 (2017).

4. *Chevron U.S.A. Inc. v. Nat'l Res. Def. Council,* 467 U.S. 837 (1984).

5. Cass R. Sunstein and Adrian Vermeule, *The Morality of Administrative Law*, 131 HARV. L. REVIEW at 1954 (2018).

6. Metzger, *supra* note 3, at 39.

7. *Id.*

8. 5 U.S.C. § 706 (2018).

9. For pragmatic criticism on this ground, *see* Jack M. Beermann, *End the Failed Chevron Experiment Now: How Chevron Has Failed and Why It Can and Should Be Overruled,* 42 CONN. L. REV. 779, 795–96 (2010); for a restatement of the separation of powers argument, *see* Philip Hamburger, Chevron *Bias,* 84 GEO. WASH. L. REV. 1187, 1233–34 (2016).

10. 5 U.S.C. § 706(2018).

11. *Id.* § 706(2)(a).

12. Cass R. Sunstein, Chevron *as Law,* 107 GEO. L.J. 1613 (2019).

13. *Id.* at 1670–72.

14. *Chevron,* 467 U.S. at 842–43.

15. *City of Arlington v. FCC,* 569 U.S. 290 (2013).

16. *Id.* at 317.

17. *United States v. Mead Corp.,* 533 U.S. 218, 229 (2001) (declining to give *Chevron* deference to a tariff designation but providing *Skidmore* deference, which will be discussed below).

18. For my discussion on this, *see* Richard A. Epstein, *Our Implied Constitution,* 53 WILLAMETTE L. REVIEW 295.

19. *Gibbons v. Ogden,* 22 U.S. (9 Wheat.) 1 (1824).

20. *Id.* at 195.

21. *Id.* at 188–89.

22. *Id.* at 204.

23. For labor, *see Nat'l Labor Relations Bd v. Jones & Laughlin Steel Corp.,* 301 U.S. 1 (1937). For agriculture, *see Wickard v. Filburn,* 317 U.S. 111 (1942). For my critique, *see* Richard A. Epstein, *The Progressives' Deadly Embrace of Cartels: A Close Look at Labor and Agricultural Markets 1890-1940* in THE PROGRESSIVES' CENTURY: POLITICAL REFORM, CONSTITUTIONAL GOVERNMENT, AND THE MODERN AMERICAN STATE 339 (Stephen Skowronek et al. eds., Yale. U. Press, 2016).

24. *Mead Corp.,* 533 U.S. at 218.

25. *Skidmore v. Swift Co.,* 323 U.S. 134 (1944)(discussed *infra* at Part 4, at 192–131.

26. For the original coinage of the term "Step Zero," *see* Thomas W. Merrill and Kristin E. Hickman, Chevron's *Domain*, 89 Geo. L.J. 833, 836 (2001); *see also* Cass R. Sunstein, Chevron *Step Zero,* 92 Va. L. Rev. 187 (2006).

27. *Chevron,* 467 U.S. at 842–44.

28. Brett Kavanaugh, *Fixing Statutory Interpretation,* 129 Harv. L. Rev. 2118, 2136 (2016) ("Unfortunately, there is often no good or predictable way for judges to determine whether statutory text contains 'enough' ambiguity to cross the line beyond which courts may resort to . . . *Chevron* deference").

29. For the best account, *see* Merrill, *supra* at note 1.

30. *Chevron,* 467 U.S. at 859–60 (interpreting 42 U.S.C. § 7502(b)(6)).

31. *See* Merrill, *supra* note 1, at 258.

32. *Id.* at 264.

33. *See* Cass R. Sunstein, Chevron *without* Chevron, Sup. Ct. Rev. 59 (2018).

34. *See, e.g., Wis. Elec. Power Co. v. Reilly,* 893 F.2d 901 (7th Cir. 1990).

35. *See* Lawrence B. Solum and Cass R. Sunstein, Chevron *as Construction* (Dec. 12, 2018), *available at* https://papers.ssrn.com/sol3/papers.cfm?abstract_id=3300626.

36. *Id.* (manuscript at 3).

37. For a more systematic analysis of how interpretation works across different legal systems, *see* Epstein, *Our Implied Constitution*, at 45–71. For an earlier version, *see* Richard A. Epstein, *A Common Lawyer Looks at Constitutional Interpretation,* 72 B.U. L. Rev. 72 (1992). For a general discussion of the police power, *see* Richard A. Epstein, Takings: Private Property and the Power of Eminent Domain, 107–145 (Harvard U. Press, 1985).

38. For an early case expanding speech protections to all forms of expression, *see* Thomas Irwin Emerson, The System of Freedom of Expression (Random House, 1970).

39. For early treatments of this subject, *see* Ernst Freund, The Police Power: Public Policy and Constitutional Rights (Univ. of Chicago Press,1904).

40. 545 U.S. 967 (2005).

41. 47 U.S.C. §§ 201–209.

42. 47 U.S.C. § 251(a)(1).

43. *Id.* § 254(d).

44. *Brand X,* 545 U.S. at 976–77.

45. *Id.* at 981.

46. *AT&T Corp. v. City of Portland,* 216 F.3d 871 (9th Cir. 2000).

47. Pub. L. No. 92-500, 86 Stat. 816 (1972), *codified at* 33 U.S.C. §§ 1251-1387(2017). For operative definition of "navigable waters" governing the jurisdiction of the Army Corps of Engineers, *see* 33 U.S.C. § 1362(7)(2017).

48. *Nat. Res. Def. Council, Inc. v. Callaway,* 392 F. Supp. 685 (D.D.C. 1975).

49. *Id.* at 686.

50. *See supra* Part 1, at 11.

51. 33 U.S.C. § 1344(2017).

52. *United States v. Riverside Bayview Homes, Inc.,* 474 U.S. 121 (1985).

53. *Id.* at 123. Note that the new regulation extended the term "waters of the United States" to include interstate waters, such as interstate wetlands, "intrastate lakes, rivers, streams (including intermittent streams), mudflats, sandflats, wetlands, sloughs, prairie potholes, wet meadows, playa lakes, or natural ponds," as well as the wetlands adjacent to these waters.

54. *Id.* at 124 (citing 33 C.F.R. § 323.2(c))(1978)(emphasis added).

55. *Id.* at 126–28 (citing *Penn Cent. Transp. Co. v. City of New York,* 438 U.S. 104 (1978)).

56. *Id.* at 127.

57. In *First English Evangelical Lutheran Church of Glendale v. County of Los Angeles,* 482 U.S. 304 (1987), the Supreme Court announced a rule that allowed for compensation in the event of temporary total takings. But that rule has, in the context of administrative review, been gutted by the broad exception precluding compensation "in the case of normal delays in obtaining building permits, changes in zoning ordinances, variances, and the like." *4 & 2 U.S. at 321.*

58. The same cycle arises in the permits needed for constructing nuclear power plants. *See* Richard A. Epstein, *The Many Sins of NEPA,* 6 Tex. A&M L. Rev. 1 (2018) (discussing *Calvert Cliffs' Coordinating Comm., Inc. v. U.S. Atomic Energy Comm'n,* 449 F.2d 1109 (D.C. Cir. 1971)). For a defense of NEPA, *see* Richard Lazarus, *The National Environmental Policy Act in the U.S. Supreme Court: A Reappraisal and a Peek Behind the Curtains,* 100 Geo. L.J. 1507, 1513–14 (2012).

59. *Solid Waste Agency of N. Cook Cty. v. Army Corps of Eng'rs,* 531 U.S. 159 (2001).

60. *Id.* at 164, 169.

61. *Rapanos v. United States,* 547 U.S. 715 (2006).

62. *Id.* at 782 (Kennedy, J., concurring).

63. *Sackett v. EPA,* 566 U.S. 120 (2012).

64. *Id.* at 124.

65. *Army Corps of Eng'rs v. Hawkes Co.,* 136 S. Ct. 1807 (2016).

66. *Id.* at 1815.

67. *North Dakota v. EPA,* 127 F. Supp. 3d 1047, 1056 (2015).

68. 33 U.S.C. § 1362(11)(2017).

69. Exec. Order 13778, *Restoring the Rule of Law, Federalism, and Economic Growth by Reviewing the "Waters of the United States" Rule,* 82 Fed. Reg. 12497 (Mar. 3, 2017).

70. *South Carolina Coastal Conservation League v. Pruitt,* 318 F. Supp. 3d 959 (D.S.C. 2018).

71. For further discussion of this point, see the discussion of NEPA in connection with pipeline approvals, *infra* at Part 5, at 192–205.

72. *Weyerhaeuser v. U.S. Fish & Wildlife Serv.,* 139 S. Ct. 361 (2018), *rev'g Markle Interests, LLC v. U.S. Fish & Wildlife Serv.,* 827 F.3d 452 (5th Cir. 2016).

73. Pub. L. No. 93-205, 87 Stat. 884 (1973), *codified at* 16 U.S.C. §§ 1531–1544.

74. *Id.* § 3(5)(A)(i), 16 U.S.C. § 1532(5)(A)(i).

75. *Markle Interests,* 827 F.3d at 459.

76. *Weyerhaeuser,* 139 S. Ct. at 366.

77. *Id.* at 368.

78. *Babbitt v. Sweet Home Chapter of Cmtys. for a Greater Oregon,* 515 U.S. 687 (1995).

79. ESA § 9(a)(1), 16 U.S.C. § 1538(a)(1)(2017).

80. *Id.* § 3(19), 16 U.S.C. § 1532(19).

81. *Id.* § 5(a)(2), 16 U.S.C. § 1534 (a)(2).

82. *Sweet Home,* 515 U.S. at 703.

83. *NBC v. United States,* 319 U.S. 190 (1943).

84. For a discussion, see Josh Blackman, *Gridlock,* 130 Harv. L. Rev. 241, 260–65 (2016).

85. *MCI Telecomms. Corp. v. AT&T,* 512 U.S. 218 (1994).

86. *Id.* at 234 (interpreting the Communications Act of 1934, Pub. L. No. 73-416, 48 Stat. 1064 (1934)).

87. *Id.* at 224 (citing § 203(b), 47 U.S.C. § 203(b))(1988)).

88. *Id.* at 226.

89. *Id.* at 225–26.

90. *Id.* at 235.

91. *FDA v. Brown & Williamson Tobacco Corp.,* 529 U.S. 120 (2000) (interpreting the Pure Food and Drug Act, Pub. L. No. 59-384, 34 Stat. 768 (1907), *codified at* 21 U.S.C.).

92. 21 U.S.C. § 321(g)(1)(c)(1994).

93. *Brown & Williamson,* 529 U.S. at 162 (Breyer, J., dissenting).

94. *See, e.g., Nat'l Nutritional Foods Ass'n v. Mathews,* 557 F.2d 325 (2d Cir. 1977).

95. *Brown & Williamson,* 529 U.S. at 131.

96. Pub. L. No. 111-31, 123 Stat. 1776 (2009), *codified at* 21 U.S.C. §§ 301–399(2017).

97. *Whitman v. American Trucking Ass'n,* 531 U.S. 457 (2001).

98. Pub. L. No. 88-206, 77 Stat. 392 (1963), *codified at* 42 U.S.C. §§ 7401–7671(2017).

99. *Id.* § 109(b)(1), 42 U.S.C. § 7409(b)(1).

100. *Id.*

101. *Whitman,* 531 U.S. at 466.

102. *Id.* at 490 (Breyer, J., concurring).

103. *Massachusetts v. EPA,* 549 U.S. 497 (2007).

104. CAA § 202(a)(1), 42 U.S.C. § 7521(a)(1)(2017).

105. *Id.* § 302(g), 42 U.S.C. § 7602(g).

106. *Id.* § 302(h), 42 U.S.C. § 7602(h).

107. I have stated my views on this topic in more extensive detail elsewhere. See Richard A. Epstein, *Regulatory Enforcement Under New York's Martin Act: From Financial Fraud to Global Warming,* 154 N.Y.U. J.L. & Bus. 805, 882–918 (2018); idem, *Carbon Dioxide: Our Newest Pollutant,* 43 Suffolk L. Rev. 797 (2010). *See also* idem, *Our Latest Global Warming Scare,* Defining Ideas, Hoover Inst., Stan. U. (Oct. 16, 2018), *available at* https://www.hoover.org/research/our-latest-global-warming-scare.

108. *Mass. v. EPA,* 549 U.S. at 508–9.

109. Samson Reiny, *Carbon Dioxide Fertilization Greening Earth, Study Finds,* NASA (Apr. 26, 2016), *available at* https://www.nasa.gov/feature/goddard/2016/carbon-dioxide-fertilization-greening-earth.

110. For a clear explanation of the problem, *see, e.g.,* Richard Lindzen, *Richard Lindzen Lecture at GWPF: "Global Warming for the Two Cultures,"* WATTS UP WITH THAT? (Oct. 9, 2018), *available at* https://wattsupwiththat.com/2018/10/09/richard-lindzen-lecture-at-gwpf-global-warming-for-the-two-cultures.

111. *See, e.g.,* Patrick J. Michaels and Ryan Maue, *The Hurricane Last Time,* CATO INST.: CATO AT LIBERTY (Sept. 11, 2018), *available at* https://www.cato.org/blog/hurricane-last-time.

112. Larry Bell, *Alarmists Are in Way over Their Heads on Rising Ocean Claims,* FORBES (Sept. 24, 2013), *available at* https://www.forbes.com/sites/larrybell/2013/09/24/alarmists-are-in-way-over-their-heads-on-rising-ocean-claims/#3c94f6121194.

113. Endangerment and Cause or Contribute Findings for Greenhouse Gases Under the Section 202(a) of the Clean Air Act, U.S. ENVTL. PROT. AGENCY, (Dec. 7, 2009) *available at* https://www.epa.gov/ghgemissions/endangerment-and-cause-or-contribute-findings-greenhouse-gases-under-section-202a-clean.

114. Paul Driessen, *Ending Obama EPA Climate Deception,* WATTS UP WITH THAT? (May 20, 2019), *available at* https://wattsupwiththat.com/2019/05/20/ending-obama-epa-climate-deception ("[T]here has never been any formal, public review of the [Endangerment Finding] conclusion or of the secretive process EPA employed to ensure the result of its 'analysis' could only be 'endangerment'—and no awkward questions or public hearings would get in the way").

115. *Regarding NASA's Claim That 97 Percent of Scientists Agree on Anthropogenic Global Warming,* COMPETITIVE ENTERPRISE INST. (July 9, 2019), *available at* https://cei.org/sites/default/files/IQA_NASA_97_Percent_Final.pdf.

116. Kauppinen and Malmi's more complete conclusion reads:

    We have proven that the [general circulation models] used in [the Intergovernmental Panel on Climate Change] report AR5 cannot compute correctly the natural component included in the observed global temperature. The reason is that the models fail to derive the influences of low cloud cover fraction on the global temperature. A too small natural component results in a too large portion for the contribution of the greenhouse gases like carbon dioxide. That is why IPCC represents the climate sensitivity more than one order of magnitude larger than our sensitivity 0.24 C. Because the anthropogenic portion in the increased CO2 is less than 10%, we have practically no anthropogenic climate change. The low clouds control mainly the global temperature.

    Jyrki Kauppinen and Pekka Malmi, *No Experimental Evidence for the Significant Anthropogenic Climate Change* (July 13, 2019), *available at* https://arxiv.org/pdf/1907.00165.pdf.

    A separate group of Japanese scientists have presented evidence similarly suggesting a natural cause of "rapid climate changes":

    Centennial-to decadal-resolution paleoceanic records recently revealed multiple suborbital-scale climate events in the marine isotope stage (MIS) 19 interglacial period, when the last geomagnetic reversal occurred. Most events were associated with sea-level changes, some possibly related to iceberg discharge. At least one event was associated with a decrease in the strength of the Earth's magnetic field. Thus, climate records from the MIS 19 interglacial can be used to elucidate the mechanisms of a variety of climate changes, including testing the effect of changes in geomagnetic dipole field strength on climate through galactic cosmic ray (GCR)-induced cloud formation, as the present evidence for this effect is weak and biased toward the oceans.

Masayuki Hyodo et al., *Intensified East Asian Winter Monsoon During the Last Geomagnetic Reversal Transition,* Scientific Reports (June 28, 2019) (citations omitted), *available at* https://www.nature.com/articles/s41598-019-45466-8.pdf. Describing his study, Professor Hyodo said: "This study provides an opportunity to rethink the impact of clouds on climate. When galactic cosmic rays increase, so do low clouds, and when cosmic rays decrease clouds do as well, so climate warming may be caused by an opposite-umbrella effect. The umbrella effect caused by galactic cosmic rays is important when thinking about current global warming as well as the warm period of the medieval era." Kobe University, *Winter Monsoons Became Stronger During Geomagnetic Reversal,* SCIENCEDAILY (July 3, 2019), *available at* https://www.sciencedaily.com/releases/2019/07/190703121407.htm.

117. The Finnish study has been attacked by various commentators in *Climate Non-Peer-Reviewed Manuscript Falsely Claims Natural Cloud Changes Can Explain Global Warming,* CLIMATE FEEDBACK(July 12, 2019), *available at* https://climatefeedback.org/claimreview/non-peer-reviewed-manuscript-falsely-claims-natural-cloud-changes-can-explain-global-warming).

118. *Mass. v. EPA,* 549 U.S. at 531 (citing 42 U.S.C. § 7521(a)(2)).

119. *Id.*

120. *Brown & Williamson,* 529 U.S. at 137.

121. *King v. Burwell,* 135 S. Ct. 2480 (2015).

122. Pub. L. No. 111-148, 124 Stat. 119 (2010), *codified as amended throughout* U.S.C.

123. Jonathan F. Gruber, quoted in Michael F. Cannon, *ObamaCare Architect Jonathan Gruber: "If You're a State and You Don't Set Up an Exchange, That Means Your Citizens Don't Get Their Tax Credits" [Updated],* FORBES (July 25, 2014), *available at* https://www.forbes.com/sites/michaelcannon/2014/07/25/obamacare-architect-jonathan-gruber-if-youre-a-state-and-you-dont-set-up-an-exchange-that-means-your-citizens-dont-get-their-tax-credits/#1ce93e895438. For a more detailed and systematic critique, see Jonathan Adler and Michael F. Cannon, King v. Burwell *and the Triumph of Selective Contextualism,* 15 CATO SUP. CT. REV. 35 (2015).

124. *King,* 135 S. Ct. at 2488.

125. *Id* at 2945.

126. *Id.* at 2489 (quoting *Util. Air Regulatory Grp. v. EPA,* 573 U.S. 302, 324 (2014)).

127. *Id.* at 2489.

128. *Id.* at 2491.

129. *Id.* at 2496 (Scalia, J., dissenting).

PART 4

CHEVRON LITE

Skidmore

If *Chevron* is incorrect, is there still a place for a more limited form of deference? Here the basic answer remains no. The only legal rules that meet the standards of the rule of law are those that use the test of ordinary meaning. This point becomes clear in connection with the so-called *Skidmore* deference,[1] which was applied by Justice Robert H. Jackson in connection with an inquiry under the 1938 Fair Labor Standards Act (FLSA) over the extent of overtime wage protections. The administrator of the program announced his conclusions on the matter in both an interpretive bulletin and informal rulings, which Justice Jackson regarded as the distillation of views by an impartial party "representing the public interest in enforcement."[2] In light of these considerations, Justice Jackson announced the standard interpretive approach as follows:

> We consider that the rulings, interpretations and opinions of the Administrator under this Act, while not controlling upon the courts by reason of their authority, do constitute a body of experience and informed judgment to which courts and litigants may properly resort for guidance. The weight of such a judgment in a particular case will depend upon the thoroughness evident in its consideration, the validity of its reasoning, its consistency with earlier and later pronouncements, and all those factors which give it power to persuade, if lacking power to control.[3]

The failure of this eloquent rhetoric to persuade becomes clear by taking a closer look at the question before the Court, which involved overtime protections applied to a group of daytime workers who agreed to work several nights a week on or near the premises, when, by contract, their sole duties were to respond to certain fire alarms, work for which they were separately compensated. When sitting idle, they received no compensation except for room, board, and a set of limited amenities. The workers had claimed overtime for the nonalarm hours for times when they were sleeping on the job, playing board games, or otherwise relaxing. A moment's reflection should indicate that this case was atypical because, as the Fifth Circuit said,[4] the workers' nighttime activities did not involve the additional "toil" that was thought to justify the time-and-a-half overtime regime in place under FLSA. Accordingly, the Court held that the overtime requirement applied only to the actual time spent working and not the remainder of hours. The secretary of labor weighed in with the Solomonic decision that the play time was compensable, but the sleep time was not. By accepting that distinction, Justice Jackson revealed that he had no grasp of the basic economic problem—namely, the poor fit between the FLSA overtime scheme and underlying contractual logic.

In an unregulated context, the contract reaches the correct solution by tying the level of compensation to the level of output. In-kind compensation—here, lodging—is sufficient when there is no particular task to be done. But explicit compensation is required on those occasions when a more concentrated effort is called for—that is, responding to fire alarms. FLSA is credible only in situations where overtime work requires a heavier effort—although it is doubtful whether the time-and-a-half rule works even then, because labor at such a high-wage level commonly results in economic losses for the employer.

Notwithstanding these problems, the Department of Labor (DOL) rule makes no economic sense because it creates intolerable incentives for men who knew that they could gain overtime pay by staying awake but idle, instead of sleeping. The decision thus distorts the relevant marginal incentives. All this material is readily available on the face of the record. When DOL invoked this rule, there was no historical practice on the matter, given that FLSA had been in effect for only six years before *Skidmore* was decided, and this ruling was issued without any effort by Justice Jackson to square this policy with the general statute. To be sure, the Supreme Court cannot fix the deep structural flaws in FLSA; but why compound them by deferring to arguments that only make a bad situation worse?

Speaking more generally, the same argument applies to *Chevron*. If government expertise promises some systematic advantage, its resulting arguments should carry the day on their merits, wholly without deference.

Seminole Rock and Auer

The last of the major heads of deference go by two names: *Seminole Rock*, a price-control case from 1945;[5] and *Auer*, an FLSA case from 1997.[6] The two cases are said to stand for the proposition that administrative agencies are afforded extensive deference in the interpretation of their own regulations.

That skin-deep conclusion misses the huge gulf between these two cases. *Seminole Rock* reads just like the pre–New Deal cases, such as *J. W. Hampton*,[7] that are concerned with incremental adjustments in technical pricing situations—in the one case, for tariffs; and the other, for maximum prices. The case for low-level continuity in accordance with customary practice would seem the best solution, but in *Seminole Rock*, the problem was compounded because the entire scheme emerged all at once by a series of complex orders that had not evolved through a process of trial and error, as would be the case with customary practices.

In contrast, *Auer* concerns a single overtly politicized effort by then–secretary of labor Robert Reich to reclassify thousands of higher-ranking officials within police departments in order to increase the scope of the overtime regulations. The regulation in *Seminole Rock* received deference only for an interpretation that the Supreme Court had independently concluded was consistent with the statute. In contrast, the blockbuster regulation in *Auer* adopted a tortured interpretation at odds with both the underlying statutory text and the principles of ordinary language. To yoke the regulations together as a uniform approach to the interpretation of disputed language is to ignore the major ground-level distinction between both cases.

The precise question for resolution in *Seminole Rock* involved the impact of a price-control scheme enacted by the federal government in April 1942, just as the military effort in World War II was reaching its fever pitch. The statute in question did not attempt to set particular prices for all the goods sold in the market. Instead, it took a more modest approach, providing that the prices for various commodities should be set by reference to the price at which those goods were sold in the previous month.[8] In fact, the text of the price-control regulations on which this case turned was a single sentence: " 'Highest price charged during March, 1942' means (i) The highest price which the seller charged to a purchaser of the same class for delivery of the article or material during March, 1942."[9]

In dealing with this provision, *Seminole Rock* claimed that the highest price should be determined by looking only at those goods that were sold and delivered in March 1942. Given that price controls were around the corner, it was easy to predict the run-up in contract prices during that period. Predictably, therefore, the seller claimed that the appropriate price was $1.50 per ton, or the amount for which a forward contract had been concluded during March 1942. The question here is not whether Congress ought to have endorsed a general regime of price controls, against which there are many powerful arguments. It is how that regime should have been construed after, as was held in *Yakus v. United States*,[10] the program had overcome all constitutional objections.

At this point, the purposivist approach to statutory interpretation, not mentioned in the case, strongly supports the government's position. The price-control system would have been wrecked on the seller's reading because the permissible prices would have been pushed upward by economic activity undertaken with knowledge that the program would go into effect. That could not happen under the government's reading, which asserted that goods delivered pursuant to contracts entered into prior to that date could not benefit from a price bump that might negate the impact of the price-control legislation. As with *Skidmore*, decided just the year before, the economics of the situation gives powerful insight into the validity of the administrative interpretation.

Even if attention is paid only to more traditional textual forms of interpretation, the result is exactly the same. Because clause (i) ties the price to the delivery date, the regulation rules out pricing based on contracts made within that period whose delivery would take place at some later time. In addressing this question, Justice Frank Murphy noted that the only two tools available for aiding interpretation in this case were "the plain words of the regulation and any relevant interpretations of the Administrator,"[11] perhaps in that order. The case for deference would have had more bite if the administrative interpretation in this case were at odds with the plain meaning of the text, but just that possibility was disclaimed when Murphy concluded that "rule (i) clearly applies to the facts of this case, making 60 cents per ton the ceiling price for respondent's crushed stone," which indeed it does. There was no implicit subtext that *any* conceivable meaning that the administrator embraced would suffice.[12]

It is against this background that the opinion's most famous passage must be read:

> Since this involves an interpretation of an administrative regulation a court must necessarily look to the administrative construction of the regulation if the meaning of the words used is in doubt. The intention of Congress or the principles of the Constitution in some situations may be relevant in the first instance in choosing between various constructions. But the ultimate criterion is the administrative interpretation, which becomes of controlling weight unless it is plainly erroneous or inconsistent with the regulation.[13]

No one can gainsay the literal force of these words, which juxtapose the "ultimate criterion" with the "plainly erroneous" view. But it is overreading the opinion to assume that it should apply in cases of evident conflict between the ordinary language interpretation of the statute and that given to it by the relevant administrator. Paul Larkin and Elizabeth Slattery have suggested: "Given the off-hand manner in which the Court adopted the rule in *Seminole Rock* and the Spartan justification that it gave, it seems that the Supreme Court could not possibly have meant what it said."[14] There was nothing in the occasion that called for a revolution in statutory interpretation. But even if the Court did intend some kind of revolution, it was a modest one, at best, given that the decision passes muster under the most rigorous standard of scrutiny.

In this regard, it is instructive to note the way in which the phrase "plainly [or clearly] erroneous" has been construed elsewhere in both civil procedure and administrative law: "A finding is 'clearly erroneous' when although there is evidence to support it, the reviewing court on

133

the entire evidence is left with the definite and firm conviction that a mistake has been committed."[15] Similarly, any findings that are credible when the record is viewed as a whole cannot be condemned as erroneous:[16] "Where here there are two permissible views of the evidence, the factfinder's choice between them cannot be clearly erroneous."[17]

None of these formulations allows an entire record to be disregarded, and a regulation upheld, because there is some isolated point that looks, at first blush, to sustain the government action. *Seminole Rock*, therefore, does not need to probe its key phrase "plainly erroneous or inconsistent with the regulation." But the phrase, like its virtual synonym "clearly erroneous," does require a court to turn somersaults to support an agency determination that refers to some finding of fact "that is not supported by substantial or competent evidence or by any reasonable inference."[18] There is not a whisper in this formulation that any agency determination should be accepted if there is some conceivable ground on which it could be supported, even when the vast bulk of evidence on the point moves in the opposite direction.

More concretely, between *Seminole Rock* and *Auer* lies a vast gulf, because *Auer* goes far beyond what *Seminole Rock* required or, indeed, even contemplated.[19] There, the Supreme Court, per Justice Scalia, afforded extensive deference to DOL's decision on whether sergeants and one lieutenant employed by the St. Louis police force were entitled to receive overtime pay under FLSA, even though they did not fall into the class of "executive, administrative, and professional employees" (EAPs) under the act.[20] Applicable DOL regulations raised the question of whether these parties were salary-based employees, given that they could suffer deductions in pay for various rule infractions. The secretary of labor refused to treat them as employees who were exempt from overtime because, in his view, such people "are not 'disciplined' by piecemeal deductions from their pay, but are terminated, demoted, or given restricted assignments."[21] The Court showed far more deference than is required under the clearly erroneous rule when it concluded that judicial deference to the secretary's interpretation was appropriate because the statute did not speak exactly to the proper treatment of offsets.

With or without deference, the decision is way off-base—that is, plainly erroneous. There is no conceivable reason to assume, a priori, that monetary sanctions should be removed from the tool kit that senior executives have for dealing with EAPs. No private firm would categorically take those sanctions off the table. Alternative disciplinary remedies require shifting around the work staff and may constitute overkill for small infractions that nonetheless deserve some sanction. There was no effort here to give, as the 19th-century cases did, some practical construction to a statute that deferred to the standard practices used in the field. The regulator, therefore, was more confident in its own judgment than the common practices of those actually charged with the supervision.

Worse still, the regulation flies in the face of all experience. The definition of "administrative personnel" usually involves their supervising other workers, which is evident for sergeants, and overwhelmingly clear for lieutenants. A one-sentence summary of the job description for a police sergeant demonstrates beyond argument that they have executive, administrative. and professional responsibilities.[22] The definition of the responsibilities of a police lieutenant is even clearer.[23] Yet the willingness to defer inspired Justice Scalia to avoid the simple test of checking a police manual to see how those job descriptions stacked up against the proffered administrative interpretation.

The only good news on *Auer* is that Justice Scalia subsequently voiced doubts in *Perez v. Mortgage Bankers Association*[24] about his earlier handiwork in a case that was every bit as easy on its merits as the former.[25] In *Perez*, the Court held that the secretary of labor could define classes of exempt employees and, more important, could reverse earlier definitions, all without the benefit of a notice-and-comment rulemaking, to determine whether the regulations promulgated under FLSA exempted mortgage loan officers as administrative employees.

The history was erratic. Democratic administrations denied the objections at issue in *Perez* in 1999 and 2001, and they were then reversed by a Republican administration in 2004. That definition was then reversed in 2006 by a Republican administration, only to be restored in a Democratic administration, without any notice and comment, in 2010.[26] These administrative flip-flops cannot happen with anything close to the same frequency when questions of statutory construction are treated as a matter of law to be decided authoritatively by a court.

Perez started off well, by rejecting the view that an extratextual requirement could be added to APA[27] without asking how the business job description squares with the statutory standard. The statutory test under FLSA requires that an exempt worker does office or nonmanual work; that the work is directly related to the management or general business operations of the employer or the employer's customers; that a primary component of the work involves the exercise of independent judgment and discretion; and that the judgment and discretion concern matters of significance. The *Investopedia* description of a "loan officer" tracks these four requirements completely:

> A loan officer is a representative of a bank, credit union, or other financial institution who finds and assists borrowers in acquiring loans. Loan officers can work with a wide variety of lending products for both consumers and businesses. They must have a comprehensive awareness of lending products as well as banking industry rules, regulations, and required documentation.[28]

Unfortunately, Professors Sunstein and Vermeule's discussion of the case does not give any specific account of the interpretive issue at stake but instead points to some temporizing language from an earlier opinion of Justice Kennedy in *Thomas Jefferson University v. Shalala*, cited by Justice Sonia Sotomayor in *Perez*,[29] suggesting that there are some constraints on deference—namely, the inconsistency between the regulation and the agency's interpretation, or findings of some lack of fair and considered judgment.[30] But once again, those cautionary words have to be taken with a grain of salt. The disregard of any effort to confront the textual issue head-on says it all. It is best to judge a court by how it behaves, not by the occasional insertion of cautionary language that never seems to bite.

Again, the canon of deference comes in a distant second-best to the rule that gives words their ordinary meaning. The deference regime gives too much running room for political appointees with partisan agendas and thus constitutes an open invitation to repeated flip-flops on the governing rules that generate major inconsistencies within short periods of time. The consistency needed to satisfy Fuller's sensible prerequisites for the rule of law is nowhere to be found. Only *Auer* deference turns *Perez* into a difficult case.

None of these refinements matters to the defense of *Auer* in the work of Sunstein and Vermeule, who continue the common, if unwise, practice of doing administrative law from a fact-free perspective at 30,000 feet. That practice is dangerous, given the reversals of opinion between Democratic and Republican administrations, which necessarily turn the law into the type of political football that Fuller deplored. Sunstein and Vermeule are far from justifying these flip-flops.

Professor Metzger sides with Sunstein and Vermeule in defending broad delegations of "binding interpretive authority" to administrative agencies, which she finds necessary because any "insistence on a firm divide between interpretation and policymaking conflicts with broadly accepted legal realist insights about the frequency of legal indeterminacy, and thus of policy-making, in judicial decision making."[31] But "accepted" by whom? The difficulty in her observation is that it implicitly adopts the legal realist position that overstates the level of ambiguity in text, which it then celebrates for its own sake. The traditional division of labor that gives agencies presumptive control over policy and the courts control over interpretive matters strikes the right balance. Agencies do have a comparative advantage, not in legal interpretation but in policymaking: linguistic relativism conflates the two. It is for this reason that the original distribution of authority found in APA Section 706(a) should continue to apply. Sadly, such common disregard of the statutory command also flouts Fuller's rule-of-law concerns while purporting to comply with them.

Gloucester County

The extent to which *Auer* deference can change the terms of a legal debate is well evidenced by the 2016 Fourth Circuit decision in *G.G. v. Gloucester County School Board*.[32] This case confronted the question of how regulations promulgated under Title IX of the Education Amendments of 1972[33] should be applied to individuals seeking assignment of sex-based facilities by gender identity rather than by biological sex. *Gloucester County* forthrightly presented this problem when G.G., a high school student born female, was diagnosed with gender dysphoria, a condition that made G.G. think of himself as an innate male trapped inside a female body. The district court rejected G.G.'s Title IX claim on a conventional reading of the applicable regulation as unambiguously allowing schools to assign bathroom access on the basis of biological sex.[34] The Fourth Circuit reversed that decision in January 2016, relying foursquare on *Auer*[35] to defer to the decision of the Obama administration, which, in an opinion letter dated January 7, 2015, explained how Title IX regulations should apply to transgender individuals: "When a school elects to separate or treat students differently on the basis of sex . . . a school generally must treat transgender students consistent with their gender identity."[36]

After the decision in *Gloucester County*, the Department of Justice (DOJ) and Department of Education (DOE) put forth the same conclusion verbatim in their "Dear Colleague" letter of May 13, 2016.[37] There were no ifs, ands, or buts in this declaration, which treated self-determined gender identity as the sole test for discrimination except perhaps in some inconsequential special circumstances. The ruling was not made conditional on a diagnosis of gender dysphoria or any other medical or psychological condition. At no point was there an analysis of the impact of this policy on the operation of schools and colleges, whether secular or religious,[38] or of any of the thousands of other matters that necessarily would have come out, had the decision gone through typical notice and comment procedures.

The obvious concern with this regulation was the impact it might have on other persons, but the Obama administration determined unilaterally to brush any such concern aside: "As is consistently recognized in civil rights cases, the desire to accommodate others' discomfort cannot justify a policy that singles out and disadvantages a particular class of students."[39] The cavalier use of the term "discomfort" conceals the weight of the interests on the other side. In the sensitivities of the high school environment, forcing girls to disrobe in the presence of classmates perceived as boys, or to compete with them in athletic events where they are inherently disadvantaged, could have serious harmful consequences. The entire structure of Title IX was meant to avoid male domination of sports to the exclusion of female athletes. Elsewhere, Title IX was meant to protect the central tenets of various religions, many of which flatly prohibit interactions between the sexes in the terms specified in the "Dear Colleague" letter. Is it mere "discomfort" if these girls and women find themselves bound to withdraw from the use of locker rooms or athletic competition? Is it really a statement of agency expertise for two political appointees—Catherine E. Lhamon at DOE and Vanita Gupta at DOJ—to inject their own value judgments into a major statutory scheme?

In their zeal, the entire history and structure of Title IX is pushed aside in exchange for another single sentence that is thought by the court in *Gloucester County*, without more explanation, to change decades of established law: "An agency may not condition access to facilities—or to other terms, conditions, or privileges of employment—on the completion of certain medical steps that the agency itself has unilaterally determined will somehow prove the *bona fides* of the individual's gender identity."[40] No independent analysis of this conclusion was offered in DOE/DOJ guidance or elsewhere.

After the 2016 election, the Supreme Court vacated and remanded *Gloucester County*'s acquiescence to the Obama administration's rule "for further consideration in light of the guidance document issued by the Department of Education and the Department of Justice on February 22, 2017."[41] In their new guidance reversing the old, DOE and DOJ made it clear that the "withdrawal of these guidance documents does not leave students without protections from discrimination, bullying, or harassment. All schools must ensure that all students, including LGBT students, are able to learn and thrive in a safe environment."[42]

Thus, for the time being, this episode has come to an end, but not before deference under *Auer* to an agency interpretation of its own regulation allowed for a major transformation of the law that commanded little support among parents and students. Even without *Auer*, any school district that chose to go down this road could do so, without opposition from Title IX on the basis of local sentiment and without imposing its wishes on other schools.

How did this confrontation arise as a matter of statutory interpretation? As a matter of ordinary interpretation and historical understanding, the distinction between the sexes is marked by obvious differences at birth. Some sex-change operations—now termed "gender reassignment surgery"—had taken place prior to the enactment of Title IX, but no legislator thought or uttered a word about how those novel cases fit within the sharply dichotomous scheme recognized by the statute.

It has always been the social practice that once gender reassignment surgery was complete, individuals used the bathroom facilities of their adopted sex, not their sex as designated at birth. But the current litigation on gender identity does not depend on any physical operation or medical diagnosis to effectuate a changed treatment of one's sex under the policy. Instead, under the proposed regime, the question is whether the switch in gender identity is covered by the sex-discrimination laws before any outwardly visible transformation has been made. The issue is especially acute in secondary education, in which students are not of age and live in a controlled environment before these operations are even allowed without parental consent.

At one point, G.G. did all his changing of clothes at home so that the issue of separate facilities at the local high school never occurred. When he began changing clothes and using the bathroom facilities at his school, he originally accepted an accommodation whereby he changed in a one-person unisex restroom. But after two months, he "found it stigmatizing to use a separate restroom," and, at his request, he was allowed to use the boys' restroom, beginning in October 2014.[43] At this point, the school was inundated with parental protests that found the new accommodation to be an invasion of privacy of the other students. The entire matter provoked a major public debate in November 2014, after which the Board of Gloucester County Public Schools (GCPS) concluded:

> It shall be the practice of the GCPS to provide male and female restroom and locker room facilities in its schools, and the use of said facilities shall be limited to the corresponding biological genders, and students with gender identity issues shall be provided an alternative appropriate private facility.[44]

It should be evident from this brief account that GCPS was attempting a reasonable solution to a difficult social issue, which took into account the interests and sensitivities on both sides. Separate bathroom facilities were a standard feature of social life everywhere long before the antidiscrimination laws were put into place and will be long afterward, such that only an overwhelming case warrants modifying the arrangement. It takes a form of willful social blindness to regard the bedrock interest in this kind of separation as either trivial or mean-spirited. GCPS did not exclude G.G. from using the girls' bathroom, and it sought to provide a reasonable alternative accommodation that avoided the unhappiness of using that facility without inconveniencing any of the boys.

This and other accommodations, including providing any desired medical or psychological support at the expense of the public, could readily be made because they touched on no strong competing interests. It takes a peculiarly dogmatic mind to be so confident that the conventional wisdom is so wrong that it should be overturned by legal compulsion. This is all the more so because the decision failed to account for the many countervailing interests, or to consider the unpleasant dangers of social disorder that could result if even a single student should decide to act out his or her frustrations in a way that resulted in physical or emotional harm.

By definition, all accommodations of competing interests leave everyone somewhat unhappy with the situation. But, as a matter of first principle, this kind of sensitive balance is what we should hope that every institution will try to achieve, based on the knowledge at its disposal. This was the perfect type of dispute for a local resolution that would avoid overblown rhetoric and polarization on both sides. But any subtle approach could not abide once the dispute was turned into a legal tussle over the meaning of Title IX, and a healthy assist from DOE that could have assured that the incremental, low-level accommodation survived a more general attack was not forthcoming.

To set out the statutory framework, Title IX provides, in relevant part: "No person in the United States shall, on the basis of sex, be excluded from participation in, be denied the benefits of, or be subjected to discrimination under any education program or activity receiving Federal financial assistance."[45] This provision is coupled with a further provision in the statute that states: "Notwithstanding anything to the contrary contained in this chapter, nothing contained herein shall be construed to prohibit any educational institution receiving funds under this Act, from maintaining separate living facilities for the different sexes."[46] DOE subsequently backstopped these provisions with regulations promulgated through a notice-and-comment rulemaking that reads, in relevant part: "A recipient may provide separate toilet, locker room, and shower facilities on the basis of sex, but such facilities provided for students of one sex shall be comparable to such facilities provided for students of the other sex."[47]

The obvious intention of these provisions was to implement a regime of "separate but equal," which makes sense in dealing with cases of discrimination by sex even if it is widely and rightly regarded as abhorrent when done on grounds of race.[48] It is for this reason that the Civil Rights Act of 1964 allows an exception to the general prohibition on employment discrimination for bona fide occupational qualifications for sex, but not for race.[49]

As a matter of ordinary language and historical understanding, there was no one at the time of the passage of Title IX or the promulgation of its implementing regulations who thought that the issue of gender identity was covered by the title. It takes little imagination to understand that the major purpose of the statute was to integrate women into schools' academic programs at a time (which I can personally remember) when many individual professors had explicit policies not to take on female graduate students in subjects like chemistry or mathematics. The situation with sex discrimination, however, has always been fraught with difficulties that are not encountered with race discrimination. Separate but equal with regard to race is an anathema upheld by *Plessy v. Ferguson*.[50] But, at the same time, the Congress that passed Title IX thought the separate-but-equal approach to be strictly required in dealing with sex discrimination in athletic programs, where, in my view, it has led to excessive intrusions of federal power into an area best governed by school districts and universities.

There is little doubt as a matter of ordinary statutory interpretation that the traditional meaning of "sex" as understood through biological markers dominates, not only as a matter of text but also as a matter of general understanding of the statute, from 1972 until the 2015 decision by DOJ and DOE to change the rules of the game. At this point, the introduction of new ambiguities became the administrator's best friend, and the Fourth Circuit majority eagerly seized on contrived interpretive difficulties to back up their joint decision. Thus, the court stretched two dictionary definitions to create some running room by pointing to unrelated and irrelevant ambiguities long associated with difficult cases: it cited the *American College Dictionary's* definition of "sex" as "the character of being either male or female" or "the sum of those anatomical and physiological differences with reference to which the male and female are distinguished"[51] and *Webster's Third New International Dictionary's* definition of "sex" as "the sum of the morphological, physiological, and behavioral peculiarities of living beings that subserves biparental reproduction with its concomitant genetic segregation and recombination which underlie most evolutionary change."[52]

Note that neither of these definitions refers to "gender identity" as a possible, let alone plausible, definition of sex, and certainly neither supports the use of that term as the sole definition for a statute enacted about 40 years before the term gained currency.[53] But no matter: the standard of review is "highly deferential," and "an agency's interpretation need not be the only possible reading of a regulation—or even the best one—to prevail."[54] After all, the case involved supposedly hard situations that Title IX does not cover, prompting the court to raise the specter of unrelated ambiguities: "Which restroom would a transgender individual who had undergone sex-reassignment surgery use?"[55] "What about an intersex individual?"[56] "What about individuals who lost external genitalia in an accident?"[57] The answer: in the absence of any sex change, they would use the restroom assigned to their original sex without any needed accommodation. "What about an individual born with X-X-Y sex chromosomes?"[58] Common practice may well supply some of these answers. But the distressing feature about the *Gloucester County* majority is that it did *not* want to examine how these questions had been answered in deciding whether to defer to the administrative decision.

What is so galling about the majority opinion is that it does not once mention the possibility of a special accommodation for difficult cases in public school settings. Instead, it takes the view that cases of gender identity should be treated as if Congress made them a civil rights imperative that brooks no opposition, even though they raise, at least in *Gloucester County*, a condition capable of accommodation like so many other individual cases of unique physical and psychological need. DOJ's Office of Civil Rights under Obama did not display the slightest level of professional expertise in presenting its solution to this particular problem, but instead made a wholly political judgment that it well knew would never be adopted by any legislature charged with deciding the issue.

Indeed, the situation is worse than this. Before the inevitable agency flip-flop after the 2016 election, against which the proponents of classification by gender identity can mount no challenge under *Auer*, there arose considerable political turmoil when this local issue became a national cause célèbre. The school board's decision provoked an immediate response from the Charlotte City Council, which, on February 22, 2016, passed by a 7–4 vote Ordinance 7056, prohibiting discrimination on the basis of sexual orientation and gender identity in all public accommodations, without giving a precise answer to the question of how best to treat changing the facilities in high schools.[59] The initial dispute over bathroom facilities should have been resolved by low-level administrative accommodations, not grand political statements. But once the issue became publicized, the political divisions grew in scope and intensity.

Thereafter, in March 2016, the North Carolina legislature rushed into law House Bill 2, grandly titled "An Act to Provide for Single-Sex Multiple Occupancy Bathroom and Changing Facilities in Schools and Public Agencies and to Create Statewide Consistency in Regulation of Employment and Public Accommodations."[60] HB2 preempted the local ordinances without making it clear exactly what conduct was prohibited or what punishments would be attached. The state legislature thus escalated matters further for no discernible reason, by issuing pronouncements that went far beyond cases of gender dysphoria in high school.

Not surprisingly, HB2 provoked a furious nationwide backlash among businesses, athletic associations, and state and city governments, many of which boycotted official travel to North Carolina except for essential state business, ostensibly because HB2 made it difficult to guarantee an "inclusive" atmosphere.[61] Credible estimates put the potential lost income for the state at about $3.76 billion over 12 years.[62] Why did these companies fear noninclusiveness when everyone in Charlotte lined up against HB2, and daily practices in the city had generated few prior difficulties? The simplest explanation is that it is regrettable but permissible to oust your friends in order to make a political point. Yet lost in all this was the original dispute, which would never have precipitated an exaggerated response if DOE had not teed up the lawsuit with its flimsy guidance that ACLU brought on behalf of G.G. The guidance, in turn, had such outsize impacts only because of the collision of *Auer* deference and the non-reviewability of guidances, both of which are ill-conceived doctrines in isolation but, when brought together, prove anathema to the steady democratic resolution of problems as they arise within the soothing procedural protections of the rule of law.

Now that the Obama guidance has been suspended, it is interesting to note several responses that were raised toward the letter. Most notably in connection with professional sports, the former tennis great and gay rights activist Martina Navratilova took a very strong stance against using acceptance of self-declared gender identity to force female tournaments to give an open invitation to physiological men.

In a series of tweets in December 2018, the 18-time Grand Slam champion wrote: "You can't just proclaim yourself a female and be able to compete against women," and, further, "There must be some standards, and having a penis and competing as a woman would not fit that standard."[63] She followed that up with a column in the *Times* of London, "The Rules of Trans Athletes Reward Cheats and Punish the Innocent."[64] That column prompted major denunciations by the gay rights group Athlete Ally, for which she had previously served as a goodwill ambassador. The group promptly dumped her from its ranks, taking the position that

> trans women are women, period. They did not decide their gender identity any more than someone decides to be gay, or to have blue eyes. There is no evidence at all that the average trans woman is any bigger, stronger, or faster than the average cisgender woman, but there is evidence that often when athletes lower testosterone through hormone replacement therapy, performance goes down.[65]

This last proposition is at least testable, and much depends on how a trans woman is defined. If it only takes a declaration to achieve that status, which was the position taken by the DOE/DOJ letter, the statement is manifestly false. Without any physiological changes of any sort, the considerable male athletic advantages remain, as evidenced by the growing number of cases in which male-to-female transgender athletes sweep female athletic competitions.

In connection with professional sports, the various associations and groups can decide rules of admission and exclusion for transgendered athletes for themselves, wholly without the direction of Title IX and the antidiscrimination laws. These organizations have a strong incentive to ensure that their participants compete on a level playing field because if event outcomes are skewed, it will negatively affect the group's bottom line, and hence the aggregate net take of all participants. The decentralization of governance decisions can resolve any latent questions of equity without government intervention. In some of these cases, the Navratilova charge of inherent unfairness may be vindicated; in others, it may not.

The situation is quite different with high school and college sports that are subject to Title IX governance, where no such corrective mechanism is available. Taking the Obama Title IX "Dear Colleague" letter at face value, there is no external check on how boys or men can activate their gender-identity claim. It is striking that none of the various decentralized approaches that have arisen since the letter's revocation follow the ostensible commands of the Obama guidance.

These multiple responses are well summarized in a student comment, *The Trans Athlete Dilemma*,[66] which sets out some of the relevant distinctions. First, it is far easier for trans boys to compete against boys, because no one thinks they have any particular athletic advantage, which also makes it less likely that they will be able to effectively compete. But allowing trans girls to compete against girls raises serious issues of competitive balance that do require some response. It seems clear that in these cases, no one takes the position that a simple declaration of a change in gender identity should be sufficient to tip the balance. There are instances of male-to-female trans competitors winning girls' races without undergoing any hormone therapy or physical operation, which happened when Andraya Yearwood won both the 100-meter and 200-meter dash in the Connecticut State Track and Field Championship. Just two months later, Yearwood finished in second place at another women's track and field competition—to another transgender competitor.

These results have to be regarded as genuinely contrary to the structure of Title IX, which was written to ensure that female athletes could receive equal support for their events. But the very fabric of these events is undermined when physiological boys can switch over the aisle to compete and, of course, to enter women's locker rooms, causing some women and girls to feel a sense of physical insecurity. It is therefore instructive that the many different solutions to this challenge do not embrace the Obama guidance position that a simple declaration will suffice. The physical differences do matter, even if the two learned women who drafted the 2016 guidance are blind to them.

Recall that the 2016 guidance used the term "discomfort" to belittle the strength of these concerns. That word makes sense if the question is whether any individual person should prevent a transgender student from taking classes in high school with other students. Of course, that has never been an issue in any of the heated debates over inclusion and diversity, which shows again that the antidiscrimination laws work best when they are not needed. But "discomfort" does not quite capture the relevant distinction here. The matter in question is now subject to proposed legislation under the Equality Act, which, in relevant part, states: "[A]n individual shall not be denied access to a shared facility, including a restroom, a locker room, and a dressing room, that is in accordance with the individual's gender identity."[67]

Abigail Shrier suggests that this legislative initiative will have the following consequences:

> Biological boys who identify as girls would gain an instant entitlement to compete on girls' teams in all 50 states. No more democratic discussion of accommodation, competing interest, sacrifice and fairness. No more debate about whether we should really allow girls' scholarships and trophies to go to male athletes who were unable to excel on the boys' teams. No more discussion about whether it's right to allow, as we have, biological men to pick off championships in women's and girls' powerlifting, cycling, wrestling and running.[68]

Surely, changes of this scope should not be decided by administrative fiat but should go through a full discussion in the political process, and overcome potential constitutional challenges suggesting that such provisions amount to an unconstitutional invasion of the privacy of girls and young men. More to the point, using the administrative process to validate the Obama guidance on transgendered students fails to comport with the minimum moral requirements of administrative law.

The key question that remains is whether *Gloucester County* can survive *Kisor*; the answer, at least in principle, seems to be no. But as this book is being published, the substantive issue regarding Title VII is now before the Supreme Court in two important cases that will be decided in the upcoming 2019–20 term, neither of which has received a small fraction of the public attention given to *Gloucester County*. In *Bostock v. Clayton Board of County Supervisors*,[69] the Eleventh Circuit issued a summary affirmance of a district court decision that rejected the claim that Title VII covered discrimination on grounds of sexual orientation: "This circuit has previously held that '[d]ischarge for homosexuality is *not* prohibited by Title VII.' "[70] In *Equal Employment Opportunity Commission v. R. G. & G. R. Harris Funeral Homes, Inc.*,[71] the Sixth Circuit found that Title VII offers protection against the use of gender stereotypes in employment and refused to accept any exception from Title VII based on the Free Exercise Clause of the First Amendment. Yet at no point in her long exposition does Judge Karen Nelson Moore cite *Auer* or *Chevron* to support the Sixth Circuit's conclusion. The same is true of the brief filed by the individual Respondent Aimee Stephens in the Supreme Court.[72] As the substantive battle reaches the Court, it appears that, if only by default, the administrative-law issue is moot, largely because of the Court's decision in *Kisor v. Wilkie*.[73]

Kisor

Kisor v. Wilkie[74] is less than an ideal vehicle through which to view *Auer* or *Perez* because the choices that it presents are less fundamental to the operation of the Department of Veterans Affairs (VA). James Kisor, a marine veteran of the Vietnam War, applied in 1982 to VA for benefits relating to what he claimed to be a case of post-traumatic stress disorder (PTSD) stemming from his participation in Operation Harvest Moon during the Vietnam War. His request was denied. In 2006, Kisor renewed his claim and got a split verdict.[75] Although Kisor insisted that he was entitled to receive benefits retroactively starting from the time of his initial 1982 application, VA held that he was eligible for benefits only from the date of his reapplication.

At issue in the case was the definition of the term "relevant" in the applicable statute. The new information that Kisor presented in 2006 gave further confirmation that he had indeed participated in military action. But the grounds for the dismissal of the case stemmed from the want of any proof that he suffered from PTSD when in active service. VA did not consider that the new evidence he presented was relevant to the medical grounds on which the original claim rested—that is, as proof that he experienced PTSD at the time he was in the military. The dispute in the case turns on whether VA's narrow interpretation of that vague term should control. The applicable administrative provision states:

> [A]t any time after VA issues a decision on a claim, if VA receives or associates with the claims file relevant official service department records that existed and had not been associated with the claims file when VA first decided the claim, VA will reconsider the claim.[76]

The precise question is how far within the applicable service record VA must go in deciding when a claim vests. VA's position is that the service record related to the "last denial" of the claim controls. Kisor argued that a service department record is relevant if it has "any tendency to make the existence *of any fact that is of consequence to the determination of the action* more probable or less probable than it would be without the evidence."[77]

Unlike *Auer* and *Perez*, *Kisor* has two instructive features. First, it is a close case on the construction of the regulation at issue; second, it is not all that important institutionally because all the determinations of VA disability benefits will, no matter what the rules on evidence, often turn on close, fact-specific cases. Indeed, in contrast to the terms at issue in *Auer* and *Perez*, neither the word "relevant" nor the phrase of which it is a part has the obvious punch attached to the categorical classification of police officers or mortgage brokers.

All this does not mean that deference should be accorded solely because the case is hard. It only means that the best possible reading should be given to regulatory language. Kisor claimed that the definition of "relevant" should be construed in light of the Federal Rules of Evidence—to wit, evidence is relevant if it has "any tendency to make a fact more or less probable" when the "fact is of consequence in determining the action."[78] In my view, that definition should not in this context supply Kisor with any assistance. The new evidence only went to a point on which Kisor had already won. How, then, is it possible that it could have made the fact more probable, when it was treated as certain at the time of the initial dispute? The only open question in 2006 was the causal status relating to Kisor's PTSD, and none of the new evidence related to that issue at all. The case should have been decided against Kisor because none of the new evidence tended to prove an earlier onset of the disease.

This is not a particularly difficult case when stated in this manner, wholly without regard to *Seminole Rock* or *Auer* deference. But the new administrative law jurisprudence never seems to look to the simple arguments first. It always goes after some institutional question of whether the type of question described here is one that should be left to the expertise of the relevant agency, which is surely relevant to the question of when the PTSD originated but not to the legal question of what counts as relevant. Rising to the bait on this question, the court of appeals invoked *Auer* deference, giving this reason: The relevant provision "does not specify whether 'relevant' records are those casting doubt on the agency's prior rating decision, those relating to the veteran's claim more broadly, or some other standard. This uncertainty in application suggests that the regulation is ambiguous."[79] At no point did the court raise the argument that further proof in support of a factual point that has already been decided in the claimant's favor is irrelevant. A bit of intellectual legwork could have gone a long way to resolve this case.

When the case got to the Supreme Court, the same charade continued. That the entire enterprise was a failure is shown conclusively by the range of opinions involved:

> KAGAN, J., announced the judgment of the Court and delivered the opinion of the Court with respect to Parts I, II–B, III–B, and IV, in which ROBERTS, C.J., and GINSBURG, BREYER, and SOTOMAYOR, JJ., joined, and an opinion with respect to Parts II–A and III–A, in which GINSBURG,

BREYER, and SOTOMAYOR, JJ., joined. ROBERTS, C.J., filed an opinion concurring in part. GORSUCH, J., filed an opinion concurring in the judgment, in which THOMAS, J., joined, in which KAVANAUGH, J., joined as to Parts I, II, III, IV, and V, and in which ALITO, J., joined as to Parts I, II, and III. KAVANAUGH, J., filed an opinion concurring in the judgment, in which ALITO, J., joined.[80]

This cacophony produces an outcome in which it is said unanimously that *Seminole Rock* and *Auer* are still the law of the land. Yet this one case gives rise to four concurrences and a thankless remand for further consideration. The affirmation of *Seminole Rock* and *Auer* might have been credible if the Court had just affirmed the rather slapdash opinion of the court of appeals. But the remand shows that something more was afoot than the routine application of a most tainted doctrine. Exactly what was it?

Both too much and too little. Justice Kagan started with the time-worn explanation for deference: it is the will of Congress, and it takes advantage of agency expertise. But why Congress could not express itself more clearly in the derogation of the judicial function was left unexplained. And nowhere did she explain why agency expertise on matters of diagnosis should carry over to statutory construction. But conscious that she was facing an insurrection, she then took the strategic step of restricting *Auer* to cases in which a rule is "genuinely ambiguous," a phrase that nowhere appears in *Auer*. To achieve that equipoise, she took a "taxing inquiry," nowhere conducted in *Auer*, in which "a court must exhaust all the 'traditional tools' of construction,"[81] citing *Chevron*, which itself is hardly the poster child for that approach. And just how is this to be done? "To make that effort, a court must carefully consider . . . the text, structure, history, and purpose of a regulation, in all the ways it would if it had no agency to fall back on."[82]

Justice Kagan's bold recharacterization of administrative law bears no relationship to what was done in *Auer*, which upheld the decision of the secretary of labor without bothering to parse the text of the statute; to give any weight to the on-again, off-again flip-flops of supposedly expert administrators; or, indeed, to provide any explanation of how the purpose of that statute, which was to give protection to low-level employees, managed to apply to police sergeants and lieutenants, whose never-discussed job descriptions fit perfectly into the statutory exemption for "executive, administrative, and professional" responsibility.

There is a familiar pathology at work here. In line with the Court's fact-free and text-free view of administrative law, Justice Kagan never once answered the question of whether *Auer* itself could have survived under the radical new reading that she gave to the case. Indeed, if she were serious that statutes and regulations should be interpreted as if there were no administrative state, she should have voted to overrule both *Chevron* and *Auer*. Put into the language of baseball, her stress on the tiebreaker image tracks the rule that "ties go in favor of the runner." But it turns out that if we use precise measuring devices, there are very few ties indeed, which is what would happen if the legal analysis were relentlessly pursued. In the end, Justice Kagan only showed disdain for the case by refusing to give her preferred reading of the relevant materials, which, if done correctly, would have driven her to affirm the decision of the federal circuit on the merits, while overruling *Auer*. As noted, *Seminole Rock* is a wholly different kettle of fish; but again, she did not dig deep enough into the details of a price-fixing scheme to reach the right result.

In light of Kagan's conceptual muddle, both the chief justice and Justice Kavanaugh are right to ask just how much daylight there is between Kagan's position and that of her now-arch-nemesis, Justice Gorsuch, who took no pains in his concurrence to conceal his total disdain for *Auer* and the fleeting but accurate recognition that the case goes beyond what was required by *Seminole Rock*.[83]

Gorsuch took the sensible position that "I would stop this business of making up excuses for judges to abdicate their job of interpreting the law, and simply allow the court of appeals to afford Mr. Kisor its best independent judgment of the law's meaning."[84] He was, moreover, surely correct to note that *Seminole Rock* is light-years removed from *Auer*, but then he insisted—wrongly, in my view— that the salvation comes in the renewed endorsement of *Skidmore*, without asking whether it does better in dealing with statutes than a rule that just asks for the best interpretation in accordance with the ordinary meaning of the text.[85] Does he really think that these workers are entitled to overtime when they play games on the job but just don't sleep?

Most disappointingly, Gorsuch did not do what had to be done in order to discredit *Auer*: apply the usual tools of statutory construction to all the relevant disputes to indicate how they should be correctly decided. If these are all questions of law, as he insisted in dealing with Section 706(a), he should have used the tools of law to demonstrate how they should be resolved so as to transform Kagan's ad hoc revision of *Auer* into a total rout. The correct response is that no matter who issues any interpretation of a legal text, it should always be treated as a question of law, without any deference at all. Gorsuch is right to think that litigation will receive a new boost after *Kisor*, but he could have done more to lay down a firmer foundation for his cause for the next time that this issue—and the only question is when—comes before the Court.

RETROACTIVITY AND THE REVERSAL OF LONG-STANDING POSITIONS

Fundamental Choices

My earlier analysis of deference explains why it is never possible under the modern administrative state to observe Fuller's concerns about long-term consistency and retroactivity in practice. Both concerns echo a position taken by Fuller in the law of contract, where he devoted extensive work to defending the power of reliance interest. The standard argument here is that change and transitions are always costly, so all public institutions should take care not to break the continuity of the law unless it is strongly necessary to do so.

Given the importance of this issue, a fair corollary is that novel departures of law should be done by legislative action, or perhaps even judicial decisions on key points of law. By the same token, an administrative agency, exercising only delegated authority, should be cautious about making those changes on its own in the two settings where the question is most likely to arise: first, in the application of novel solutions in individual cases; and second, in a wholesale change of a rule.

Those rule changes, in turn, could be of two sorts. The first is strongly retroactive in the sense that they apply new rules to actions done in reliance on earlier rules. The second is weakly retroactive, insofar as the changes do not seek to judge old cases by the new rules, even as they indicate that, going forward, a thoroughgoing change in legal position should be made—and if such a change is made, it should be done through legislation, given the enormity of the consequences. The strength of these concerns can, of course, differ by cases, for in some situations a shift in legal rule requires relatively little change in institutional behavior or private practice. Yet now that industry regulation is the target of many administrative agencies—FCC, SEC, and FDA, among others—in many cases, the size of the reliance interest is likely to prove substantial.

Defenders of modern administrative law do not look at matters first from the perspective of the regulated party. Rather, their basic claim is that administrative agencies need the ability to adapt to changed circumstances, and it is said that by doing so, reversals of their own previous rules will be enabled, even in the face of what could be an interim authoritative judicial interpretation of the same materials.[86] The system thus protects the discretion of administrators but only at the cost of increasing the risk necessarily placed on the private parties governed by these rules. It is hard to find any reason that an agency, with its greater knowledge of the regulatory, administrative, and policymaking process, should be allowed to fob this risk off onto private parties, given these parties' lesser knowledge about agency activities.

At this point, it is critical to again note that the early administrative law decisions previously discussed did not survive the advent of the Progressive Era, in which far less respect was held for the prohibitions dealing with retroactivity and consistency. Progressives thought, and still think, that it is appropriate to give more discretion to government officials because of an underlying belief that these officials would turn their expertise only to appropriate ends. Thus, the traditional uneasiness with retroactive legislation gave way to a more positive view of state action. The point here is of great importance because, a generation after

Fuller wrote his book, the general restriction on retroactive law has been sharply limited by the Court. Its basic premise has been that retroactive impositions are permissible so long as individuals are on notice that Congress, or its administrative agencies, may decide to reverse its position. Naturally, given the frequency of reversals, all private parties are on notice that they could happen, rendering this constraint on government action largely worthless.

Before the advent of the New Deal, it was clear that courts took a dim view of any retroactive behavior. Just that view was maintained in *Railroad Retirement Board v. Alton Railroad Co.*,[87] which held that no legislation could extend a railroad's liability beyond its original contractual boundaries. That decision did not survive the New Deal revolution, as *Alton Railroad* was effectively overruled by the 1976 decision *Usery v. Turner Elkhorn*.[88] There the Supreme Court sustained the retroactivity of a black-lung-disease compensation program by focusing on the benefits to recipients and ignoring the costs for the mining companies forced to shoulder the burden of the program.[89] At no point did the case consider that general government revenues should be used to fund the system of payments put into place.

Thereafter, in *Pension Benefit Board Corp. v. R. A. Gray & Co.*,[90] the Court found no violation of the Due Process Clause in the imposition of retroactive restrictions on the right to withdraw from a government pension board, even though affected companies had obtained by contract an explicit guarantee of that exit right.[91] No private party could ever breach its contracts with such impunity. Subsequently, in *Connolly v. Pension Benefit Guaranty Corp.*,[92] the Court held that the Takings Clause also afforded no protection against a calculated reversal of government policy.[93] These decisions, both on procedure and substance, were not flashes in the pan but rather relied on the Court's earlier decision in *Turner Elkhorn*, which declared: "[O]ur cases are clear that legislation readjusting rights and burdens is not unlawful solely because it upsets otherwise settled expectations . . . This is true even though the effect of the legislation is to impose a new duty or liability based on past acts."[94] The basic conceit is that private parties are on "notice" that they are at risk of expropriation whenever they enter a heavily regulated industry.[95] In these cases, the law has traveled a long distance from the categorical stance against retroactive adjustments defended so tenaciously in *Arizona Grocery v. Topeka, Atchison & Santa Fe Railway Co.*[96]

Note the switch in the use of the twin concepts of notice and foresight. The early cases opposed retroactive legislation because they foresaw its occurrence and sought to prevent it. Today, foresight serves a very different function. It explains why private parties should proactively mitigate their losses because they are on notice of the risk of this form of surprise government action. Fuller would shudder.

Nor would Fuller be pleased with the modern effort to accommodate the old ban on retroactive legislation, which cashes out as a presumption against retroactivity whenever the organic statute is silent on the question. Sunstein and Vermeule think that this accommodation supports the internal morality of administrative law, when they write: "In 1988, the Supreme Court announced a new canon of construction, forbidding administrative retroactivity unless Congress has explicitly authorized it. Though the announcement came very late in the twentieth century, the Court purported to speak for a tradition and for the presumptive morality of administrative law."[97] The difficulty with this defense is not that it came too late but that it came at all, for this presumption still leaves Congress and, by implication, all administrative agencies, with the kind of discretion that is utterly inconsistent with the rule of law. It is the counsel of despair to hope that any administrators would not use all the weapons that Congress has placed in their arsenal.

The deviations from the earlier principles of *Arizona Grocery* and *Board of Public Utility Commissioners v. New York Telephone Co.*[98] are also evident in the rate-regulation cases.[99] In this regard, it is useful to note that the rate-regulation cases in some situations tend to adhere to the earlier rules in which efforts were made to guard against confiscation. One such troublesome modern case is *Duquesne Light Co. v. Barasch*,[100] where the question was whether Duquesne Light could include in its rate base the costs of designing nuclear power plants that were reasonable when made but became worthless when the government withdrew its permission to continue with the program. At one level, the administrative decision looks as though it clearly violates Fuller's command against retroactive readjustments. In this view, the utility should stop work but could recover additional funds for its reasonable past expenditures and the costs of mitigating going forward, which fits well within the standard model of mitigation of damages in the law of contract.

After a careful review of earlier cases, however, Chief Justice Rehnquist disallowed the recovery of expenditures by including those expenditures in the general operating costs of the utility. At this point, two pre-1937 rules were still operative in the area.[101] *Smyth v. Ames*,[102] under which the only assets that fell into the rate base were those that were used and usable in the business, excluded some expenditures but compensated the utility for its smaller rate base by offering it a higher rate of return on the residual assets used in the business. The alternative method adopted in *Hope Natural Gas v. Federal Power Commission*[103] included all expenditures in the rate base but reduced the rate of return because the ratepayers, rather than the shareholders, now took the risk of poor investments. Under the *Hope* formula, the reviewing court looked to see only if the "bottom line" rate of return met constitutional standards. That bottom line was not a single number but a range, and to Chief Justice William Rehnquist, no compensation was owed in this case because the rate of return after the special charges was sufficient to meet the *Hope* standard. In principle, the sounder form of regulation treats separately all special charges, especially when they reflect political risk beyond the control of the utility, because these charges always exert a negative effect on return rates. Indeed, after the decision, the Pennsylvania legislature authorized the utility to recover those expenditures.

Duquesne Light represents, at best, the outer limit of correct regulation within Fuller's general framework. In the subsequent case of *Verizon Communications Inc. v. FCC*,[104] the Court examined, within the context of the Telecommunications Act of 1996, a system that reimbursed the incumbent local exchange carriers (ILECs) for the unbundled network elements (UNEs) that they were required to supply to the competitive local exchange carriers (CLECs).[105] UNEs can be defined as "a part of a telecommunications network that [ILECs] are required to offer on an unbundled basis under the U.S. Telecommunications Act of 1996."[106]

Forcing the sale of individual components of a particular switch or device allows the new entrant to build out its own network by purchasing particular elements at prices set by FCC. From a rule-of-law perspective, there are two highly dubious consequences of this system.

The first is that it is imposed retroactively on facilities that ILECs made prior to the change in the statute, leading to an inconsistent treatment of long-term investment. Second, the rule gives a free option to CLECs, which fabricate their own elements when the cost of production is lower than the purchase price. The 1996 Act does not require CLECs or the government to compensate ILECs for the costs that the option imposes on them, which are not trivial, given that multiple CLECs were able make simultaneous demands on ILECs.

The question then arose as to how to price these UNEs. After much deliberation, FCC settled on a system known as the total element long-run incremental cost (TELRIC), which disclaimed any reliance on the "historical cost" needed to assemble the network. The TELRIC system, in effect, required the pricing at each point in time to reflect the interim technological improvements in a falling cost industry, so that, over the life of the particular project, the ILEC could not recover its overall historical cost.

In effect, the system combined the two least favorable elements from *Smyth* and *Hope*: the smaller base of the former and the lower rates of the latter. *Verizon v. FCC* was decided on grounds of statutory construction, but the writing was on the wall. No court that praised administrative discretion under the statute was going to strike down the statute on constitutional grounds. In effect, therefore, this last rate case shows that the constitutional discipline imposed in the pre–New Deal cases would be eroded in subsequent years. The decline is not, perhaps, as precipitous as it has been with respect to retroactive rate-making in general. But it remains clear that the protection afforded public utilities today is below what would be required under the principles that Fuller announced in *The Morality of Law*.

Fuller's general view of the rule of law paid large respect to the gradual evolution of common law norms to deal with individual cases. Those same concerns should attend administrative rulemaking, a topic that did not attract his attention in *The Morality of Law*. It is therefore instructive to see how in both individual cases and rulemaking contexts, rule-of-law principles survive in the administrative context by looking at two episodes involving securities law. *SEC v. Chenery Corporation (Chenery I)*[107] and *SEC v. Chenery Corporation (Chenery II)*,[108] a second case by the same name that was decided four years later, deal with individual proceedings at the dawn of the administrative state. A contemporary illustration of the basic problem is found in *Chamber of Commerce v. United States Department of Labor*,[109] where the capacity for mischief is mightily increased because of the vast number of individual cases that fall under any given rule.

Chenery I and *Chenery II*

The gutting of the anti-retroactivity norm was accomplished through several major decisions. The first of these decisions came about in two related cases arising out of actions of the Securities and Exchange Commission: the first case, *Chenery I*, was decided in 1943; the second case, *Chenery II*, was decided after World War II, just after the passage of APA. The standard account of these two cases celebrates their willingness to allow for administrative discretion to institute new principles of legal enforcement by either rulemaking or case-by-case decisions, all at the option of the agency. The Court couched its argument for this point by noting that, in some instances, case law development could prove superior to rulemaking:

> Since the Commission, unlike a court, does have the ability to make new law prospectively through the exercise of its rule-making powers, it has less reason to rely upon *ad hoc* adjudication to formulate new standards of conduct within the framework of the Holding Company Act. The function of filling in the interstices of the Act should be performed, as much as possible, through this quasi-legislative promulgation of rules to be applied in the future. But any rigid requirement to that effect would make the administrative process inflexible and incapable of dealing with many of the specialized problems which arise . . . Not every principle essential to the effective administration of a statute can or should be cast immediately into the mold of a general rule. Some principles must await their own development, while others must be adjusted to meet particular, unforeseeable situations. In performing its important functions in these

respects, therefore, an administrative agency must be equipped to act either by general rule or by individual order. To insist upon one form of action to the exclusion of the other is to exalt form over necessity.

In other words, problems may arise in a case which the administrative agency could not reasonably foresee, problems which must be solved despite the absence of a relevant general rule. Or the agency may not have had sufficient experience with a particular problem to warrant rigidifying its tentative judgment into a hard and fast rule. Or the problem may be so specialized and varying in nature as to be impossible of capture within the boundaries of a general rule. In those situations, the agency must retain power to deal with the problems on a case-to-case basis if the administrative process is to be effective. There is thus a very definite place for the case-by-case evolution of statutory standards. And the choice made between proceeding by general rule or by individual, *ad hoc* litigation is one that lies primarily in the informed discretion of the administrative agency.

Hence we refuse to say that the Commission, which had not previously been confronted with the problem of management trading during reorganization, was forbidden from utilizing this particular proceeding for announcing and applying a new standard of conduct.[110]

The principle as stated has wide acceptance in the modern canon of administrative law, and the previous passage, or some portion of it, is cited with favor by each of three authors whose work I have commented on in this book: Metzger,[111] Pojanowski,[112] and Sunstein and Vermeule.[113]

What is distinctive about the Sunstein and Vermeule effort is that they realize that there is an evident tension between *Chenery II* and Fuller's stern injunction against retroactive lawmaking, for, as they rightly point out, the gist of *Chenery II*'s opposition to the new SEC rule was that "the SEC had violated core Fullerian principles of nonretroactivity by issuing a disgorgement order based on previous conduct not covered by an administrative rule."[114] At this point, the authors do not seek to explain that this evident tension does not exist. Instead, they invoke the implicit norm of happy endings, to assume that Fuller, writing a decade after the case was decided, would have agreed with *Chenery II* anyway:

> Chenery II offers a broad lesson: Fullerian principles, however valid and appealing, have limits of both scope and weight. They must inevitably be traded off against the agency's institutional role and capacities, resource limitations, and programmatic objectives. Chenery II's lesson became the consensus view among administrative lawyers of the post-war era, as reflected in the magisterial treatise by Louis Jaffe, Fuller's colleague. We like to think that Fuller, who understood that law's morality hardly exhausts the domain of what government does, that his principles had an aspirational dimension, and that a valid legal system might instantiate them only partially, would be the first to agree.[115]

Fuller would have done no such thing. But to see why, it is necessary to unpack the two *Chenery* decisions because the objection to SEC's conduct does *not* turn on the supposed inability of the common law to develop new ideas out of established principles without offending the rules of retroactivity. There are many cases in which adjudication has had just that effect, and to good purpose. To give but one famous example of this problem that also deals with various issues of fraud, recall the situation in the great English decision of *Pasley v. Freeman.*[116] *Pasley* arose when the plaintiffs asked the defendants about the credit condition of one John Christopher Falch. They received a reply that he was creditworthy, when, to their knowledge, he was not. Large sums were advanced, and when Falch defaulted, the plaintiffs sued the defendant for fraud in the inducement, and were met with the objection that the defendant did not make the fraudulent representations to advance his own interests but to help an independent third party who was not even indebted to him.

It should be evident that the extension of liability in this case amounts to an explication of the scope of the fraud principle and thus falls clearly within the scope of adjudication, which is the proper scope to deal with the matter. On behalf of the defendant, it has been argued that the older cases had not shown any instance where a defendant was held responsible for fraud in the absence of privity of contract. It has further been argued that heavy liabilities of this sort should not be imposed without an explicit guarantee. But the lone dissenting judge lost out when his three peers (on a four-panel bench, no less) came down the opposite way.

It is for these purposes necessary only to consult the decision of Judge William Henry Ashhurst, who adequately summed up the moral issue in the case when he wrote: "And it should seem that it ought more emphatically to lie against [the defendant], as the malice is more diabolical, if he had not the temptation of gain."[117] He then articulated the basic legal principle in terms that would have brought a smile to Fuller's face:

> Where cases are new in their principle, there I admit that it is necessary to have recourse to legislative interposition in order to remedy the grievance: but where the case is only new in the instance, and the only question is upon the application of a principle recognized in the law to such new case, it will be just as competent to Courts of Justice to apply the principle to any case which may arise two centuries hence as it was two centuries ago; if it were not, we ought to blot out of our law books one fourth part of the cases that are to be found in them.[118]

The situation in *Pasley* was indeed new, but the legal principle was not changed because there was no effort to attenuate the meaning of the term "fraud" or to apply it to conduct—rightly condemned as diabolic—that was not worthy of legal sanction. What is so clear about the fuller—no pun intended—account of *Chenery* is that SEC did exactly what the English court refused to do in *Pasley*: it took traditional conceptions of fiduciary responsibility out of context, such that its conclusion was wholly unwarranted *whether done by common law judicial decision or by administrative regulation*. This agency failure cannot be detected solely by looking at broad statements of administrative law principles but instead must be assessed considering the underlying facts.

The two *Chenery* cases involved a complex transaction under the Public Utility Holding Company Act of 1935 (PUCHA).[119] That decision was, in turn, challenged by the respondents under Section 24(a) of the act. As stated by Justice Frankfurter in *Chenery I*, SEC brought an enforcement action against certain officers, directors, and controlling stockholders of the Federal Water Service Corporation to exclude these individuals from sharing in the gains with other shareholders from a proposed set of reorganizations. The respondents had, at various times, purchased preferred stock in the company in a set of open-market transactions. The reorganization essentially gave all the new common stock of the company to the old preferred shareholders. Nonetheless, SEC decided to limit the respondents, who were preferred shareholders in the corporation, to a more limited payout, equaling only the purchase price of their shares plus the accumulated dividends. All the excess appreciation in their shares necessarily would go to the other preferred shareholders. SEC did not find fraud or nondisclosure. It recognized that the respondents did not trade on inside information. Instead, its assigned reason for stripping the respondents of their pro-rata gains was that they owed an unspecified fiduciary duty to the other shareholders, and their breach of the duty justified the penalties imposed against them.

Justice Frankfurter held that SEC had gone too far in excluding the respondents from their share of the gain. He did not contest that these parties owed the other shareholders a fiduciary duty, but instead insisted that there was no breach of fiduciary duty under the recognized heads of that obligation:

> The Commission did not find that the respondents as managers of Federal acted covertly or traded on inside knowledge, or that their position as reorganization managers enabled them to purchase the preferred stock at prices lower than they would otherwise have had to pay, or that their acquisition of the stock in any way prejudiced the interests of the corporation or its stockholders.[120]

In sum, the commission conceded: "In its own words, 'honesty, full disclosure, and purchase at a fair price' characterized the transactions."[121] The clear implication is that the recognized heads of the fiduciary duty obligation were exhaustive, so the commission's extension of the duty had to be rejected. Indeed, no court prior to or after *Chenery I* has found a breach of fiduciary duty by parties who acted as the respondents had done here. Accordingly, Frankfurter chastised the commission for claiming that they followed traditional principles: "As the Commission concedes here, the courts do not impose upon officers and directors of a corporation any fiduciary duty to its stockholders which precludes them, merely because they are officers and directors, from buying and selling the corporation's stock."[122]

Frankfurter was open to the possibility that the commission could have found a newer standard, akin to *Pasley v. Freeman*, but SEC had made no such effort, and the clear findings of fact precluded any such novel departure of the sort that would not require legislation. But no statute imposed an absolute duty on fiduciaries never to trade at all. As Frankfurter noted, PUCHA also imposed a special duty on company insiders holding more than 10% of the firm's stock to return to the corporation any "short swing" profits that they realized based on the purchase and sale of stock within a six-month period.[123]

The situation was further clouded by Frankfurter's noting that the law also conferred on the commission broad powers to oversee "unlawful security transactions by registered holding and subsidiary" companies covered under Section 6 of PUCHA.[124] Thus, Section 7, Parts (d) (6) and (e) of the act together imposed restrictions on transactions that were, first, "detrimental to the public interest or the interest of investors or consumers,"[125] and, second, under Section 11(e), that were not, all things considered, "fair and equitable" to all shareholders.[126] Frankfurter thought that these sections could be the source of additional authority, but he did not explain exactly how those novel powers would work. Instead of facing that hard question, he refused to extend a lifeline to the commission if it did not choose to exercise its administrative powers under PUCHA, at which point it could only rely on "its special administrative competence" to support its chosen outcome.

The change in mood at the end of his argument is what would follow. Intellectually, Frankfurter was still the New Deal progressive who, in many other areas, was a consistent and enthusiastic champion of the broad administrative state.[127] He did not see administrative law as did 19th-century judges: as a way to bolster the enforcement of common law rights when private rights of action proved incapable of dealing with systematic losses—for example, systematic frauds on the stock market. He often voiced deep dissatisfaction with the coherence or utility of such key common law terms as "negligence."[128] Frankfurter's general skepticism about key standard common law terms caused him to overlook the inherent merit of key common law conceptions that could operate as an open invitation to the commission to get its act together. Instead of relying on common law principles, according to Frankfurter, the commission just had to make clear that it was explicitly relying on its statutory authority and the situation would change. Just that course of action was taken, which led to the commission's explicit reliance on Sections 7 and 11 of PUCHA to justify the same result that it had reached in the earlier case.

However, SEC ran into headwinds in the District of Columbia Circuit Court, which did not share Frankfurter's implicit nominalism on the possible meanings of "fiduciary duty." In an insightful opinion that Fuller would have endorsed, Chief Judge David L. Groner thought that this new source of authority under PUCHA could not cure the enormous gaps in the administrative record:

> The Commission's position actually amounts to neither more nor less than a definite holding that purchases of stock of a corporation in process of reorganization are unlawful, when made by officers or employees of the corporation—and this without regard to any factor of good or bad faith, or any other factor which might impute special knowledge, secret information, or indeed anything tending to show a lack of bona fides in the transaction . . .

> But the Commission has made no additional findings and disclosed no additional considerations to justify its adherence to its former order. In short, its attitude seems to be that Section 11(e) of the Act, confers a purely discretionary power not subject to judicial review. But we are referred to nothing and can find nothing in the Act to sustain this view. Nor is it sustainable on the theory of Congressional intent, for as we pointed out in our earlier opinion, the Senate Committee's report on submission of the bill declared that the authority of the Commission must be administered within the well-defined limits of the Act; and the Act itself certainly confers no such grant of general power.

> Considered in this view, we think that the Commission has failed to interpret correctly the limits prescribed for its

guidance by the Supreme Court. It is true, as the Commission now asserts, that the Supreme Court recognizes that the Act and its provisions confer upon it broad powers for the protection of the public and that this authority was intended to be responsive to the demands of the particular situations with which the Commission might be faced. But it is also true that the Court recognized that the Commission, like the ocean, has its appointed bounds, and lest it break through its limits and engulf a continent,—spoke these words of caution: "The Commission's action cannot be upheld merely because findings might have been made and considerations disclosed which would justify its order as an appropriate safeguard for the interests protected by the Act." And the Court added this further caution that the grounds upon which the administrative agency acts must be clearly disclosed and adequately sustained.[129]

Groner's view is no crabbed reading of the powers of the administrative state, but he well understands that the incorporation of common words into a statute does not give any administrative agency the power to promulgate rules that make otherwise lawful conduct unlawful. If the commission had its way, there would be nothing to limit the respondents to a loss of future profits. It could order the parties to surrender all their shares without any compensation at all. To be sure, prophylactic rules are always fair game to control fraud. Indeed, the rule under PUCHA dealing with short-swing profits is one such rule directed against potential insider abuse that might be hard to detect. There is no sensible constitutional challenge to this provision.

But it is one thing to enact that rule by statute and quite another for the commission to impose a rule like the short-swing profit rule under Sections 17(a) and (b) of PUCHA absent any statutory support. Such behavior would be a manifest abuse of discretion, as would be an attempt to strengthen the provision by shortening the relevant period to five months by administrative order. In this regard, the general observations of Judge Ashhurst in *Pasley* are right on the mark. It is one thing to go after novel forms of fraud through common law development and quite another to take conduct that is otherwise legal and make it illegal by an administrative agency's appeal to notions of the public interest or fair and equitable behavior. It is never in the public interest to under-mine confidence in the market by allowing the commission to convert retroactively legal activity into illegal conduct. And it is the height of inequitable behavior to hold that some shares of any given class of stock are more (or less) equal than any other. The central purpose in creat-ing SEC was to strengthen investor confidence in markets riddled with dubious schemes by fly-by-night operators. An effort by SEC to use a scheme or artifice to shut out shareholders from the market is plainly contrary to this purpose. That purpose is made clear in the Securities and Exchange Act of 1934,[130] passed just the year before PUCHA, when it addresses the "Necessity for regulation." The section states:

> Frequently the prices of securities on such exchanges and markets are susceptible to manipulation and control, and the dissemination of such prices gives rise to excessive specula-tion, resulting in sudden and unreasonable fluctuations in the prices of securities which . . . cause alternately unreasonable expansion and unreasonable contraction of the volume of credit available for trade, transportation, and industry in interstate commerce.[131]

No one could claim that the purpose of this statute was to un-dermine the efficiency of competitive markets. The purpose of the full range of securities laws was to rid markets of the wrong kinds of ma-nipulation and control so that various market participants could have confidence that they were trading on a level playing field.

This statute was wholly unlike the National Labor Relations Act and the Fair Labor Standards Act, both of which explicitly went beyond common law notions of fairness because of fears that excessive market power by employers would result in unfair labor deals justifying strong government action. Under neither of those acts could anyone claim that the failure to limit regulations to common law definitions of unfair-ness constituted an abuse of administrative discretion. Both statutes were open invitations to correct supposed market failures beyond what would be allowed under common law notions.

But that novel conception of fairness has nothing to do with PUCHA, so it is utterly inconsistent with the purpose of that act to go beyond such common law limits. Chief Judge Groner understood that point, but the Supreme Court wholly missed it. No one should attack *Chenery II* based on the proposition that it is impossible for administrative agencies to make new law through incremental decisions without going through the rulemaking process. It is equally important to understand that *Chenery II* represents yet another instance of abuse of discretion by an administrative agency that does not respect the substantive limitations in its authorizing statute. It is wrong to think that unconstrained discretion is needed to deal with unforeseen situations and novel circumstances. The facts in *Chenery II* were ordinary, and the action that SEC took was a profound abuse of discretion whether it proceeded by case-by-case adjudication or rulemaking. Fuller would have understood that common law decisions that violate every settled legal expectation constitute an illegal form of retroactive decision making. It is a pity that both the relevant case law and the learned commentators of administrative law miss this obvious point.

Chamber of Commerce v. United States Department of Labor

The discretion of administrative agencies is not exercised only in individual cases. It is also exercised through general rulemaking, where changes are intended to reverse past practices, without making illegal any conduct undertaken before the promulgation of the rule. The stakes in these cases are far higher than they are in one-off decisions like *Chenery II*, although, for the most part, the same framework governs such discretion. One notable case that has resisted the common trend is *Chamber of Commerce v. United States Department of Labor*,[132] in which the Fifth Circuit invalidated by a 2–1 vote a major fiduciary rule that DOL under the Obama administration finalized in April 2016.[133] The purpose of the regulation was to introduce a new regime to govern the conduct of broker-dealers. The fiduciary rule consisted of a set of seven different rules, which in combination sought to offer a new rendition of the statutory phrase "investment advice fiduciary" as it appears in both the Employee Retirement Income Security Act of 1974 (ERISA)[134] and the Internal Revenue Code (IRC).[135] Together, the seven rules proposed were intended to impose on broker-dealers the same onerous standard that the Investment Advisers Act of 1940 imposes on investment advisers.[136] The stated justification for the new rule was the need to bolster protection against potential conflicts of interest in the dispensing of investment advice: "Unless they are fiduciaries . . . these consultants and advisers are free under ERISA and the Code, not only to receive such conflicted compensation, but also to act on their conflicts of interest to the detriment of their customers."[137]

Much therefore turns on the coverage offered by these two statutes. Under both ERISA and IRC,

> a person is a fiduciary with respect to a plan to the extent he . . . renders investment advice for a fee or other compensation, direct or indirect, with respect to any moneys or other property of such plan, or has any authority or responsibility to do so.[138]

The key question is what counts as "investment advice" under this statutory regime. In 1975, shortly after ERISA was enacted, DOL promulgated this five-part test for deciding who falls within the statutory scope. As Judge Edith H. Jones explained, under the test, an investment-advice fiduciary is a person who: (1) "renders advice . . . or makes recommendation[s] as to the advisability of investing in, purchasing, or selling securities or other property"; (2) "on a regular basis"; and (3) "pursuant to a mutual agreement . . . between such person and the plan." The advice must: (4) "serve as a primary basis for investment decisions with respect to plan assets"; and (5) be "individualized . . . based on the particular needs of the plan."[139]

That definition remained in effect for over 40 years before the Obama administration sought to broaden its reach by making two critical changes. The first was to eliminate the second requirement calling for the professional to provide services "on a regular basis"; the second was to remove the term "primary" from the fourth requirement. These are not small or incremental changes, given that they sweep all broker-dealers into the class of investment advisers. The prior law had sharply distinguished between investment advisers, on the one hand, and broker-dealers, on the other, with the latter including only those persons whose advice is "solely incidental to the conduct of his business as a broker or dealer and who receives no special compensation therefor."[140]

The new DOL fiduciary rule imposed a set of onerous fiduciary duties on covered parties, including an extensive set of "prohibited transactions" that the newly minted fiduciaries could not enter into unless they fell within a newly created Best Interest Contract Exemption (BICE). BICE protected certain of the newly minted fiduciaries if they confirmed that they were fiduciaries and agreed to incorporate into their work certain "impartial conduct standards" to accept duties of loyalty and prudence that normally attached to such fiduciaries. Their purpose for taking these steps was to avoid making certain misleading statements and to limit themselves to accepting no more than "reasonable compensation" for the services they rendered.[141] It should be clear that BICE was itself the source of additional duties not formerly imposed on broker-dealers.

In his dissent in *Chamber of Commerce*, Chief Judge Carl E. Stewart started by insisting that under *Chevron*, the statute contained sufficient ambiguity to uphold the regulation. He then found no reason that, in construing the statutory language, DOL was bound by the common law definitions of "fiduciary duty" if it concluded that the sterner protections were necessary to deal with the conflicts of interest in question, which are, of course, ubiquitous in all agency relationships. Judge Stewart argued that "the panel majority disregard[ed] the requirement of showing judicial deference under *Chevron*," pointing out various difficulties with the way in which the new fiduciary duty standard fit within the overall framework of the statute.[142]

There is little doubt that under the current law, there is much to support in the fiduciary rule on these grounds. On the face of the statute, the term "fiduciary" is not defined, and a key feature of the modern administrative state is that it does not treat common law definitions as having dispositive weight when other interpretations are possible.[143] Under *Chevron*, the dictionary definitions of a "fiduciary" are certainly permissible, even if they conflict with the relevant common law rules. It is also the case that curing a conflict of interest is always a sufficient justification for regulation, and Judge Stewart's dissent took the view that it is up to the agency to decide, under the familiar doctrine of deference, what the remedy for such a conflict should be. The dissent noted that there had been a major revolution in dealing with ERISA plans and individual retirement accounts since the earlier regulation was promulgated in 1975, which made it sensible for DOL to update the regulation.[144] Accordingly, it made no effort to weigh the costs of the regulation against the benefits, thinking that this task was one to be resolved by agency expertise. The dissent might have added a citation to *FCC v. Fox Television Studios*,[145] in which the Supreme Court dealt with FCC's first declaration that a broadcasting company was liable for airing a program that included fleeting and isolated expletives. Writing for the majority, Justice Scalia announced that the government bears no special burden of justification when it changes long-established rules. As he explained, the agency

> need not demonstrate to a court's satisfaction that the reasons for the new policy are *better* than the reasons for the old one. It suffices that the new policy is permissible under the statute, that there are good reasons for it, and that the agency *believes* it to be better, which the conscious change adequately indicates.[146]

In my view, Judge Stewart's dissent in *Chamber of Commerce* represents a defensible approach that may well be correct—subject to the caveats that follow—within the *Chevron* framework.

It is therefore instructive to see the multiple ways in which Judge Jones's majority opinion in *Chamber of Commerce* sought to avoid the application of *Chevron*, with her methods mirroring the attitudes toward administrative law that governed in the pre-*Chevron* era. One point that she stressed is that the regulation that was abruptly changed by the fiduciary rule had been in place for 45 years and that it had been applied consistently, even as the practices within the investment and securities industry had changed dramatically over that period. She might have added, but did not, that the fiduciary rule required undoing years of established practice, which would have been much more onerous than the relatively minor agency change at issue in *Fox*. She could have also noted that DOL did not offer any estimate as to the potential harm caused by the application of the old rule in order to assess whether the costs of the proposed changes were justified. Indeed, the rapid growth in the industry while the earlier rule was in effect is potent evidence that no such harm was caused by the earlier regulation, partly because reputation matters in the industry and skittish customers can be counted on to withdraw from funds operated by any firm suspected of engaging in improper practices with or without any regulatory determination in place. If any abstract concern with conflicts of interest is sufficient to justify a change in regulatory policy, the fiduciary rule and virtually any other regulation—even those that are far more draconian—will pass muster.

Judge Jones homed in on the magnitude of the proposed shift in regulatory policy and its consequences for the entire financial-services industry: "The stated purpose of the new rules is to regulate in an entirely new way hundreds of thousands of financial service providers and insurance companies in the trillion dollar markets for ERISA plans and individual retirement accounts (IRAs)."[147] She noted: "DOL estimates that compliance costs imposed on the regulated parties might amount to $31.5 billion over ten years with a 'primary estimate' of $16.1 billion."[148] Based on this information, she outlined a tale of woe that the dissent did not see fit, given its deferential view, to address. This tale is worth quoting in full:

> The Fiduciary Rule has already spawned significant market consequences, including the withdrawal of several major companies, including Metlife, AIG and Merrill Lynch from some segments of the brokerage and retirement investor market. Companies like Edward Jones and State Farm have limited the investment products that can be sold to retirement investors.
>
> Throughout the financial services industry, thousands of brokers and insurance agents who deal with IRA investors must either forgo commission-based transactions and move to fees for account management or accept the burdensome regulations and heightened lawsuit exposure required by the BICE contract provisions.
>
> Further, as DOL itself recognized, millions of IRA investors with small accounts prefer commission-based fees because they engage in few annual trading transactions. Yet these are the investors potentially deprived of all investment advice as a result of the Fiduciary Rule, because they cannot afford to pay account management fees, or brokerage and insurance firms cannot afford to service small accounts, given the regulatory burdens, for management fees alone.

The Fiduciary Rule's expanded coverage is best explained by variations of the following hypothetical advanced by the Chamber of Commerce: a broker-dealer otherwise unrelated to an IRA owner tells the IRA owner, "You'll love the return on X stock in your retirement plan, let me tell you about it" (the "investment advice"); the IRA owner purchases X stock; and the broker-dealer is paid a commission (the "fee or other compensation"). Based on this single sales transaction, as DOL agrees, the broker-dealer has now been brought within the Fiduciary Rule. The same consequence follows for insurance agents who promote annuity products.[149]

On economic grounds, her logic is impeccable. There is no reason to disrupt a stable system under which broker-dealers are regulated under the Dodd-Frank Act, which contains specific provisions empowering SEC to promulgate enhanced, uniform standards of conduct for broker-dealers and investment advisers who render "personalized investment advice about securities to a retail customer."[150] The fiduciary rule would unnecessarily reduce the set of consumer options by eliminating the distinction between investment advisers and broker-dealers. SEC is positioned to handle the latter. Indeed, in June 2019, SEC finalized the Regulation Best Interest, which stiffens the standards of disclosure applicable to broker-dealers, without going as far as the fiduciary rule.[151] Judge Jones opted for a mode of statutory construction that stresses the continuity between Roman and common law definitions of a "fiduciary" that concentrate on the reliance of trust and confidence. These definitions were embodied in the 1975 regulations, in which the requirements of the second (regular advice) and fourth (primary purpose) provisions are needed to implement that view.[152] A narrow form of textualism is displaced by a concern with history and context. The judge disputed the proposition that this regulation is ambiguous under Step One of the *Chevron* test on the basis that

DOL's interpretation of an "investment advice fiduciary" relies too narrowly on a purely semantic construction of one isolated provision and wrongly presupposes that the provision is inherently ambiguous. Properly construed, the statutory text is not ambiguous. Ambiguity, to the contrary, "is a creature not of definitional possibilities but of statutory context."[153]

She goes on: "Moreover, all relevant sources indicate that Congress codified the touchstone of common law fiduciary status—the parties' underlying relationship of trust and confidence—and nothing in the statute 'requires' departing from the touchstone."[154] This point is, of course, contestable because there is nothing in the *Chevron* test that dictates the choice between textualism and contextualism in the construction of statutes. In a system of de novo review, the court can adopt its preferred method of construction. But under *Chevron*, a narrower form of textualism is a much harder sell.

That said, the strongest argument in favor of Judge Jones's opinion is that the law makes far more sense if it has two distinct models to which parties can gravitate, rather than a single model that is, as she notes, ill-suited for a large range of transactions. However, the difficulty of deciding the case under the *Chevron* test should count as a strong indictment of the rule. Indeed, every argument that Judge Jones made in her effort to wiggle free from *Chevron*'s clutches is entirely consistent with the 19th-century version of administrative law that understood the need to preserve continuity between the common law and its administrative implementation—recognizing that long usage was entitled to a strong presumption, that major deviations from previous policy should not be made by an agency without some compelling reason to do so, and that questions of law should be decided by courts rather than administrative agencies. Major changes in policy have to be implemented by legislation. Applying those rules, Judge Jones's opinion is clearly correct. But if you apply the current rules of administrative law—including *Chevron*—agencies have an open invitation to overreach. When administrative agencies are confined to a more modest role, something like the fiduciary rule never gets off the ground.

ENDNOTES

1. *Skidmore v. Swift Co.,* 323 U.S. 134 (1944).

2. *Id.* at 138.

3. *Id.* at 140. The test receives a qualified endorsement in Cass R. Sunstein and Adrian Vermeule, *The Morality of Administrative Law*, 131 HARV. L. REV., at 1950 (2018), without any awareness of the substantive argument.

4. *See Skidmore,* 323 U.S. at 113 ("The vice of long hours of toil is not present here").

5. *Bowles v. Seminole Rock & Sand Co.,* 325 U.S. 410 (1945).

6. *Auer v. Robbins,* 519 U.S. 452 (1997).

7. *J. W. Hampton, Jr. & Co. v. United States,* 276 U.S. 394 (1928).

8. Emergency Price Control Act of 1942, Pub. L. No. 77-421, 56 Stat. 23, 24 (1942), § 2(a).

9. Maximum Price Regulation No. 188, § 1499.163(a)(2), 7 Fed. Reg. 7957, 7968–69 (Oct. 8, 1942). The remaining two subsections describing the meaning of the highest price charged read: "(ii) If the seller made no such delivery during March 1942, such seller's highest offering price to a purchaser of the same class for delivery of the article or material during that month; or (iii) If the seller made no such delivery and had no such offering price to a purchaser of the same class during March, 1942, the highest price charged by the seller during March, 1942, to a purchaser of a different class, adjusted to reflect the seller's customary differential between the two classes of purchasers." *Id.* at § 1499.163(a)(2).

10. *Yakus v. United States,* 321 U.S. 414 (1944).

11. *Seminole Rock,* 325 U.S. at 413–14.

12. *Id.* at 415.

13. *Id.* at 413–14.

14. Paul J. Larkin, Jr. and Elizabeth H. Slattery, *The World After* Seminole Rock *and* Auer, 42 HARV. J. L. & PUB. POL'Y 625, 634 (2019).

15. *United States v. Gypsum Co.,* 333 U.S. 364, 395 (1948).

16. *Anderson v. City of Bessemer,* 470 U.S. 564 (1985).

17. *Id.* at 574 (citing *United States v. Yellow Cab Co.,* 338 U.S. 338, 342 (1949)).

18. *Merriam-Webster,* https://www.merriam-webster.com/legal/clearly%20erroneous, last visited Aug. 11, 2019. For application, see Federal Rules of Civil Procedure Rule 52(a).

19. On the gulf, *see* Larkin and Slattery, *supra* note 14, at 635–36 (citing Jonathan H. Adler, *Auer Evasions,* 16 GEO. J. L. & PUB. POL'Y 1 (2018)(For a detailed account of the doctrinal revolution).

20. *Auer,* 513 U.S. at 461.

21. *Id.* at 456.

22. A Sergeant "[s]upervises Police Officers and other department employees in enforcement of local, state, and federal laws and in provision of personal, real property, and equipment security throughout campus. Supervises investigation and documentation of crimes and incidents. Documents and presents evidence; provides legal testimony." *Position Classification Description: Police Sergeant,* U. OF NEW MEX. (last updated June 19, 2018), *available at* https://jobdescriptions.unm.edu/detail. php?v&id=X6003.

23. A Police Lieutenant "[p]lans, organizes, oversees, and coordinates the daily activities of a designated operational entity of the Police Department. Manages supervisory personnel and police officers who provide personal, real property, and equipment security throughout campus, ensuring consistent and equitable enforcement of local, state, and federal laws and university regulations. Reviews and approves reports on incident and crime investigations." *Position Classification Description: Police Lieutenant,* U. OF NEW MEX. (last updated June 19, 2018), available at https://jobdescriptions.unm.edu/detail.php?v&id=X6015.

24. *Perez v. Mortg. Bankers Ass'n,* 135 S. Ct. 1199 (2015).

25. *Id.* at 1211–13 (Scalia, J., concurring).

26. Richard A. Epstein, *Structural Protections for Individual Rights: The Indispensable Role of Independent Federal Courts in the Administrative State,* 26 GEO. MASON L. REV. (forthcoming 2019).

27. *Id.* at 1206 (citing *Vermont Yankee Nuclear Power Corp. v. Nat. Res. Def. Council,* 435 U.S. 519 (1978)).

28. *Loan Officer,* INVESTOPEDIA (last updated Apr. 14, 2019), *available at* https://www.investopedia.com/terms/l/loanofficer.asp.

29. *Perez,* 135 S. Ct. at 1208 n.4 (citing *Thomas Jefferson Univ. v. Shalala,* 512 U.S. 504, 515 (1994)).

30. Sunstein and Vermeule, *supra* note 3, at 1948 (citing *Christopher v. SmithKline Beecham Corp.,* 567 U.S. 142, 155 (2012)).

31. Gillian Metzger, *1930s Redux: The Administrative State Under Siege, 131* HARV. L. REV., at 40 (2017).

32. *G.G. v. Gloucester Cty. Sch. Bd.,* 822 F.3d 709 (4th Cir. 2016).

33. 20 U.S.C. § 1681–1688(2017).

34. *Gloucester Cty.,* 822 F.3d at 719 (citing *G.G. v. Gloucester Cty. Sch. Bd.,* 132 F. Supp.3d 736 (2015)).

35. *Id.* at 720–21.

36. *Id.* at 718–19.

37. Catherine E. Lhamon, Assistant Secretary for Civ. Rts., Off. for Civ. Rts., U.S. Dep't of Educ., and Vanita Gupta, Principal Deputy Assistant Att'y Gen. for Civ. Rights, Civil Rts. Division, Dep't of Just., *Dear Colleague Letter on Transgender Students* (May 13, 2016), *available at* https://www2.ed.gov/about/offices/list/ocr/letters/colleague-201605-title-ix-transgender.pdf.

38. Title IX covers public institutions as well as those private institutions that receive federal financial assistance from a variety of sources, which, as a practical matter, include virtually all schools, colleges, and universities. *See* 20 U.S.C. § 1681(a)(2017) ("under any educational program or activity receiving Federal financial assistance").

39. Lhamon and Gupta, *supra* note 37, at 2.

40. *Id.* at 2 n.6 (citing EEOC, Appeal No. 0120133395, 9 (2015).

41. *Gloucester Cty. Sch. Bd. v. G.G.,* 137 S. Ct. 1239 (2017).

42. Sandra Battle, Acting Assistant Secretary for Civ. Rts., U.S. Dep't of Educ., and T. E. Wheeler II, Acting Assistant Att'y General for Civ. Rts., U.S. Dep't of Justice, *Dear Colleague Letter,* at 2 (Feb. 22, 2017), *available at* https://www2.ed.gov/about/offices/list/ocr/letters/colleague-201702-title-ix.pdf.

43. *Gloucester Cty.,* 822 F.3d at 732 (Niemeyer, J., concurring in part and dissenting in part) (internal quotation marks omitted).

44. *Gloucester County Public Schools Minutes* (Nov. 11, 2014), at 4.

45. 20 U.S.C. § 1681(a)(2017).

46. *Id.* § 1686.

47. 34 C.F.R. § 106.33.

48. For discussion, *see* Richard A. Epstein, Forbidden Grounds: The Case Against Employment Discrimination Law 269–83 (Harv. U. Press, 1992).

49. 42 U.S.C. § 2000e-2(e)(2017)(allowing for discrimination "in those certain instances where religion, sex, or national origin is a bona fide occupational qualification reasonably necessary to the normal operation of that particular business or enterprise"). The provision has been largely gutted through statutory interpretation, which reads it as narrowly a "business necessity" test. *See, e.g., Chambers v. Omaha Girls Club,* 840 F.2d 583 (8th Cir. 1988), *criticized in* Epstein, *supra* note 48, at 283–90.

50. *Plessy v. Ferguson,* 163 U.S. 537 (1896).

51. *Gloucester Cty.,* 822 F.3d at 721 (citing *Sex, American C. Dictionary* (1970)).

52. *Id.* (citing *Sex, Webster's Third New Int'l Dictionary* (1971)).

53. The dissent gave a more plausible treatment of the dictionary definitions and contemporary meaning. *Id.* at 736 (Niemeyer, J., concurring in part and dissenting in part) ("virtually every dictionary definition of 'sex' referred to the *physiological* distinctions between males and females").

54. *Id.* at 721 (internal citation and quotation marks omitted).

55. *Id.* at 720–21.

56. *Id.* at 721.

57. *Id.*

58. *Id.*

59. Charlotte, N.C., Ordinance 7056 (2016), *available at* https://charlottenc.gov/NonDiscrimination/Documents/NDO%20Ordinance%207056.pdf.

60. An Act to Provide for Single-Sex Multiple Occupancy Bathroom and Changing Facilities in Schools and Public Agencies and to Create Statewide Consistency in Regulation of Employment and Public Accommodations, H.B. 2, 2016 Gen. Assemb., 2d Spec. Sess. (2016), N.C. Gen. Stat. §§ 143–760, *repealed by* 2017 N.C. Sess. Laws 1 (2017).

61. Paul Blake and Will Gretsky, *ACC Pulls Championships from North Carolina over Anti-LGBT Bathroom Law,* ABC News (Sept. 14, 2016), *available at* https://abcnews.go.com/US/acc-pulls-championships-north-carolina-anti-lgbt-bathroom/story?id=42089282; Dan Schulman, *PayPal Withdraws Plan for Charlotte Expansion,* Charlotte Observer (Apr. 15, 2016), Reuters, *available at* https://www.reuters.com/article/idUSFWN1780GG. Several highlights: NCAA (National Collegiate Athletic Association) stripped North Carolina of hosting rights for seven tournaments, and other sports associations followed suit. The loss of business included PayPal's withdrawal of a plan to introduce 400 jobs, worth about $20 million in total payroll. For an exhaustive list of private- and public-sector responses, *see Public Facilities Privacy & Security Act,* Wikipedia, *available at* https://perma.cc/W46H-7VSY (last visited Apr. 10, 2019).

62. Emery P. Dalesio and Jonathan Drew, *"Bathroom Bill" to Cost North Carolina $3.76B,* Associated Press (Mar. 30, 2017), *available at* https://www.apnews.com/e6c7a15d2e16452c8dcbc2756fd67b44.

63. Martina Navratilova, quoted in Rob Goldberg, *Martina Navratilova: Transgender Athletes in Women's Sports Is Insane, Cheating,* Bleacher Report (Feb. 18, 2019), *available at* https://bleacherreport.com/articles/2821380-martina-navratilova-transgender-athletes-in-womens-sport-is-insane-cheating.

64. Martina Navratilova, *The Rules on Trans Athletes Reward Cheats and Punish the Innocent,* The Times (Feb. 17, 2019), *available at* https://www.thetimes.co.uk/article/the-rules-on-trans-athletes-reward-cheats-and-punish-the-innocent-klsrq6h3x.

65. Joanna Hoffman, *Athlete Ally: Navratilova's Statements Transphobic and Counter to Our Work, Vision and Values* (Feb. 19, 2019), Athlete Ally, *available at* https://www.athleteally.org/navratilovas-statements-transphobic-counter-to-our-work-vision (citing Joanna Harper, *Race Times for Transgender Athletes,* 6 J. Sporting Cultures & Identities 1 (2015)).

66. Michael J. Lenzi, Comment, *The Trans Athlete Dilemma: A Constitutional Analysis of High School Transgender Student-Athlete Policies,* 67 American U. L. Rev. 841 (2018).

67. Equality Act, H.R. 5, 116th Cong. § 9 (2019), *available at* https://www.congress.gov/bill/116th-congress/house-bill/5/text.

68. Abigail Shrier, *The Transgender War on Women: The Equality Act Sacrifices Female Safety in Restrooms, Locker Rooms and Even Domestic-Violence Shelters,* Wall St. J. (Mar. 26, 2019), *available at* https://www.wsj.com/articles/the-transgender-war-on-women-11553640683.

69. 723 F. App'x 964 (11th Cir. 2018).

70. *Id.* at 964 (emphasis in original).

71. 884 F.3d 560 (6th Cir. 2018).

72. Brief for Respondent Aimee Stephens, *R. G. & G. R. Harris Funeral Homes, Inc. v. EEOC,* 139 S. Ct. 2049(2019)(No. 18-1807), *available at* https://www.supremecourt.gov/DocketPDF/18/18-107/104141/20190626105814174_No%2018-107%20RG%20and%20GR%20Harris%20Funeral%20Homes%20v%20EEOC%20and%20Aimee%20Stephens%20Brief%20for%20Respondent%20Aimee%20Stephens.pdf.

73. *Kisor v. Wilkie,* 139 S. Ct. 2400 (2019).

74. *Id.*

75. *Id.* at 2409.

76. 38 C.F.R. § 3.156(c)(1)(2013).

77. *Kisor v. Shulkin,* 869 F.3d 1360, 1366 (Fed. Cir. 2017).

78. Fed. R. Evid. 401(a)–(b).

79. *Shulkin,* 869 F.3d at 1367.

80. *Kisor v. Wilkie,* 139 S. Ct. at 2403.

81. *Id.* at 2415.

82. *Id.*

83. *Id.* at 2425.

84. *Id.* at 2426.

85. *Id.* at 2427–28.

86. *See Nat'l Cable & Telecomm. v. Brand X Internet Servs.*, 545 U.S. 967 (2005).

87. *R.R. Bd. v. Alton R.R. Co.*, 295 U.S. 330 (1935).

88. *Usery v. Turner Elkhorn*, 428 U.S. 1 (1976).

89. *Id.* at 19.

90. *Pension Benefit Board Corp. v. R. A. Gray & Co.*, 467 U.S. 717 (1984).

91. *Id.* at 718.

92. *Connolly v. PBGC*, 475 U.S. 211 (1986).

93. *Id.* at 224.

94. *Turner Elkhorn*, 428 U.S. at 16.

95. *Connolly*, 475 U.S. at 227 ("Prudent employers then had more than sufficient notice not only that pension plans were currently regulated, but also that withdrawal itself might trigger additional financial obligations [citing *Gray*, 467 U.S. 717, 752 (2984)]. Those who do business in the regulated field cannot object if the legislative scheme is buttressed by subsequent amendments to achieve the legislative end."). (citation and quotation marks omitted)

96. *Arizona Grocery v. Topeka, Atchison & Santa Fe Ry. Co.*, 284 U.S. 370 (1932).

97. Sunstein and Vermeule, *supra* note 3, at 1944 (referring to *Bowen v. Georgetown Univ. Hosp.*, 488 U.S. 204 (1988)).

98. *Bd. of Pub. Util. Comm'rs v. New York Tel. Co.*, 271 U.S. 23 (1926).

99. On this problem, *see generally Richard A. Epstein*, Principles for a Free Society: Reconciling Individual Liberty with the Common Good 307–18 (Perseus, 1998).

100. *Duquesne Light Co. v. Barasch*, 488 U.S. 299 (1989).

101. For an excellent discussion of the relative merits of the many permutations of rules for rate regulation, *see* Michael W. McConnell, *Public Utilities' Private Rights: Paying for Failed Nuclear Power Projects*, 12 Regulation 35 (1988).

102. *Smyth v. Ames*, 169 U.S. 466 (1898).

103. *Hope Natural Gas v. Fed. Power Comm'n*, 320 U.S. 591 (1944).

104. *Verizon Communic'ns Inc. v. FCC*, 535 U.S. 467 (2002).

105. The relevant material is collected at *Telecommunications Act of 1996*, FCC (last updated June 20, 2013), *available at* https://www.fcc.gov/general/telecommunications-act-1996.

106. *Unbundled Network Element (UNE)*, Technopedia, *available at* https://www.techopedia.com/definition/26165/unbundled-network-element-une (last visited Apr. 10, 2019).

107. *SEC v. Chenery Corp.*, 318 U.S. 80 (1943).

108. *SEC v. Chenery Corp.*, 332 U.S. 194 (1947).

109. *Chamber of Commerce v. United States Dep't of Labor*, 885 F.3d 360 (5th Cir. 2018).

110. *Chenery II*, 332 U.S., at 202–3.

111. Metzger, *supra* note 31, at 87.

112. Jeffrey A. Pojanowski, *Neoclassical Administrative Law*, 133 Harv. L. Rev. (forthcoming 2019).

113. Sunstein and Vermeule, *supra* note 3, at 1977–78 (referring to *Chenery II*, 332 U.S., at

199–200, where the Court noted: "Under *Chenery II*'s view, the Commission would be free only to promulgate a general rule outlawing such profits in future utility reorganizations; but such a rule would have to be prospective in nature and have no retroactive effect upon the instant situation.").

114. *Id.* at 1977.

115. *Id.*

116. *Pasley v. Freeman* (1789), 100 Eng. Rep. 450.

117. *Id.* at 456.

118. *Id.*

119. Ch. 687, 49 Stat. 803, 15 U.S.C. § 79. [hereinafter PUCHA]

120. *Chenery I,* 318 U.S. at 85.

121. *Id.* at 86.

122. *Id.* at 87–88.

123. *Id.* at 91.

124. *Id.*

125. PUCHA, at § 7(d)(6).

126. PUCHA, at § 11(e).

127. *See, e.g., FCC v. Nat'l Broad. Co., Inc.,* 319 U.S. 239 (1943) (upholding the broad delegation of authority that allowed FCC to adopt rules of spectrum allocation that served the public, interest, convenience and necessity, which spawned many difficulties in the area); Coase, *The Federal Communications Commission,* Hazlett, *The Rationality of U.S. Regulation.*

128. *See, e.g., Wilkerson v. McCarthy,* 336 U.S. 53, 56 (1949) ("These observations are especially pertinent to suits under the Federal Employers' Liability Act. The difficulties in these cases derive largely from the outmoded concept of 'negligence' as a working principle for the adjustments of injuries inevitable under the technological circumstances of modern industry. This cruel and wasteful mode of dealing with industrial injuries has long been displaced in industry generally by the insurance principle that underlies workmen's compensation laws.") Frankfurter never addressed the serious issues that can arise under workmen's compensation laws in a wide range of areas. The case law on this subject is every bit as complex as that under the negligence system with the difficulties merely emerging different places. For the complexity of the case law, see the multivolume treatise, Lex K. Larson and Arthur Larson, Larson's Workers' Compensation Law, 5th ed. (Matthew Bender, 2013).

129. *Chenery Corp. v. SEC,* 154 F.2d 6, 9–10 (D.C. Cir. 1946).

130. 48 Stat. 881 (1934), *codified as amended at* 15 U.S.C. § 78b § (2017).

131. *Id.* § 3 § 78b(3).

132. *Chamber of Commerce,* 885 F.3d 360 (5th Cir. 2018), *rev'g Chamber of Commerce of the United States v. Hugler,* 231 F. Supp.3d 152 (N.D. Tex. 2017). The challenge to the new fiduciary rule was also rejected in *Nat'l Ass'n for Fixed Annuities v. Perez,* 217 F. Supp.3d (2016).

133. Fiduciary, 81 Fed. Reg. 20,946 (Apr. 8, 2015).

134. Employee Retirement Income Security Act of 1974, Pub. L. No. 93-406, 88 Stat. 829, *codified as amended at* 29 U.S.C. §§ 1001–1003(2017).

135. Internal Revenue Code, 26 U.S.C. § 4975(2017).

136. Investors Advisers Act of 1940, 16 U.S.C. §§ 80b-1–80b-21(2017).

137. 81 Fed. Reg. at 20956.

138. 29 U.S.C. § 1002(21)(A)(ii)(2017).

139. *Chamber of Commerce,* 885 F.3d at 354–65 (citing 29 C.F.R. § 2510.3-21(c)(1) (2015)).

140. 15 U.S.C. § 80b-2(a)(11)(C)(2017).

141. *Chamber of Commerce,* 885 F.3d at 391.

142. *Id.* at 395.

143. *Id.* at 391–92.

144. *Id.* at 389.

145. *FCC v. Fox Television Studios,* 556 U.S. 502 (2009).

146. *Id.* at 515 (emphasis in original).

147. *Chamber of Commerce,* 885 F.3d at 362.

148. *Id.* at 366 (citing Department of Labor, Employment Benefits Security Administration, Definition of the Term "Fiduciary"; Conflict of Interest Rule—Retirement Investment Advice, 81 Fed. Reg. 20946, at 20951)(Apr. 8, 2016)).

149. 885 F.3d at 369.

150. *Id.* at 385 (citing Dodd-Frank Wall Street Reform and Consumer Protection Act, Pub. Law. No. 111-203 § 913(g)(1), 124 Stat. 1827–28 (2010)).

151. Regulation Best Interest: The Broker-Dealer Standard of Conduct, 17 C.F.R. Part 240 (2019), *available at* https://www.sec.gov/rules/final/2019/34-86031.pdf (containing an exhaustive rule running 771 triple-spaced pages). For a spirited defense of that rule, see Editorial, *Fiduciary Rule Fixer-Upper,* WALL ST. J. (June 9, 2019), *available at* https://www.wsj.com/articles/fiduciary-rule-fixer-upper-11560118310. The new rule does require disclosures of conflicts of interest on fees and commissions. It prohibits broker-dealers from getting bonuses for the sale of specific products but does not require them to register under the 1940 Investment Advisers Act or bar commission payments, which are favored by individuals who make relatively few transactions annually.

152. *Chamber of Commerce,* 885 F.3d at 370.

153. *Id.* at 369 (citing *Brown v. Gardner,* 513 U.S. 115, 118 (1994)).

154. *Id.* at 369.

PART 5

QUESTIONS OF FACT UNDER THE ADMINISTRATIVE PROCEDURE ACT

Arbitrary, Capricious, or an Abuse of Discretion

With the completion of the discussion of APA's approach to matters of law, it is now necessary to turn to the second major division of administrative law, which involves the question of judicial review on matters of fact. On this question, APA clearly considers that the administrative agency should have some running room that it is denied on questions of law. That position is, of course, consistent with the general view of appellate review on matters that fall outside the field of administrative law. Trial courts and juries are given greater leeway on questions of fact, where determinations about credibility and demeanor are at stake. In every legal proceeding, the higher that one proceeds up the decision tree, the fewer and more important are the decided issues.

The use of the three terms in "arbitrary, capricious, [or] an abuse of discretion"[1] connotes the opposite of de novo review for legal questions. These three terms in sequence reinforce the basic distinction. As a matter of ordinary English, the term "arbitrary" is not associated with every instance of the drawing of sharp lines, for unless some clear demarcations of classes are permitted, routine administration becomes impossible.

Under 18 years of age, one cannot vote; under 16, one cannot drive. It is sometimes the case that someone under 18 is a better citizen than someone over 18, just as someone under 16 may be a better driver than someone over 16. Nonetheless, the use of this and countless other hard demarcations is not arbitrary in the negative sense of the word, which asks a different question: Is the hard stop put in the right place, and do the delineations that follow run in the right direction? Hence, a rule that allows people to vote only upon reaching age 65 would be both clear and arbitrary, even though the vesting of retirement benefits at that age is both clear and sensible. Similarly, allowing people to vote *under* the age of 18 while denying that privilege to those *over* that age is perverse, given the need to encourage the existence of an informed electorate. But there is normally no incentive anywhere in the political arena for these odd inversions. Instead, the usual question is whether to draw the line for voting somewhere between 18 and 21, or for driving somewhere between 15 and 18. There are pros and cons to each of the points within the customary ranges, so the requirement of non-arbitrariness is satisfied so long as reasonable arguments can be made for the selected point, even if, with the fullness of time, someone could conclude that another point was correct.

The term "capricious" has even less bite in these cases. To do something on a caprice is to act on a whim or a lark without having given the question any thought. It is highly unlikely that any professionalized administrative body acts in that fashion, so the scope of review under this term is rightly limited.

The notion of "abuse of discretion" as used in ordinary cases where it is asked whether an appellate court should override a district court again contemplates a very narrow scope of judicial oversight. Hundreds of cases stress these recurrent themes. The abuse of discretion standard may only be invoked on a "firm conviction" that the court that lies below committed a clear error of judgment in weighing the relevant factors.[2] The three terms thus work together to create fewer systemwide errors by avoiding exacting scrutiny of findings of fact without insisting on total abnegation on these questions. The standard represents the cumulative judgment in appellate procedures for ordinary litigation. Administrative law does well when it follows this customary norm, particularly since the norm is incorporated into APA Section 706(a) in three different ways.

The issue here has some real difficulties in interpretation because of the two important contexts in which it can arise. In the first, the question is how the test applies in connection with traditional regulation where some administrative agency threatens to impose sanctions on private parties that do not meet appropriate standards, usually on questions of safety or financial soundness. Second, APA also applies the "arbitrary and capricious" standard to major administrative decisions in the executive branch to set policy on key public issues, dealing with such vital matters as immigration and the construction of the census. Everyone concedes that the executive branch, including its highest cabinet officials, receives broad delegations from Congress to run these large programs, a proposition confirmed by a divided Supreme Court in *Trump v. Hawaii*,[3] dealing with the exclusion of certain groups from the United States, and in *Department of Commerce v. New York*,[4] dealing with the enumeration of the census. The decisions in both these separate areas are deeply fractured. As a rough, but only rough, approximation, the liberal bloc on the Court tends to be more tolerant of administrative discretion in the regulatory context, while the conservative bloc tends to take that same attitude in connection with high-stakes decisions made as a matter of executive policy. Yet, as is so often the case, the particulars of any given statutory scheme may, in principle, make any such generalizations difficult to sustain.

Traditional Agency Action

In most instances, the phrase "arbitrary and capricious," as noted, has been read to be in contrast with the notion of de novo review, requiring some measure of judicial deference to administrative expertise on matters of fact. But this topic was made far more difficult to understand because the most authoritative interpretation of that phrase was offered in *Motor Vehicle Manufacturers Association v. State Farm*,[5] which moved sharply in favor of a higher standard of review. Justice White, ignoring the phrase "abuse of discretion," gave this rendition of arbitrary and capricious:

> Normally, an agency rule would be arbitrary and capricious
> if the agency has relied on factors which Congress has not

intended it to consider, entirely failed to consider an important aspect of the problem, offered an explanation for its decision that runs counter to the evidence before the agency, or is so implausible that it could not be ascribed to a difference in view or the product of agency expertise. The reviewing court should not attempt itself to make up for such deficiencies; we may not supply a reasoned basis for the agency's action that the agency itself has not given.[6]

Unfortunately, this statement references two wholly inconsistent standards of review. On the one hand, it is common to say that the "arbitrary and capricious" standard is "extremely limited and highly deferential,"[7] which is in line with its standard usage. On the other hand, it is commonly said that the "arbitrary and capricious" standard requires that a reviewing court take a "hard look" at the underlying record to see if any of the named defects have occurred, a standard against which few administrative rulings on matters of fact can survive in a court hostile to the underlying enterprise.[8] Virtually all modern administrative determinations require complicated decisions about approval for new projects or products that will necessarily give rise to a welter of conflicting considerations. To hold that a decision is arbitrary and capricious because, as part of its overall analysis, the agency relied on a single factor that Congress had not intended it to consider effortlessly transforms a once-deferential standard into one of exacting scrutiny. No agency's record is perfect, and nothing is more common than for any agency to overlook some relevant factor or to consider some errant factor in its analysis. But the sensible reading of this "arbitrary and capricious" standard would allow the agency to prevail unless it engaged in a wholesale and knowing disregard of large masses of relevant information. Similar strictures should apply to any agency that misses some important aspect of a problem or offers an explanation that is counter to the evidence.

The dangers of overreading this phrase were all too evident in the facts of *State Farm*, which arose when the Reagan administration rescinded a mandate that one of two kinds of passive restraint devices—airbags—be installed in all automobiles by 1982. Justice White listed some of the reasons that led to the administration's decision in this passage:

In a statement explaining the rescission, NHTSA [National Highway Traffic Safety Administration] maintained that it was no longer able to find, as it had in 1977, that the automatic restraint requirement would produce significant safety benefits. This judgment reflected not a change of opinion on the effectiveness of the technology, but a change in plans by the automobile industry. In 1977, the agency had assumed that airbags would be installed in 60% of all new cars and automatic seatbelts in 40%. By 1981 it became apparent that automobile manufacturers planned to install the automatic seatbelts in approximately 99% of the new cars. For this reason, the lifesaving potential of airbags would not be realized. Moreover, it now appeared that the overwhelming majority of passive belts planned to be installed by manufacturers could be detached easily and left that way permanently. Passive belts, once detached, then required "the same type of affirmative action that is the stumbling block to obtaining high usage levels of manual belts." For this reason, the agency concluded that there was no longer a basis for reliably predicting that the Standard would lead to any significant increased usage of restraints at all.[9]

Why should the agency have decided this case otherwise? Indeed, that short summary gives only a partial list of the relevant concerns that led to the decisions. Other highly relevant evidence supported the decision: the evidence was still unclear as to whether the airbags would function correctly, especially with children in the front seat; the overall cost was sufficiently high that mandatory incorporation could raise the price of new cars and thereby leave potential buyers exposed to greater risks in the older vehicles they continued to use; and the estimates of net social savings were contingent on the anticipated use of restraints by consumers, which was itself in doubt.[10]

Nonetheless, Justice White took the doctrinal position that the same standards had to be applied to the rescission of a proposed standard as were applied to its promulgation.[11] In so doing, he ignored a large difference between the two situations. If the promulgation of a new standard is set aside, the technology that remains in use has already been vetted and approved. But if the rescission is undone, the pressures to implement a new standard remain, even if there are serious doubts about its proper implementation, which creates serious risks of accidents and mishaps that could, in turn, result in personal injuries and product liability litigation. Justice White suggested that the agency could have considered requiring all vehicles to be equipped with airbags, a proposal that is just plain dumb if there were any serious doubts remaining about their safety and effectiveness.[12] Any private manufacturer that made the choice to equip its vehicles with questionable technology on its own would certainly have faced a bevy of class action and product liability lawsuits.

The great flaw in *State Farm* is that the Supreme Court thought that searching review on matters of process could be successfully separated from a substantive review on the merits. To be sure, appellate courts do not decide these cases on the merits. Instead, they remand the decisions to lower courts for further consideration of the apparent procedural shortfalls committed by the agency. And the interim delays caused by these ostensible procedural shortfalls operate as a powerful form of injunctive relief, even in cases where there is no sign of imminent peril to the affected parties, which courts typically require to justify preliminary relief in tort cases, an anomaly that becomes all too evident in the pipeline cases discussed below.

Doctrinally, it is hard to underestimate the influence of *State Farm*, which has been cited more than 11,000 times in the 36 years since it was handed down. But as Professors Jacob Gersen and Adrian Vermeule have rightly observed, it is not the only authoritative decision on the proper interpretation of the phrase "arbitrary and capricious."[13] Indeed, they further claim that the government has won what they figure is 92% of the arbitrary and capricious cases before the Supreme Court between 1982 and 2016.[14] Of that mass of cases, they point to the important, if somewhat neglected, case *Baltimore Gas & Electric Co. v. Natural Resources Defense Council, Inc.*,[15] which was decided only weeks before *State Farm* but with a totally different orientation toward the "arbitrary and capricious" standard.

At issue in *Baltimore Gas* was a challenge by the Natural Resources Defense Council (NRDC) to a "generic procedure" adopted by the Nuclear Regulatory Commission (NRC) for the approval of new nuclear plants. These procedures set out the proper treatment of waste products generated by light-water nuclear power plants. To expedite the proceedings, NRC adopted Table S-3, which features "a numerical compilation of the estimated resources used and effluents released by fuel cycle activities supporting a year's operation of a typical light-water reactor."[16] The saving of time and energy was supposed to come from the use of this table, so that "[n]o further discussion of such environmental effects should be required" for dealing with the storage of solidified transuranic and high-level waste.[17] Accordingly, it held that all future evaluations should operate on what was known as a "zero-release" assumption for the assessments of individual plants, even though "the risks from longterm repository failure were uncertain, but suggested that research should resolve most of those uncertainties in the future."[18] NRC offered this explanation for its decision:

> In view of the uncertainties noted regarding waste disposal, the question then arises whether these uncertainties can or should be reflected explicitly in the fuel cycle rule. The Commission has concluded that the rule should not be so modified. On the individual reactor licensing level, where the proceedings deal with fuel cycle issues only peripherally, the Commission sees no advantage in having licensing boards repeatedly weigh for themselves the effect of uncertainties on the selection of fuel cycle impacts for use in cost-benefit balancing. This is a generic question properly dealt with in the rulemaking as part of choosing what impact values should go into the fuel cycle rule. The Commission concludes, having noted that uncertainties exist, that for the limited purpose of the fuel cycle rule it is reasonable to base impacts on the assumption which the Commission believes the probabilities favor, *i.e.,* that bedded-salt repository sites can be found which will provide effective isolation of radioactive waste from the biosphere.[19]

In *Natural Resources Defense Council, Inc. v. Nuclear Regulatory Commission,*[20] the action was challenged under the National Environmental Policy Act (NEPA)[21] because, among other reasons, "the record indicates that serious concerns were raised over the likelihood of developing the human institutions or political consensus necessary to establish and maintain the hypothesized facilities." The judge "somewhat belatedly" acknowledged that "the Commission's own recent statements indicate the existence of such uncertainty concerning permanent disposal of high-level and transuranic wastes that the zero-release assumption, taken as a finding of fact, cannot stand."[22]

Note that nowhere in this condemnation was there any effort to quantify the time that it would take for these supposed risks to manifest themselves, nor the likelihood of their occurrence. In addition, the statement made it clear that this determination was only for a "limited purpose," so that the defects could be considered to exist elsewhere in the cycle. Nor did the opinion mention the huge logistical advantage that comes from applying a generic rule on low-risk issues, in that it can conserve resources for dealing with more important risks. Finally, in light of the rapid advances in nuclear technology in the generation or so in which it has been introduced, it is only sensible to assume that even with political pitfalls, further advances will be made. It may well be that the decision was wrong, but I think that Judge David L. Bazelon, who wrote this opinion, was in way over his head and manifested more of his ill-concealed hostility to nuclear technology than any credible form of expertise.

In this regard, a bit of history matters, for *Baltimore Gas* was not the first case that dealt with the issue of controlling nuclear waste. Thus, an earlier opinion of Judge Bazelon in the same line of cases, *Natural Resources Defense Council, Inc. v. United States Nuclear Regulatory Commission*,[23] received an exceptionally harsh rebuke from Justice Rehnquist when he reversed that decision on appeal: "But this much is absolutely clear. Absent constitutional constraints or extremely compelling circumstances the administrative agencies should be free to fashion their own rules of procedure and to pursue methods of inquiry capable of permitting them to discharge their multitudinous duties."[24]

There is, accordingly, no way in which that decision, which rested on a detailed analysis of the major pluses and minuses, could be dismissed as arbitrary and capricious just because the D.C. Circuit Court, when the 1982 case was before it, had attached a different weight to the residual uncertainties from the chosen procedures than did NRC. It should come as no surprise that the Supreme Court reversed the D.C. Circuit Court,[25] relying in part on *Vermont Yankee*, concluding: "Resolution of these fundamental policy questions lies . . . with Congress and the agencies to which Congress had delegated authority." It refused to overturn the agency's determination in light of the fact that NRC, in formulating the rule, "has made careful consideration and disclosure require[d] by NEPA."[26]

That should have been the end of it, unless careful determinations could in the next breath be regarded as arbitrary and capricious. Unfortunately, Justice O'Connor went on to conclude that, on the one hand, "Congress intended that the 'hard look' be incorporated as part of the agency's process of deciding whether to pursue a particular federal action,"[27] only to announce in the next breath that in "examining this kind of scientific determination, as opposed to simple findings of fact, a reviewing court must generally be at its most deferential."[28] The best response is that both these extremes are misguided, in that some standard of intermediate scrutiny seems to be appropriate on these mixed questions of law and fact, which, in this case, NRC passed with flying colors. One might think that *Baltimore Gas* would have inclined the Supreme Court in *State Farm* to back off its tough version of the same hard look doctrine that is qualified in *Baltimore Gas*. But *Baltimore Gas* was nowhere mentioned in *State Farm*; so in the single month of June, the Court committed itself to two versions of the hard look doctrine.

The divergence between *State Farm* and *Baltimore Gas* is rightly stressed by Gersen and Vermeule in their law review article with the provocative title "Thin Rationality Review." They are right to insist that the tough rendition of *State Farm* was far too unyielding. But they make the opposite mistake by bending over backward to ensure that the "arbitrary and capricious" standard has no teeth at all, for as the article's title hints, they lurch hurriedly to the opposite extreme by urging "a much less demanding and intrusive interpretation of the 'arbitrary and capricious' standard." Thus the centerpiece of their article is this striking claim about all courts: "[T]hey have failed to grasp a crucial twist: under a robust range of conditions, *rational agencies may have good reason to decide in a manner that is inaccurate, nonrational, or arbitrary.*" They go on to explain this position:

> Although this claim is seemingly paradoxical or internally inconsistent, it simply rests on an appreciation of the limits of reason, especially in administrative policymaking.

Agency decisionmaking is nonideal decisionmaking; what would be rational under ideal conditions is rarely a relevant question for agencies. Rather, agencies make decisions under constraints of scarce time, information, and resources. Those constraints imply that agencies will frequently have excellent reasons to depart from idealized first-order conceptions of administrative rationality.[29]

They conclude: "Forced to pick one case to encapsulate the Court's approach to rationality review, the best choice would be the powerfully deferential opinion in *Baltimore Gas*, decided in the same term as *State Farm*."[30]

But that account has no resonance. There is not the slightest hint that NRC labored under any time or resource constraint, or that it had to resort to unhappy compromises to reach its decision. Instead, its statement of reasons and its response to uncertainty were the kind of exemplary decisions that set a role model for how these decisions should be made.

Justice O'Connor knew full well that NRC had given a good account of itself, so there was no reason for her to bend over backward to make all sorts of allowances that NRC did not need. Recall that in the earlier discussion of deference, it was clear that *Seminole Rock* was worlds apart from *Auer v. Robbins*,[31] in that the former did very well under any standard of intermediate scrutiny, whereas the latter failed. What is needed on these ultimate questions of fact is a move toward the middle. But that turns out to be not what we get. Neither *State Farm* nor *Baltimore Gas* attached any weight to whether the agency upheld the challenge to the new development or rejected it, which becomes, in many cases, the legal realist's takeaway from the splitting of standards on "arbitrary and capricious." It is impossible to deal with what are thousands of applications of that standard. But it is instructive to see the bifurcation of that standard in the pipeline cases to which I shall now turn.

The Pipeline Cases

When the government agency allows the pipeline to be built, the hard look standard emerges as the dominant standard. But where the agency denies the application to build a pipeline, extreme deference is very much the order of the day. The consequences are not trivial. It is well understood that to shut down pipelines is to compromise the transmission of fossil fuels, which is exactly what the pipeline opponents want. It should be understood that the oscillation in standards is, of course, inconsistent with Fuller's vision of the rule of law.

To set the stage, the basic statutory framework requires that new pipelines meet the performance standards specified in the Clean Water Act,[32] which, in turn, requires that the various disclosures made in connection with the applications for new pipelines meet NEPA's requirements. NEPA does not impose any substantive standards and, at its inception, did not appear to call for any form of judicial review. Rather, NEPA's basic plan was to require agencies to consult with various parties and consider their positions before making any decision. In that way, a broad spectrum of groups could add their different perspectives into the mix—a perfectly sensible procedure.[33]

But the entire enterprise took a dramatic turn in *Calvert Cliffs' Coordinating Committee v. U.S. Atomic Energy Commission.*[34] Here, Judge J. Skelly Wright held that the high objectives of the statute—"to use all practicable means and measures, including financial and technical assistance, in a manner calculated to foster and promote the general welfare, to create and maintain conditions under which man and nature can exist in productive harmony, and fulfill the social, economic, and other requirements of present and future generations of Americans"[35]— required much greater judicial oversight. With evident glee, he wrote: "These cases are only the beginning of what promises to become a flood of new litigation—litigation seeking judicial assistance in protecting our natural environment."[36] In effect, his decision allowed *any* party who was unhappy with the outcome of an administrative decision to challenge it in court.

The *Calvert Cliffs* decision thus introduced two major revolutions in administrative law. First, it got the courts involved in the merits of these administrative cases. Second, its standing rules made sure that the parties most likely to appear in court were those most opposed to the administrative decision, which, in practice, then and now, meant that groups of staunch environmentalists would dominate the proceedings, targeting issues such as nuclear power, as in *Calvert Cliffs*, or pipeline construction. This framework, which has no legislative foundation, provides fertile ground for the "hard look" at various processes under *State Farm*—a hard look that has been adopted in many other cases.[37]

What really twists this standard is the form in which challenges are presented. As a general matter, low levels of scrutiny are applied when private applicants are denied administrative permissions. But far higher levels of scrutiny are applied when permissions are granted.

Let's start with an instance of extreme and indefensible discretion. In *Constitution Pipeline Co. v. New York State Department of Conservation*,[38] Constitution Pipeline (CP) applied for a permit to construct a 121-mile pipeline between Pennsylvania and New York, of which about 98 miles were to be inside New York State. Under the applicable rules, CP could obtain a federal certificate of "public convenience and necessity" only if it first obtained project approval from the New York State Department of Environmental Conservation.[39] The department issued a set of demands for detailed information on a broad swath of issues: the construction methods and site-specific project plans for stream crossings; alternative routes; pipeline burial depth in stream beds; procedures and safety measures that CP would follow in the event that blasting was required; and CP's plans to avoid, minimize, or mitigate discharges to navigable waters and wetlands and the cumulative impacts.[40] Notably, all these requests were made on an individual case basis, and there was no effort to devise or apply the kind of generic standards developed by NRC in *Baltimore Gas*. The obvious cost inefficiencies of the case-by-case approach were intended to slow the process down and make it more costly.

That objective was doubly ironic because, as noted in *Baltimore Gas*, technology has been on an upward arc. Pipeline construction has been a developing industry for many years, and its associated technologies have improved in every dimension: smaller footprints, superior design, better monitoring, better construction, fewer leaks, and faster response times. The American Petroleum Institute summarized the basic position: "[A] comparison of three-year spill averages for the periods 1999–2001 and 2009–2011 shows a 60% decrease in the number of spills per 1,000 miles of pipeline and a 43% decrease in the volume spilled per 1,000 miles of pipeline."[41] These are nontrivial improvements, and that rate of progress has continued apace.

The alternative modes of shipment of oil and gas, whether by rail, truck, or ship, are all more dangerous. The dangers of existing modes of transportation are most acute in the Northeast,[42] where the state-level opposition to new pipeline construction is the most intense and part of the campaign to discredit the use of fossil fuels—a policy issue that is orthogonal to the approval process and wholly irrelevant to it.

The critical point: in this and similar contexts, the government's informational demands are not made to facilitate empirical assessments of the kinds of multiple trade-offs that were raised on the record in *State Farm* and *Baltimore Gas*. Indeed, these agencies make no empirical judgments of any sort. Rather, their requests for information are in the nature of a request for discovery, where the applicable rule in ordinary civil litigation is not deference to findings of fact but special rules that govern the use and abuse of discovery procedures to unearth facts relevant to these proceedings. Under the Federal Rule of Civil Procedure 26(b)(1), such requests have a broad general scope subject to limitations on frequency and extent provided in Rule 26(b)(2). One of those critical discovery limitations arises when "the discovery sought is unreasonably cumulative or duplicative, or can be obtained from some other source that is more convenient, less burdensome, or less expensive."[43] This provision is necessary because it is far cheaper for litigants to pose questions than it is for their opponents to answer them, so the imposition of excessive costs via litigation remains a constant threat requiring judicial oversight.

Unfortunately, nothing in APA addresses the same problem in administrative law, when a government agency demands exhaustive information before it is willing to decide anything. Judicial control of these burdensome delay tactics is needed to counteract the massive risk of strategic behavior by the agencies.

The point here is no idle consideration because the duplicative nature of most of these requests is evident in the pipeline context. The location, design, construction, and maintenance of pipelines follow standard protocols on virtually all topics. The industry works best when accumulated wisdom is used and updated with each project. For most of the agencies' inquiries, there are standard responses and customary practices that give all the information needed to solve any particular problem. There is no point in gathering this information from scratch in each individual case. There is often good reason, as part of standard oversight, to require supplementation of the common information, but only when site-specific problems are identified. In addition, many standard inquiries turn out to be premature—such as asking today for definitive answers about problems whose solutions are sure to take shape tomorrow, as is commonly the case with strategies for leak containment and pipeline repairs. As I have written elsewhere:

> NEPA makes a further serious structural error insofar as it insists that in major cases *all* information be gathered and evaluated by the relevant agency before it can take *any* action. The agency could well deal with information by resisting the temptation to pack everything into the initial analysis, for there is no need to rely on imperfect information to resolve the many remote and improbable contingencies that are better fixed when they occur, if at all, down the road.[44]

The evolution observed in *Baltimore Gas* should not encourage government administrators to front-load their review of all potential issues that could arise out of any environmental hearing. The initial hearings should deal with those matters that will occur at the inception of the project with a high degree of probability. Other issues, such as the mitigation questions post-leak, should, in any event, be updated with new technologies; and a commitment by any applicant to make those adjustments should obviate the need to speculate about the future course of technology at the time of the initial application.

The general deference needed for the hard evaluation of trade-offs between rival courses of action is appropriate in cases like *State Farm*, where the question concerns the development of new state-of-the-art technology that poses serious design and implementation challenges. In that vein, the situation in *Constitution Pipeline* presents important issues on the siting of the particular pipeline, which can never be perfect but has shorter paths that are generally more desirable, especially if some previous pipeline has been laid through the same territory. But for virtually all the other issues specified in the case, the best explanation for the detailed and repetitive information requests is that they were intended to cause a simple delay in the effort to raise costs or block the project—both abuses of the regulatory scheme.[45]

Yet pipeline cases are not cases in which delays are appropriate under the maxim "Better safe than sorry." The refusal to expedite approvals for a new pipeline leaves in place pipelines and other modes of oil and gas transportation that pose greater risks to human safety and the environment alike. It also results in systematic shortages, which make it difficult to open new businesses in a state, such as has been the case with New York City's key natural gas provider, Con Edison, which can barely obtain enough energy to supply natural gas to its existing customers in such major locations as Westchester County.[46] Nonetheless, New York continues to block modest projects such as a proposed 37-mile pipeline that would link New York to natural gas fields in Pennsylvania and New Jersey, both of which are open to fracking, where New York is not.[47]

As is common, the fear of global warming is often cited in review proceedings under the Clean Water Act, which should be confined to the issues of water. I believe that the case that links carbon dioxide to global warming is tenuous, at best. The most recent data show a decline in global temperatures of about 0.56° centigrade between February 2016 and February 2018, even as carbon dioxide concentrations continue to rise.[48] To put that point in perspective, any effort to get the United States to zero emissions would reduce temperatures by only 0.137°C and, if done on a global level, would reduce temperatures by only 0.278°C.[49] But even if carbon dioxide does play some larger role in global warming, these puny regulatory efforts do not target the major sources of carbon dioxide emissions in the United States, and they ignore the simple fact that total emissions from China are twice those of the United States. Those from India are about half those of the United States and are rising at a far more rapid rate: the United States has had virtually no increase in carbon dioxide emissions between 1990 and 2018. India has had a 405% increase, and China a 453% increase.[50] A sensible cost-benefit analysis would not let a minuscule effect, from an uncertain cause, drive decision making. A far more sensible approach to the cost-benefit analysis would take into account the evidence on the magnitude of the risks of preserving the status quo, which means, in virtually all cases, setting the background presumption *in favor* of the issuance of a pipeline permit in order to reduce the stress on alternative forms of oil and gas transportation. We need to concentrate on the local, not the global, although that is typically not the accepted approach.

Here is one illustration of how New York's permitting process—upon which federal permissions for New York's pipelines are conditioned—goes awry. One barrage of questions that the New York authorities asked CP pertained to how the new pipeline would traverse certain small streams, for which two methods were available. The trenched method requires the creation of a dry open-cut crossing, which necessitates diverting the stream, burying the pipeline under the waterway, and then restoring the stream to its original condition. The system obviously creates potential risks from both diversion and restoration during the construction project. The alternative method, called horizontal directional drilling (HDD), involves boring holes under the existing stream and running the pipeline through the holes without diverting the stream. CP prepared studies that indicated at which spots it thought the various techniques should be used, taking the position that HDD should be used for smaller bodies of water where the risks were lower. Nonetheless, this approach was rejected in favor of an approach that required individualized determinations for each river, stream, or creek. It seems as though delay was the dominant motivation of the program. On review, the Second Circuit did not give a hard look at the result in this case but veered off in the opposite direction. The court noted that its current rule held that the deference was "due [to] an agency's determination that it should not grant a permit application where it has already determined that additional information is needed, and the applicant refuses to supply it."[51] The earlier reference to the hard look doctrine was no longer applicable, and no effort was made to assess whether the demands made by the New York authorities were an abuse of the discovery process.

We can generalize from this example the institutional weaknesses that pervade the entire administrative process. In ordinary civil litigation, magistrate judges are called in on a regular basis to review objections to discovery requests long before any final judgment is made by a district court judge. But the administrative process has no comparable institution for an interim review of these discovery-type requests, which means that disputes over the requests immediately go to some appellate court.

The ability to make these challenges should be facilitated on an interim basis so as to avoid the expense and delay of requests that demand information that will never figure in the ultimate decision. That oversight can be made continuous so that further inquiries are submitted based on changed circumstances. The ability to use this oversight process makes it clear that only in extraordinary cases should any court upset a pipeline application at the outset, when remediation is routinely available during the construction and the operation periods. The deference given the New York agency in *Constitution Pipeline* missed the point that excessive discovery requests should, under the current framework, be treated as arbitrary and capricious, at least until some relief is supplied on an interim basis.

The hard look doctrine, however, has sprung to life in other pipeline cases—most notably, in the disputes dealing with the Army Corps of Engineers approvals for the Dakota Access Pipeline (DAPL), which now runs 1,172 miles from North Dakota to Illinois and which was met with protracted resistance by the Standing Rock Sioux Tribe, whose lands lay close to the pipeline's path.[52] By the time of the litigation, the relevant agencies, including the Army Corps of Engineers and the state public utility commissions of North Dakota, South Dakota, Nebraska, Iowa, and Illinois, had approved the project.[53] But no deference was accorded in these approvals, where the so-called "procedural" dimension of NEPA "places upon an agency the obligation to consider every significant aspect of the environmental impact of a proposed action, and it ensures that the agency will inform the public that it has indeed considered environmental concerns in its decisionmaking process."[54]

The results of this lack of deference were gargantuan hearings and long delays in the approval process, where the basic result should have been ordained from the outset: the new technology beats the old, and most of the objections were frivolous in connection with various environmental issues.

In these cases, the critical issue is whether a preliminary report, known as an environmental assessment (EA), is sufficient to cover the case, or whether a longer environmental impact statement (EIS) is needed. The difference between the two forms of documentation can add years to any construction process, and the greater the number of relevant substantive issues, the larger the scope of the review.

With DAPL, the process lasted for years, and even after issuing a preliminary permit indicating that all the location and design issues were satisfied, Judge James E. Boasberg still expressed reservations that the agencies did not consider the impact that potential leaks could have on tribal fishing rights. He expressed this reservation even though he had already found that there was, at most, only a remote possibility that any leak of significant magnitude could occur. There were further concerns about environmental justice[55]—that is, the risk that the pipeline would have a disproportionately negative impact on poor and minority groups, a consideration that makes sense with respect to, for example, the location of a garbage dump in a specific community, but not for pipelines that can function only if they are of uniform quality across tens or hundreds of miles and near many diverse communities.

Suffice it to say that all the initial design and construction decisions could have been backed up by a requirement that firms take out insurance against leaks, for which they could be held strictly liable, except perhaps in cases of sabotage, where criminal charges would be appropriate against the saboteur. Front-loading these costs in the approval process was a serious error. There would have been lower costs and lower risks of error if the environmental oversight had been continuous, which is how complex projects are always governed in the private sector. The key saving grace in Judge Boasberg's opinion came in his remedial decision. The usual rule for NEPA violations is to suspend the operation of a project, no matter how far along it is in construction, which ignores any sensible effort to balance the equities between stopping a project and going forward, perhaps on some limited basis. Stopping a project is dangerous in practice because half-completed pipelines not in use present serious engineering and safety problems.

Fortunately for the DAPL litigation, under *Allied-Signal, Inc. v. U.S. Nuclear Regulatory Commission*, a district court retains some discretion on the type of relief that is afforded.[56] The relevant test for the decision to vacate "depends on the seriousness of the order's deficiencies (and thus the extent of doubt whether the agency chose correctly) and the disruptive consequences of an interim change that may itself be changed."[57] Given that all the essential questions dealing with route, construction, and operational safety had been satisfactorily answered, Judge Boasberg refused to stop construction and asked for more information on specific issues. Eighteen months later, nothing much happened on these submissions, and the pipeline has gone into operation without incident. It may well be that the system backed into the correct solution by an utterly convoluted process. Indeed, to shut down the pipeline now would massively rattle the entire oil economy, disrupt long-term contracts, and force various parties to scramble to reestablish the older modes of transportation, all of which have been long discarded. The outcome of this case should have been evident from the outset, which makes it clear that the hard look approach is utterly inappropriate for these managerial issues.

Nonetheless, the hard look approach continues to dominate. Thus, in *Atchafalaya Basinkeeper v. U.S. Army Corps of Engineers*,[58] the district court issued an injunction against the completion of a 163-mile, 24-inch pipeline with a carrying capacity of some 480,000 barrels of crude oil that runs from Nederland, Texas, to Lake Charles and St. James, Louisiana, both major oil transportation hubs.[59] Once again, the construction plans were state of the art, fully appropriate for pipelines that run through sensitive sites that are home to many forms of fish, plants, and other wildlife. The basic plan necessarily removed about 142 acres of habitat—of a total of nearly 900,000 acres—from permanent circulation and another 300 acres on a temporary basis. These are rock-bottom minimums, and if such losses count as "irreparable harm," no pipeline could be built anywhere, ever. The pipeline builder offered to replace the lost habitat through the creation and acquisition of new wetlands. Nonetheless, Judge Shelly Dick held that, under the hard look doctrine, getting approval from the Army Corps of Engineers was arbitrary and capricious because there might have been better methods for mitigation available. The decision never paused to consider that the mitigation question could be addressed anew, if need be, when construction took place.[60] As before, all the difficulties in the case were on collateral matters, so it was a stroke of good fortune that the completion of the pipeline was allowed when the Fifth Circuit summarily reversed Judge Dick's decision under the *Allied-Signal* doctrine.[61]

That same approach should be applied to the most recent decision in this tradition, *Indigenous Environmental Network v. U.S. Department of State*,[62] in which an injunction against the completion of the Keystone XL Pipeline was granted by Judge Brian Morris. Judge Morris invoked hard look review to issue an injunction for perceived collateral weaknesses in a Supplemental Environmental Impact Statement

(SEIS).[63] Once again, the issue did not turn on the basic design of the pipeline but instead focused on four areas: the effects of current oil prices on the viability of the Keystone pipeline; the cumulative effects of greenhouse gas emissions from a nearby pipeline expansion and the Keystone pipeline; a survey of potential cultural resources contained in the 1,038 acres not addressed in the 2014 SEIS; and an updated modeling of potential oil spills and recommended mitigation measures. A few brief comments help explain why these requests are utterly beside the point.

First, the determination of price sustainability is one that the company can make better than any court. And there are no clear inferences that could be drawn from the price information provided. The lower prices could lead to a greater quantity of oil shipped through the pipeline, or soft demand could lead to a decline in price, at least in the short run. So much depends on a welter of other factors that are difficult to forecast that it becomes hard to see why this issue should ever matter to a court whose major concern is safety and environmental impact. In addition, the pipeline is a long-term asset whose life could exceed 20 or 30 years. Long-term projections are hard to make. But there is no reason to stop construction until revised estimates can be made, since those estimates will soon become obsolete in the next cycle of review.

Second, the supposed cumulative effect of the emission of greenhouse gases in this context is, at best, a rounding error. Pipelines are not plants (which should be separately regulated); they are designed in their normal operations to move, not leak, gas. Nor is there any reason to worry about the supposedly interactive effects from the leakage from multiple lines, for there is no reason that any such interconnections should exist, given that there are other far larger emitters of greenhouse gases. The known effects are dwarfed by those of other activities, and to the extent that some unforeseeable issue might arise in the future, it can be dealt with at that time. The basic theme holds: don't try to resolve these issues today when better information will be available tomorrow.

Third, any supposed concern with cultural resources can be handled when the problems arise. The ostensible concern identifies 1,038 acres, or about one acre per mile of pipeline, much of which runs through relatively barren territory. The pickings are likely to be slim. But even if these resources could be identified, there is no reason to stop the project now. The sensible procedure is to ask the objectors to identify resources that they think are worthy of protection and then address them as the project goes forward. Surely the one form of relief that should never be required is to relocate the pipeline at immense cost after construction has begun, when the new location could be stopped on the grounds that some different set of cultural resources will have to be addressed. Again, there is no reason to stop construction on a 1,000-plus-acre pipeline to deal with these issues.

Finally, mitigation techniques in the event of leaks must always be updated. But it is currently known that the pipeline control systems already in place are effective in controlling major breaks, so there is no reason to stop construction until these systems are further refined, which will happen as a matter of course during and after pipeline construction. Pipelines are long-term capital assets that no company wants to destroy.

In sum, there is not a single issue raised in *Indigenous Environmental Network* to justify blanket injunctive relief. The appropriate response is identical to what should be applied to the Bayou Bridge pipeline. The government and the pipeline company should request immediate emergency relief, as the grounds given for halting the project are woefully inadequate—yet this case represents another instance of how the hard look approach can seriously misfire. It seems all too clear today that the judicial applications of this doctrine have been erratic. Even those most favorable to pipeline construction show an undue reticence in their magnification of small and remote risks into major potential hurdles. The only possible solution is to clarify the law legislatively, administratively, or both.

One recent step in that direction comes with two executive orders issued by President Trump. The first contains these general injunctions: promote "efficient permitting processes and procedures" so as to eliminate waste and duplication; adopt regulations that "reflect best practice"; and "encourage timely decision making" and "increased regulatory certainty." There is so much flab and duplication that it should be easy to advance pipeline safety and energy efficiency at the same time. Those general injunctions are sadly not operative, so that the power, if there is any power in the executive order, will come from the command to EPA to rethink the division of authority over pipeline approvals after consultation "with States, tribes, and relevant executive departments and agencies."[64] Consultations are always risky, and it is unclear exactly what guidance will come out of these procedures.

Nonetheless, it is all too clear that some action is needed to prevent the unfortunate outcome in cases like *Constitution Pipeline*, where a deadly combination of administrative rigidity and low-level rational basis review has created chronic energy shortages in the Northeast, to the point where Con Edison imposed, as of March 15, 2019, a moratorium on applications to obtain new natural gas service in southern Westchester County.[65] The answer to this problem that was offered by New York was to apply $250 million in state subsidies to encourage various forms of energy efficiency and to develop secondary energy sources. The New York approach encapsulates a major blunder of regulatory policy. Instead of removing senseless roadblocks at no cost, the state has tried to offset a major regulatory blunder by creating a costly and unfocused subsidy. That second move will only extend the distortion into other markets, while offering, at best, a glimmer of some insufficient regulatory relief down the road. The president's executive order provides a far better response, by working to remove the initial distortion. But that order will certainly be challenged, so the precarious condition of pipeline construction in the Northeast will remain unresolved.

Trump's second executive order is equally welcome. The decision in *Indigenous Environmental Network* represents the worst form of NEPA abuse. With moral certainty, we know that emissions from pipeline activities are negligible. We also know that it makes no sense to try to regulate different forms of end-use by the blunderbuss technique of slowing down pipeline development. Those sources should be regulated separately and independently. Hence, the president is on solid ground in issuing an executive order intended to expedite the approval of pipelines that cross international boundaries, like the Keystone XL Pipeline.[66] That order requires the secretary of state to adopt procedures that allow for the decision on pipeline approval (along with approval for facilities dealing with water, sewage, and bridges) to be made within 60 days of the filing of a completed application. The order contains provisions for consultation with state, tribal, and local governments, and claims that the president has sole decision-making authority, so a clash with NEPA is likely to come.

As with all such orders, they last only as long as the current administration desires and, in any event, have uncertain influence in judicial proceedings. Again, the challenges that have been created with respect to pipeline construction can be addressed only through a legislative change. Fossil fuels will long remain the dominant source of energy in the United States, providing at least 80% of total energy supplies for the foreseeable future. No system of wind and solar energy, with their serious limitations, will be able to take their place.[67]

ENDNOTES

1. 5 U.S.C. § 706(2)(A)(2018).

2. *See, e.g., SEC v. Coldicutt,* 258 F.3d 939, 941 (9th Cir. 2001).

3. *Trump v. Hawaii,* 138 S. Ct. 2392 (2018).

4. *Dep't of Commerce v. New York,* 139 S. Ct. 953 (2019).

5. *Motor Vehicles Mfrs. Ass'n v. State Farm Ins.,* 463 U.S. 29 (1983).

6. *Id.* at 43.

7. *Gulf Restoration Network v. McCarthy,* 783 F.3d 227, 243 (5th Cir. 2015) (internal quotation marks omitted).

8. For the origin of the term "hard look," *see Greater Boston Television Corp. v. FCC,* 444 F.2d 841, 851 (D.C. Cir. 1970) (Leventhal, J.) ("Its supervisory function calls on the court to intervene not merely in case of procedural inadequacies, or bypassing of the mandate in the legislative charter, but more broadly if the court becomes aware, especially from a combination of danger signals, that the agency has not really taken a 'hard look' at the salient problems, and has not genuinely engaged in reasoned decision-making.") For further discussion, *see* Merrick B. Garland, DEREGULATION AND JUDICIAL REVIEW, 98 HARV. L. REV. 505 (1985).

9. *State Farm,* 463 U.S. at 38–39.

10. For these concerns and much more, *see* Martin Albaum, *Safety Sells: Market Forces in the Development of Airbags,* Insurance Institute for Highway Safety (2005), *available at* https://www.iihs.org/media/186adabe-9ef4-479c-ad37-36b9f0e7fca1/Ka0wWQ/Albaum_Safety_Sells.pdf.

11. *State Farm,* 463 U.S. at 41.

12. *Id.* at 48 ("Given the effectiveness ascribed to airbag technology by the agency, the mandate of the Act to achieve traffic safety would suggest that the logical response to the faults of detachable seatbelts would be to require the installation of airbags. At the very least this alternative way of achieving the objectives of the Act should have been addressed and adequate reasons given for its abandonment.") There is a vast difference between an effective technology and its uniform implementation by all companies.

13. Jacob Gersen and Adrian Vermeule, *Thin Rationality Review,* 114 MICH. L. REV. 1355 (2016).

14. *Id.* at 1358.

15. *Baltimore Gas & Elec. Co. v. Nat. Res. Def. Council, Inc.,* 462 U.S. 87 (1983).

16. *Id.* at 91.

17. *Id.* at 92.

18. *Id.* at 93.

19. *Id.* at 94–95 (quoting 44 Fed. Reg. 45362 (Aug. 21979)).

20. *Nat. Res. Def. Council, Inc. v. Nuclear Regulatory Comm'n,* 685 F.2d 459 (D.C. Cir. 1982).

21. National Environmental Policy Act, 42 U.S.C. §§ 4321–4347 (1970).

22. *NRDC v. NRC,* 685 F.2d 459, 480–81.

23. *NRDC v. NRC,* 547 F.2d (D.C. Cir. 1976).

24. *Vermont Yankee Nuclear Power Corp. v. Nat. Res. Def. Council,* 435 U.S. 519, 543 (1978), (internal quotation marks omitted).

25. *Baltimore Gas,* 462 U.S. at 92–94, 97.

26. *Id.* at 98.

27. *Id.* at 99.

28. *Id.* at 103.

29. Gersen and Vermeule, *supra* note 13, at 1356–57 (emphasis in original).

30. *Id.* at 1359.

31. See Part 4, at 123–129; *Bowles v. Seminole Rock & Sand Co.,* 325 U.S. 410 (1945); *Auer v. Robbins,* 519 U.S. 452 (1997).

32. 33 U.S.C. § 1341 (2017)(dealing with § 401 certifications).

33. For discussion *see* Richard Lazarus, *The National Environmental Policy Act in the U.S. Supreme Court: A Reappraisal and a Peek Behind the Curtains,* 100 GEO. L.J. 1507, 1513–14 (2012)

34. *Calvert Cliffs' Coordinating Comm. v. U.S. Atomic Energy Comm'n,* 449 F.2d 1109 (D.C. Cir. 1971). It is worth noting that Judge Bazelon in his decision in *Baltimore Gas* relied explicitly on *Calvert Cliffs. NDRC v. NRC,* 685 F.2d at 476–77.

35. 42 U.S.C. § 4331(a)(2017).

36. *Calvert Cliffs',* 449 F.2d at 1111.

37. *See, e.g., Robertson v. Methow Valley Citizens Council,* 490 U.S. 332, 350 (1989).

38. *Constitution Pipeline Co. v. New York State Dep't of Conservation,* 868 F.3d 87 (2d Cir. 2017).

39. *See* 15 U.S.C. § 717f(c) (1988).

40. *Constitution Pipeline,* 868 F.3d at 102.

41. *Improving Liquid Pipeline Safety,* ENERGY API, *available at* https://www.api.org/oil-and-natural-gas/wells-to-consumer/transporting-oil-natural-gas/pipeline/improving-liquid-pipeline-safety (last visited Aug. 12, 2019).

42. Jude Clemente, *What Happens When You Don't Build Natural Gas Pipelines,* FORBES (Jan. 7, 2018), *available at* https://www.forbes.com/sites/judeclemente/2018/01/07/what-happens-when-you-dont-build-natural-gas-pipelines/#5d67a5e05fd6 (noting that in New York, New Jersey, and New England, where a pipeline shortage is particularly prominent, "a natural gas shortage is created, prices for both natural gas and electricity skyrocket, and CO_2 emissions go up because more carbon-intensive fuels are forced to compensate").

43. Fed. R. Civ. P. 26(b)(2)(C)(i).

44. Richard A. Epstein, *The Many Sins of NEPA,* 6 TEXAS A & M L. REV. 1, 2 (2018).

45. For one such statement, *see* Jan Hasselman, *Fighting Fossil Fuels in the Era of Trump,* EARTHJUSTICE (Aug. 21, 2018), https://earthjustice.org/from-the-experts/fighting-fossil-fuels-in-the-era-of-trump ("Achieving a clean energy economy will require a top-to-bottom transition of our entire energy and transportation sectors. The first critical step is to prevent major infrastructure investments that would 'lock in' fossil fuel use—investments like new pipelines, power plants, and export terminals. These projects, if built, would operate for decades and make phasing out fossil fuels even harder to achieve than it already is. We may not be able to phase out fossil fuel use overnight, but we can block multi-billion-dollar investments that commit us to these approaches

for the next 50 years. And the good news is that many of these projects are decided at the state and local level, where decisions can be influenced by local communities despite a federal government that will aggressively support such projects").

46. *See, e.g., No New Natural Gas Hookups in New York's Westchester County, Con Ed Says,* REUTERS (Mar. 15, 2019), *available at* https://www.reuters.com/article/ us-consolidated-edi-natgas-new-york/no-new-natural-gas-hookups-in-new-yorks-westchester-county-con-ed-says-idUSKCN1QW2IS.

47. Vivian Wang and Michael Adno, *New York Rejects Keystone-Like Pipeline in Fierce Battle over the State's Energy Future,* N.Y TIMES (May 15, 2019), *available at* https:// www.nytimes.com/2019/05/15/nyregion/williams-pipeline-gas-energy.html.

48. Editorial, *Don't Tell Anyone, but We Just Had Two Years of Record-Breaking Global Cooling,* INV. BUS. DAILY (May 16, 2018), *available at* https://www.investors.com/ politics/editorials/climate-change-global-warming-earth-cooling-media-bias.

49. David Kreutzer et al., *The State of Climate Science: No Justification for Extreme Policies,* HERITAGE FOUND. (Apr. 22, 2016), *available at* https://www.heritage.org/ environment/report/the-state-climate-science-no-justification-extreme-policies#_ ftnref57.

50. *See* M. Munean et al., FOSSIL CO_2 EMISSIONS OF ALL WORLD COUNTRIES—2018 REPORT (European Union, 2018), *available at* https://edgar.jrc.ec.europa.eu/overview. php?v=booklet2018. The key comparisons: China's emissions rose from 2397048.05 kt (kilotonnes of CO_2 equivalent) in 1990 to 10877217.94 in 2018, for a 453% increase. In that same period, India went from 605968.42 to 2454773.80, for a 405% increase. In that same period, the U.S. went from 5085896.78 to 5107393.21, for a 0.05% increase.

51. *Constitution Pipeline,* 868 F.3d at 103.

52. Robinson Meyer, *The Legal Case for Blocking the Dakota Access Pipeline: Did the U.S. Government Help Destroy a Major Sioux Archeological Site?,* ATLANTIC (Sept. 9, 2016), *available at* https://www.theatlantic.com/technology/archive/2016/09/dapl-dakota-sitting-rock-sioux/499178.

53. *The Dakota Access Pipeline Route Was Created Through a Careful and Collaborative Process,* DAKOTA ACCESS PIPELINE FACTS, *available at* https://perma.cc/MN94-VSLT (last visited Aug. 19, 2018).

54. *Standing Rock Sioux Tribe v. U.S. Army Corps of Eng'rs,* 255 F. Supp.3d 101, 112–13 (D.D.C. 2017). For other decisions in this line of cases, *see Standing Rock Sioux Tribe v. U.S. Army Corps of Eng'rs,* 282 F. Supp.3d 91, 96 (D.D.C. 2017); *Standing Rock Sioux Tribe v. U.S. Army Corps of Eng'rs,* 301 F. Supp.3d 50, 58 (D.D.C. 2018).

55. *See* Federal Actions to Address Environmental Justice in Minority Populations and Low-Income Populations, Exec. Order No. 12,898, 59 Fed. Reg. 7629 (Feb. 11, 1994).

56. *Allied-Signal, Inc. v. U.S. Nuclear Regulatory Comm'n,* 988 F.2d 146 (D.C. Cir. 1993).

57. *Id.* at 150–51.

58. *Atchafalaya Basinkeeper v. U.S. Army Corps of Eng'rs,* 310 F. Supp.3d 707, 740–41 (M.D. La. 2018), *rev'd* 894 F.3d 692 (5th Cir. 2018).

59. *Bayou Bridge Pipeline: Fact Sheet* (March 2018), *available at* https://perma.cc/QJG3-SHZ4.

60. *Atchafalaya Basinkeeper,* 310 F. Supp.3d at 727.

61. 894 F.3d at 704.

62. *Indigenous Envtl. Network v. U.S. Dep't of State,* 317 F. Supp.3d 1118 (D. Mont. 2018).

63. *Id.* at 1123.

64. Executive Order 13868 of Apr. 10, 2019, Promoting Energy Infrastructure and Economic Growth, 84 Fed. Reg. 15495 (Apr. 15, 2019), *available at* https://www.federalregister.gov/documents/2019/04/15/2019-07656/promoting-energy-infrastructure-and-economic-growth.

65. Marie J. French, *Con Edison Imposes Gas Moratorium in Westchester County,* Politico (Jan. 18, 2019), *available at* https://www.politico.com/states/new-york/albany/story/2019/01/18/con-edison-imposes-gas-moratorium-in-westchester-county-802490.

66. Executive Order 13867 of Apr. 10, 2019, Issuance of Permits with Respect to Facilities and Land Transportation Crossings at the International Boundaries of the United States (84 Fed. Reg. 15491)(Apr. 15, 2019), *available at* https://www.govinfo.gov/content/pkg/FR-2019-04-15/pdf/2019-07645.pdf.

67. Mark Mills, *Moonshot Madness,* RealClearPolicy (Apr. 18, 2019), *available at* https://www.realclearpolicy.com/articles/2019/04/18/moonshot_madness_111166.html.

CONCLUSION

The academic study of administrative law in the United States too often dissolves an abstract inquiry into the formulation of legal doctrine, wholly divorced from any knowledge of how the doctrinal commands work out in the context of the substantive dimensions of the underlying dispute. Most administrative lawyers ignore both the intersection between their doctrines and the relevant substantive legal fields. They also fail to compare their forms of adjudication with the procedural rules that govern the review of ordinary civil litigation. I take the opposite approach. I believe that only after the relevant substantive and procedural disciplines are mastered is it possible to get an intelligent take on how administrative law should operate. Conceptual speculation alone should never carry the day.

The verdict is clear. *Not one* area of modern administrative law meshes well with the substantive concerns of the underlying organic statutes. And *not one* area of modern administrative law meets the standard requirements of the rule of law. Sadly, the ultimate evaluation is clear: we have strayed a long way from Fuller's conception of the morality of law.

Modern administrative law bears little or no resemblance to historical administrative law, which raised few, if any, rule-of-law questions. The difference in outcomes between then and now cannot be waived away on the supposed grounds that times were simpler then than they are now.

In truth, all periods are very complex; what matters is the attitudes that are brought to them. It is not just an accident that the older administrative law dealt with statutory schemes that lacked the modern law's ambitions. It was because of a built-in reluctance to try out grand schemes that were likely to fail. Many modern disputes, on the other hand, are the result of a dangerous overambition with matters that have a simpler and more direct solution. Lacking that kind of institutional hubris, most earlier disputes were directed to matters of contract law that arose in connection with government employment or property grants in both land and patents. These areas are sensibly governed by the usual rules of contract interpretation that look to the course of dealing or industry practice. The regulatory side of the older administrative law dealt with such issues as imposing compensating tariffs on foreign imports. Judges did not spend much time worrying about the inherent ambiguity of ordinary language. They tended to decide cases without using any overwrought methodological apparatus. Those earlier judges did well because the test of ordinary meaning may not have been perfect—nothing is—but it removed the need to figure out which kind of ad hoc adjustment should be made in what direction, and why. The lower the level of intellectual angst, the more accurate and reliable will be the interpretations given.

With modern administrative systems, the reverse is true. The statutes have a far greater level of ambition to impose comprehensive systems of government control on the environment, drug development, telecommunications, and labor relations, among other fields. At every point, the new systems are put into place with one of two objectives: to weaken the operation of competitive markets; or to displace the common law rules of nuisance and trespass that are commonly used to control harmful externalities.

The weak set of protections for private property rights necessarily gives administrative agencies far greater discretion in the selection of the targets of regulation and the regimes to which these targets are subject. There is no way that any statute can simultaneously achieve two competing goals—to give concrete direction while also allowing for a broad scope of application. Thus, phrases like "public interest, convenience, and necessity" invariably creep into the language. But judges are hard-pressed to rule these rubbery phrases out of bounds, since no obvious narrower set of terms can cover the range of issues for which regulation via the administration is now deemed appropriate. It is no longer possible to put sharp limitations on delegated authority that could cabin administrative efforts. It is simply too hard to clamp down on administrative agencies that Congress has tasked with such an extensive set of substantive issues.

These matters are only made worse by the current attitudes taken on various questions under APA. The difficulties here do not relate to the statute's text, which is best read to give the same kind of judicial oversight to administrative agencies as is given to trial courts. Questions of law are always decided de novo on appeal. Questions of fact are generally reversed only if clearly erroneous. Ultimate questions of fact and mixed questions of fact and law have some intermediate standard, as with the nuclear waste issues addressed in *Baltimore Gas*. But the fatal combination of *State Farm* and *Chevron* put the courts on the wrong course—often inverting the sensible order of things. Factual questions are given a hard look review—sometimes; yet strategic requests for information by agencies are allowed to multiply without apparent limit for the want of judicial oversight, while the rejection of permits continues to get kid-glove treatment, even as approvals of useful projects are subject to the third degree.

Decisions rejecting permissions seem to be subject to less stringent review than are decisions to approve economically beneficial projects. Questions of law are subject to deference, but the level of deference varies with different kinds of proceedings, with one constant: agencies make an effort to duck review on matters of principle that are of consequence by avoiding notice and comment hearings, and by expanding, often dangerously, their jurisdiction by issuing nonbinding guidances, which fly under the judicial radar because they are not said to be "final."[1] Lost in the shuffle is the simple proposition that all these differences vanish under a uniform rule that leaves all questions of law to be decided by the courts de novo.

The consequences of these major administrative law commitments are far from pretty: administrative procedures are often prone to bias;

levels of delegation are often excessive and difficult to control; deference on questions of law leads to an acceptance of retroactive and inconsistent rules; and the complexity of the process makes it hard to give clear notice of the legal system to ordinary businesses and individuals, leaving them uninformed on how to deal with a welter of impenetrable and inconsistent rules.

In the end, claims by scholars such as Professor Metzger that defend the administrative state fail to come to grips with the powerful objections against its current operation. It is also hard to accept the claims of Professors Sunstein and Vermeule that somehow this ill-conceived body of modern rules comports with the rule of law as understood by Lon Fuller or, indeed, anyone else. The modern failures of administrative law are a necessary consequence of the progressive mind-set that has ushered in its modern interpretation.

At the outset, I mentioned the grave constitutional doubts about the entire system that have been expressed by Justices Gorsuch and Kavanaugh. It may well be too late to have a constitutional revolution that will so limit the size of government that administrative law accordingly becomes more coherent. But the simple decision to follow the text of the 1946 Administrative Procedure Act gets us a long way in that direction. Thus, I present a simple suggestion: forget all the fancy Supreme Court gloss that has gutted APA, and return the law to its original design, meaning, and structure. The constitutional questions will then largely take care of themselves.

ENDNOTE

1. *See, e.g., Pac. Gas & Electric Co. v. Fed. Power Comm'n,* 506 F.2d 33, 39 (D.C. Cir. 1974) ("A general statement of policy [in contrast with a rule] does not establish a 'binding norm.' It is not finally determinative of the issues or rights to which it is addressed.").

TABLE OF CASES

GENERAL INDEX